FROM THE IVORY TOWER
TO THE SCHOOLHOUSE

From the Ivory Tower to the Schoolhouse

How Scholarship Becomes
Common Knowledge in Education

JACK SCHNEIDER

Harvard Education Press
Cambridge, Massachusetts

Library of Congress Control Number 2013952613

Paperback ISBN 978-1-61250-669-2
Library Edition ISBN 978-1-61250-670-8

Published by Harvard Education Press,
an imprint of the Harvard Education Publishing Group

Harvard Education Press
8 Story Street
Cambridge, MA 02138

Cover Design: Ciano Design
Cover Photo: © Michele Constantini/PhotoAlto/Corbis
The typefaces used in this book are Adobe Garamond Pro, Futura, and Indispose

CONTENTS

Over half of U.S. public school teachers have master's degrees. Many courses that these teachers took to earn their degrees included reading and analyzing research studies. And many of these teachers wrote a master's thesis or research papers to complete the requirements for the degree. Among those teachers without an advanced degree, most have been exposed to recent research in their discipline or educational specialty through professional development workshops, media articles, or classroom research projects. And whatever their undergraduate or graduate-level coursework, many teachers search restlessly in academic journals and professional literature for studies that will point to ways that they can improve what they do daily in classrooms. So most teachers have been either consumers or creators (or both) of research.

But that familiarity with research seldom stills the frequent and intense rhetoric from policy makers, researchers, administrators, and lay reformers who ask teachers to use "evidence-based practice" and "best practices" identified in research studies. They want teachers to incorporate results of scientific studies into their lessons on fractions and decimals, phonics, photosynthesis, and the causes of the Civil War.

Moreover, since the passage of the No Child Left Behind Act in 2001—which mentions variations of "scientifically based research" over 100 times—the calls upon teachers to use research in classroom practice have multiplied. The federally funded What Works Clearinghouse, founded in 2002 to "provide educators, policy makers, and the public with a central and trusted source of scientific evidence of what works in education," concentrates on empirical studies meeting rigorous standards of effectiveness as measured by standardized test scores. It's no surprise, then, that interest in getting teachers to use knowledge harvested from research literature, especially from experimental and quasi-experimental studies, has increased dramatically in the past decade.

Yet despite so many teachers being exposed to research in their graduate programs, an expanding empirical base for effective programs, and a large population of teachers familiar with the ins and outs of research, little of that knowledge has filtered into classroom practice. Decade after decade, critics have characterized teacher use of research as slim.

This marginal use of research by classroom teachers, however, has not occurred for lack of trying. For decades, university teacher educators have taught undergraduates and graduates how research studies are put together, identified studies that can improve practice, and assigned research projects. State, federal, and private efforts over decades have spread the results of research studies to teachers. Consider, for example, the Education Resources Information Center (ERIC) that began in 1966. It contains more than a million documents, most of which are studies freely available to anyone. The National Diffusion Network (NDN) disseminated research on programs that worked in classrooms between 1974 and 1995. The American Federation of Teachers (AFT) started its Educational Research and Dissemination program for classroom teachers in 1981.

Here, then, is a puzzle: we have highly educated teachers familiar with research joined to mighty efforts to channel scholarship into practice, and yet the bulk of the nation's teacher corps seemingly ignores scholarship easily accessible to it.

There are reasons galore for this puzzle's existence. For some critics of academic research, the primary reason is that most studies answer questions teachers seldom ask. So many studies are largely irrelevant to those issues that plague teachers daily. Other critics see the reason in teachers themselves, who are so immersed in a culture of practice where experience and stories carry far more weight than findings from scientific studies. And then there are those who point to the age-graded school and the structural constraints (e.g., schedules that leave little time for teachers to meet and discuss instructional issues, number of students taught) that fix teachers' attention on daily logistics rather than applying results of scientific studies.

Whatever the reasons, most teachers, critics say, ignore the fruits of research studies that could be used to enhance both teaching and student learning. Instead, most teachers rely on experience-based practice—that is, the authority that comes from the knowledge and skills they've gained through prior experience and the wisdom of respected colleagues.

The situation, however, is not as grim as critics imply. Those familiar with the history of teaching know that certain ideas shaped and baked in academia, have, indeed, been adopted and adapted by teachers and put into practice in their classrooms. And that fact is an important clue to unraveling the conundrum.

Jack Schneider, a historian of education, has turned that clue into an eye-opening book. He does what gifted songwriters do: create a new melody or rearrange a familiar one, add fresh lyrics, and enthrall listeners. He does so by artfully building an original interpretation about teacher use of research. And his "song" will surprise teacher educators, policy makers, researchers, and lay reformers baffled over the puzzle of teachers who are knowledgeable about research yet seldom adopt scientific findings to improve their classroom practice.

The central question that drives *From the Ivory Tower to the Schoolhouse* is straightforward: what explains the fact that some scholarly ideas, and not others, have appeared in classrooms practices? Schneider answers that question by examining Bloom's taxonomy, multiple intelligences, the project method, and Direct Instruction—concepts stamped "Made in Academia." Schneider travels through time, from a century ago to the recent past, to identify the features of those ideas that have made them accessible and useful to teachers in their daily work.

Not only does Schneider make the case for the key features of those four ideas that tie together their successful research-to-practice journey, but he also takes four very similar research-driven concepts—the affective taxonomy, the triarchic theory, project-based learning, and behavioral analysis, also baked in the ivory tower—that stumbled on their way into classrooms, seldom making it past the classroom transom. He shows that some features characterizing the successful transplant of research findings were missing in action in these comparable ventures.

In clear, crisp prose enlivened by spot-on quotes, richly detailed examples, and flashes of humor, Schneider offers readers—particularly teacher educators, researchers, policy makers, practitioners, and lay reformers—a fresh historical explanation for the puzzle of teachers and their uneven use of research to improve classroom practice.

In this fine book, Schneider shows how historical research not only begins unlocking policy conundrums but also can inform policies that might well bring teachers and scholars together to deal with the complexities of classroom practice. Whether the suggestions he offers in the closing pages, based on those research ideas that have informed and changed classroom practice, will indeed alter the historic breach between the ivory tower and the schoolhouse, I cannot say. But these suggestions surely got me thinking that they are worth trying in order to mend the unfortunate gap that persists between researchers and classroom teachers.

—Larry Cuban
Professor Emeritus
Stanford University

Ask teachers if they use university-produced scholarship in their class-rooms, and you are likely to generate a range of reactions—pride, discomfort, curiosity—highlighting the complexity of the question. Many will reluctantly indicate that they probably should, but because of limits on time or training, do not. Others, answering in the affirmative, will tell stories of personal struggles locating relevant research, engaging busy colleagues, wrangling administrative support, or adapting materials for classroom use. Some who say they *do* use educational scholarship in the classroom will actually bristle at the notion, expressing discomfort with top-down mandates to do so, or voicing doubt about the usefulness of the venture. And still others will answer a question with a question: "What do you mean by scholarship?" After all, educational scholarship runs the whole gamut of methodologies and can take a seemingly endless variety of forms.

Those studying K–12 education from the outside generally have a simpler answer: "No." Insofar as scholarship ever travels beyond the ivory tower, they argue, it does so in a world parallel to the classroom—a world populated not by teachers and students, but by policy wonks and research-ers. Occasionally, it is translated into action via structural or programmatic changes like class size reductions or the adoption of a new curriculum. To the extent that such moves impact teacher work, they can shape the pro-cesses of teaching and learning. Yet rarely do scholarly ideas actually pen-etrate the *instructional core* of the school by affecting what teachers know and how they behave.[1] And when they do, by means of professional devel-opment seminars or district guidelines, the impact is usually short-lived. Like names written on a steam-covered window, they fade from view.

Scholars have offered a host of explanations for why educational re-search—or at least the large cross-section that strives to affect teacher knowledge and action—persistently fails to penetrate classroom practice.[2] And such accounts, when taken collectively, do a great deal to explain this phenomenon. Still, they cannot completely account for the messier reality that plays out in classrooms. And perhaps more significantly, they fall particularly short in explaining the surprising success of several notable exceptions to this general rule of failure. As nearly any K–12 educator can affirm, some products of educational scholarship have entered the world of practice and taken root. Such ideas have become property of the schoolhouse commons—concepts that teachers recognize, reference, and even use.

Amid the constant chorus of complaints about the irrelevance of educational scholarship, these prominent exceptions demand explanation. To put it another way: while we know a great deal about why scholarship does not enter practice, we know very little about why sometimes it *does*. Hence, this book asks two central questions:

- What characterizes the scholarly ideas that practitioners have adopted in the classroom?
- What do those particular characteristics reveal about the nature of American education and the hope for connecting research and practice?

In an effort to answer the book's core questions, the first four chapters each examine a major idea that, despite the obstacles, moved from the ivory tower into the professional knowledge base of teachers: Bloom's taxonomy, Howard Gardner's theory of multiple intelligences, the project method, and Direct Instruction. These particular pieces of scholarship, as exceptions to the rule that research does not enter teacher practice, deserve our careful attention.

Now, some might quibble with the degree to which these cases truly bridged the divide. Those oriented toward fetishized forms like large-scale randomized trails, for instance, might argue that these four examples are merely *ideas* rather than research. And those focused on the extent of their uptake might point out that these concepts have not been universally adopted by educators. Yet such claims reflect a constricted form of reasoning. Each of these ideas was the product of scholarship conducted at large research universities; the scholars in question published in leading journals; and the ideas were subsequently debated among specialists in the field. And, while none of the ideas is universally known, each has won recognition—across grade levels and regions—among classroom teachers who are often unfamiliar with any other piece of educational scholarship.[3] In short, these cases serve as evidence of the fact that research can enter classrooms and take hold.

Before we examine what makes some ideas exceptional, however, it is worth briefly discussing why the vast majority of educational scholarship fails to gain traction in the teacher knowledge base. After all, each year thousands of projects are initiated and funded with the intention of affecting classroom practice. Few, however, manage to win anything resembling a foothold with teachers.

One common explanation for this failure is that there is no "practice ready" scholarship. As many have argued, those working in higher education are frequently more interested in theory development than in practical solutions.[4] Accordingly, they write more for one another than they do for practitioners, delving into esoteric subjects divorced from the realities of real classrooms. Yet while this may be true, it is also true that a broad cross-section of scholars—researchers in policy, teacher education, educational technology, school culture, curriculum design, and the like—are deeply interested in improving K–12 teaching and learning. Look closely at the membership of the American Educational Research Association (AERA), for instance, and you will see that roughly one-quarter of the approximately 160 AERA special interest groups (SIGs) are practice-oriented. That means for every SIG on "Foucault and Contemporary Theory in Education," there is a SIG on "Classroom Management," or "School Effectiveness and School Improvement," or "Teaching History." There is even a SIG on "Multiple Intelligences: Theory and Practice." Seeking further evidence, one might also look beyond professional organizations to the content of periodicals in the field. Many outlets for education scholarship, like *American Educator* and *Education Week*, are predominantly concerned with the world of practice; and even among publications less oriented toward the classroom—including several AERA journals—articles dealing with practice are hardly novelties.

But though affecting teaching and learning remains a central aim in educational scholarship, it is rarely achieved. Why?

Another explanation is that teachers are antagonistic to new ideas. Those who take this position argue that educators have collectively worked to make the profession as comfortable for themselves as possible and are determined to protect the status quo.[5] Though teachers are not especially well remunerated, such critics argue, they earn a decent living and—often after only two years on the job—are nearly impossible to fire. Consequently, even incentive programs have fallen short in motivating teachers to stay up to date on scholarship or grow professionally.

What such arguments neglect, however, is the fact that teachers stand to benefit in a number of ways from implementing the fruits of research. Possessing specialized domain-specific knowledge would raise teacher professional status and, perhaps more importantly, improved effectiveness in the classroom would yield the rich psychic rewards associated with accomplishment. Further, teachers have virtually nothing to lose from the venture, given the fact that the financial costs of professional development are borne largely by schools and districts, which also spend millions of dollars annually on bonuses for teachers who have completed professional training and coursework. Resistance to research, we might conclude, is hardly a compelling explanation.

The real force keeping educational scholarship from entering K–12 classrooms, it turns out, is not the absence of practicable knowledge or a lack of teacher interest. Instead, it is rooted in a fundamental separation of the capacities and influence needed to move research into practice. Specifically, while American teachers are in a perfect position to influence the instructional core of the classroom, they generally lack the capacity to engage with educational scholarship. And for policy makers, the opposite is true: they are well situated to connect with the ivory tower and evaluate its products, but they are quite poorly positioned to affect the instructional core. Each half of the puzzle, in other words, exists separately from the other.

Several different factors explain this state of affairs. Consider, for instance, the culture of classroom instruction. Undergirded by many generations of American history—to say nothing of inherited European intellectual, social, and religious traditions—the work of the teacher is commonly understood to be content delivery.[6] Specifically, teachers are expected to monitor and evaluate students as they collectively engage with culturally valued texts and seemingly objective knowledge. They are not, however, expected to manage their own professional growth, develop new practices, or tap scholarship for their own use.

This cultural bequest, in turn, is reflected and strengthened by the structure of teacher training and development. Teachers are prepared for tasks like the design of curricula and assessments, and they receive substantial instruction in their content areas. But they are not trained to scrutinize research or transform the profession. Once on the job, teachers face similar limitations. Professional development is conducted on rare occasions when students stay home for the day, or in the week leading up to the opening of the school year. And when it does happen, it usually takes the form of "one shot" workshops commonly found by educational researchers to be ineffective.[7]

The cultural inheritance of the teaching profession also manifests in the structure of the teacher workday. Teachers are commonly responsible for five classes, as well as a set of supervisory tasks, with only one "prep" period left for lesson planning, grading assignments, or meeting with students. Time is rarely carved out for teachers to meet, whether by academic department or as a whole faculty, and when meetings do occur they are largely for the purpose of administrative communication.

These structural constraints, while not entirely unique to American schools, are far from an international norm. Teachers in Japan, South Korea, and Singapore, for instance, spend roughly one-third of the workday teaching, freeing up sizeable blocks of time for professional development opportunities. And in many nations, teachers participate in ongoing professional development for up to one hundred hours each year.[8]

All of this means that American teachers, who are quite capable in a number of important respects, have relatively low capacity for consuming university-produced scholarship. But that alone is not a full explanation. After all, that is true in many countries with similar cultural traditions and structural frameworks. Yet it is also frequently the case in such countries that central ministries of education control key aspects of the system like preservice preparation, the K–12 curriculum, and teacher evaluation. The state exerts a great deal of control over what educators know and how they teach—offering a clear mechanism for channeling research into practice.[9]

In the United States, however, the legacy of local control and systemic decentralization is strong, severely limiting the control that policy makers might hope to gain over the instructional core. Without a doubt, much has changed over the last quarter-century. In the past two decades, states have asserted significant authority over schools and districts. And more recently, the federal government has extended its reach in education—even suggesting incursions into teacher training. Nevertheless, local control over education remains powerfully rooted in policy structures, as well as in the American imagination.

The American culture of local control, in turn, is reflected in physical and policy structures. The standards and accountability movements, for instance, may have changed power structures vis-à-vis *what* is taught, but school-level actors continue to exercise great autonomy with regard to *how* things are taught. And when teachers close their classroom doors, they are the ultimate arbiters of teaching method. They control the core.

Collectively, these structural and cultural components foster an environment highly inhospitable for moving educational scholarship—whether quantitative or qualitative, theoretical or empirical—into teacher practice. And the upshot is that those with the least capacity to critically consume research have the greatest power to implement it. That, obviously, is a problem. But changing this particularly problematic state of affairs would require extensive, extended, and coordinated effort. It would require not just restructuring American education, but also—and simultaneously—*re-culturing* it. It's no wonder, then, that so much educational research fails to dent the common knowledge base of working K–12 teachers.

But what if moving educational scholarship into practice were not entirely dependent on such radical transformation?

As the cases in this book reveal, scholarship can move from the ivory tower into the professional knowledge base of teachers if it possesses a unique set of attributes—attributes that would be unnecessary were there greater overlap between those with the capacity for consuming research and those with control over implementation. Such qualities give teachers greater access to research without altering fundamental conditions like their training, their proximity to scholarship, their professional dispositions, their working conditions, or their peer networks. These characteristics function like genetic mutations in an adaptive organism struggling for survival in an inhospitable environment.

FOUR KEY CHARACTERISTICS

If educational scholarship is to overcome the barriers keeping it out of K–12 classrooms, it must possess a core of crucial characteristics that compensate for the lack of a research-to-practice pathway. It must, in other words, do for *itself* what in more conducive systems would be done for it.

This does not mean that all pieces of boundary-crossing research look identical; the characteristics can be brought to life in different forms or amounts. It does mean, however, that whatever the strength of its research base, a scholarly idea must possess all four attributes in some robust way if teachers are to notice, accept, use, and share it.

So what are these attributes?

The first is what might be termed *perceived significance*. In a sea of possibilities, teachers are interested in research that matters—research that seems to deal with crucial topics and appears to have produced robust findings. Given the specificity and theoretical orientation of most educational scholarship, however, very little of it tends to meet the former of those two criteria. And although teachers are concerned with research quality, they rarely have the time or training to track recent developments, assess methodologies, or critically evaluate findings. Consequently, in order for scholarship to gain traction with teachers, it must send a clear signal that it answers a question central to the profession—offering a big-picture understanding rather than merely one small piece of a larger puzzle. And it must send a practitioner-friendly signal of its scholarly merits—something often, if poorly, measured by proxies like the prestige of a scholar's university affiliation.

The second characteristic highlighted in this book is *philosophical compatibility*. Given the lack of overlap between those with the capacity to consume research and those with the power to implement it, a divide exists between outsiders and insiders. With few exceptions, scholars develop different kinds of professional identities than classroom teachers do, they are drawn to their work for different reasons, and they face different realities each day. Such beliefs are the product of different forms of professional socialization, and different personal and work-specific experience.[10] The result is that teachers generally possess a common core of interests, anxieties, attitudes, and values distinct to them as a group and that organize the way they see the world. Scholars, as outsiders to this world, all too often fail to send the right signals in their research. In fact, potentially relevant scholarship is frequently rejected on its premises, or even perceived as offensive, because it violates certain fundamental beliefs. A signal of philosophical compatibility, conversely, can function like a secret handshake—entrance into the club. For scholarship to bridge the divide, then, it must clearly jibe with closely held beliefs like the idea that teachers are professionals, or that all children can learn. Only then does the difference between insiders and outsiders dissolve enough for scholarship to become tenable among practitioners.

The third crucial characteristic detailed here is *occupational realism*— the degree to which research is easily put into immediate use. Were there a stronger structural connection between scholarship and practice, occupational realism would be a nonissue; research would be tailored thoughtfully for classrooms, and practice would be shaped around the aim of utilizing scholarship. In lieu of that, however, research must fit the occupational constraints within which teachers operate, particularly those related to time. According to the National Education Association, teachers work an average of fifty-two hours per week—thirty-seven during the required school day and the rest in lesson planning, grading student work, and performing administrative duties.[11] And according to the Organisation for Economic Co-operation and Development, American educators teach an average of 25–30 percent more hours than their counterparts in member nations.[12] Consequently, if research is going to be put to classroom use, it must take shape in a form that does not require extensive training or an overhaul of existing practices. A set of new questions for use alongside an established curriculum, for instance, is far more likely to gain traction than, say, an entirely new set of instructional objectives.

The fourth and final characteristic that this work identifies is what might be called *transportability*. In the absence of more centralized and top-down conduits for moving research into practice, this trait is what allows ideas to move—from research into practice, but also from teacher to teacher. Without it, only the most diligent educators gain access to research, poring over complex scholarship and spending long hours in working to share it with others. When an idea is transportable, though—because of a simple core easily conveyed to teachers, because of accessible language, or because of the ability to translate it into lasting structures like curriculum frameworks—it can travel through preservice coursework, professional development seminars, independent study, and peer networks. It exists, as Cynthia Coburn and colleagues put it, in a form teachers "can access and use at the time that they need it."[13] A concept made up of five simple elements, in other words, is far more likely to move across settings than one made up of fifty, or even fifteen, richly described parts.

Possessing these four characteristics does not guarantee that an idea will move beyond rhetoric and achieve a life in classrooms. As the subsequent case studies in this book reveal, there is still an element of luck, accident, and effort involved in any complex process. Yet these traits are crucial for moving scholarship into practice in the American educational system because they compensate for weak linkages between the ivory tower and the schoolhouse. Without question, these four characteristics do so imperfectly. But they are promising enough to warrant closer attention—not only with regard to how they function currently, but also with an eye toward how they might be developed and enhanced.

THE ORGANIZATION OF THE BOOK

The heart of this book is an examination of four exemplary ideas—scholarship generated in the research university—that gained a foothold in the knowledge base of classroom teachers. *Exemplary*, in this usage, should not be taken to mean that these ideas have been implemented with perfect faithfulness in the K–12 environment, or that they have always made instruction better. They have not, and this book considers several explanations for why that is. Still, a strong argument can be made for the status of these as exemplars, particularly given the context of widespread failure in which they must be viewed. When so much research goes completely unrecognized by working educators, these four ideas have penetrated the professional knowledge base of classroom teachers and persisted.

As readers will quickly notice, the book is organized around case studies. There are two reasons for this. The first is that the ideas at the heart of this project are, in a number of important ways, quite different from one another and must be recognized as such. They are the products of highly distinct histories spanning the twentieth century, reflecting different time periods as well as unique historical contingencies. They also represent different kinds of research ideas. Bloom's taxonomy, for instance, focuses on the nature of knowledge, while Howard Gardner's theory of multiple intelligences focuses on cognition. The project method addresses what students should be doing in the classroom, while Direct Instruction addresses what *teachers* should be doing in the classroom. Other differences—regional origins, teacher cooperation, and methodological underpinnings, to name a few—abound. Thus, if we are to learn anything from these cases, and if their lessons are to be persuasive, we must consider them in sufficient depth and detail.

The second reason for such organization is that while this book is primarily concerned with the connection between research and practice, these cases may also serve additional purposes. They offer particular insight, for instance, into the structure and culture of the teaching profession—the daily demands of the job, the opportunities for professional growth, the ways that teachers see the world, and the way that teachers exert authority. The cases are also revealing about the nature of professional development—why it looks the way it does, why it so often disappoints, and why it might succeed. They provide a window into educational policy making, as well as a perspective on why policy so frequently fails to penetrate the black box of the classroom.[14] And they delineate the powers and limitations of various actors—at the school, district, state, and federal levels—for affecting the inner worlds and outward actions of teachers. In short, these cases can teach us much about the systems, structures, and actors shaping K–12 education in the United States.

Whatever its various potential uses, this book focuses primarily on the connection between educational scholarship and the knowledge base of teachers. Therefore, while it offers detailed case studies of several exemplary ideas, it also presents a distinct analysis across chapters. Specifically, it highlights the importance of the four key characteristics outlined in this introduction, detailing their role in moving ideas from research into practice. Accordingly, the first four chapters of the book—on Bloom's taxonomy, the theory of multiple intelligences, the project method, and Direct Instruction, respectively—illustrate how each idea gained traction in the world of practice as a product of its perceived significance, philosophical compatibility, occupational realism, and transportability.

To better understand the characteristics crucial for moving scholarship into practice, this book also looks at another set of ideas: those that, surprisingly, did *not* gain traction in practice. After all, if certain characteristics are indeed crucial, then their absence will be as telling as their presence. The fifth chapter of the book, consequently, examines several ideas that, though similar in many ways to the ideas explored earlier in the work, failed to penetrate practice. The Taxonomy of Educational Objectives for the Affective Domain (Krathwohl's taxonomy), for instance, was a companion volume to Bloom's taxonomy, and yet is rarely recognized by teachers and seldom mentioned in curriculum guides or assessment frameworks. Robert Sternberg's triarchic theory, though similar in nature to Howard Gardner's theory of multiple intelligences and often taught alongside it in departments of education, has made only shallow inroads into schools. Generative learning, despite its similarity to the equally constructivist project method, can hardly be said to have impacted instructional practice. And, the behavior analysis model, unlike its fellow "basic skills model" Direct Instruction, never moved much beyond the experimental federal research program of which both were a part.

These eight ideas, as most scholars and educators will quickly recognize, are not encyclopedic in their breadth. Nor do they constitute the sum total of all educational scholarship to gain, or fail to gain, traction in the schoolhouse. They are, however, exemplary cases that reveal a great deal about classroom teachers, educational researchers, and policy elites. And, perhaps more significantly, they offer an extraordinarily clear view of the research-to-practice pathway in education—highlighting not just problems, but also possibilities.

LOOKING BACKWARD, MOVING FORWARD

As this brief introduction should make clear, the most upbeat explanation for why some ideas migrate into classrooms and take hold—"cream rises to the top"—is inaccurate. In a different system—one with clear and robust links between the worlds of research and practice—such an ideal scenario might play out. Reality, however, is more complex.

In the American educational system, those with the greatest capacity for consuming research inhabit a circle almost entirely separate from that occupied by those with the power of classroom implementation. As a result, educational scholarship moves into practice only if it possesses certain characteristics that function like genetic mutations—fortuitous and often unplanned elements that enable an idea to move across a hostile terrain despite the absence of a clear research-to-practice pathway.

The hazard in this, of course, is that the ideas most likely to enter into practice are not necessarily the best products of scholarship. And conversely—as well as more commonly—the best products of scholarship may not possess the characteristics crucial for movement into practice. Additionally, given that the characteristics are rarely cultivated intentionally and energetically, scholarship may enter classrooms only to be watered down or shallowly implemented.

Still, while no streamlined conduit exists to move scholarship into the classroom, the cases considered in this work also reveal that the most downbeat explanation—"never the twain shall meet"—is also inaccurate. Educational research can enter the common knowledge base of teachers if the right conditions are met, even if the fundamental conditions separating the two worlds remain unchanged. Unintended consequences certainly abound, with shallow understandings of ideas and dubious reinterpretations of them raising important questions about whether research actually *does* enter into practice. Yet such side effects are not preordained, and there's much that scholars, educators, and policy makers can do to mitigate unintended consequences. Working together, they might promote a stronger and more sustained connection between scholarship and the knowledge base of practitioners.

Coordinated action among scholars, teachers, and policy makers might seem improbable. At a time of great discord in American education—when teachers and their unions are often presented as the enemies of reform, policy makers are viewed by teachers as out of line and out of touch, and scholars are seen by both parties as irrelevant—the coordination required for such a venture represents both a practical and a political challenge. Yet all parties stand to benefit from effectively moving research beyond the walls of the ivory tower and into the schoolhouse, and insofar as that is the case, it may represent a realm of potential consensus.

Thus, although this book is informed by the past, it is oriented toward the future. Structured around historical case studies, it looks back across the previous century, documenting problems and possibilities, and seeking to draw from it some kind of order. At the same time, this book seeks to chart a path ahead—describing the kinds of practices and perspectives that can connect scholars and teachers, and in so doing enrich the work of both groups. This is the chief aim of the book's concluding chapter.

To be clear: linking research and practice is not a panacea for all that complicates the work of educating the nation's millions. Yet the ability to move university-produced scholarship into classrooms does hold the potential to promote change in a positive direction. It might, for instance, help teachers develop new practices by giving them new ideas and providing them with a strong justification for violating tradition. It might serve as a mechanism for filtering the floods of reform that emanate from federal, state, and district offices—curtailing ineffective proposals and generally reducing volume. And it might even revitalize the work of other parties involved in the process: scholars, labor unions, professional development providers, and teacher education programs.

Perhaps more importantly, though, moving research into practice has the potential to shift the dominant narrative around American education from one of swift regress to one of slow and steady progress. The notion that schools are stuck in the past, resistant to change, and inept at innovation is a powerful validation for an aggressive reform movement initiated by outsiders in top-down fashion. Such efforts invariably fail, provide the basis for further indictments of the schools, and lead inexorably to more policy churn. These repeated assaults on the public schools, whatever their intended consequences, also result in significant collateral damage to teacher morale, administrator autonomy, and parental commitment.

The project of exploring the connection between research and practice, then, is not merely a matter of fiddling around the margins of K–12 education. Rather, it is at the core of the broader effort to reconceptualize the nature of school reform. Research-informed practice represents a way to renew a sense of common purpose in the enterprise of American public education, and it offers a means of moving incrementally forward. And, insofar as that is the case, it may also represent our best hope of restoring the long-eroding public faith in our nation's schools—a faith without which our schools simply cannot succeed.

"I Have Heard the Phrase Quite a Bit"

Bloom's Taxonomy

W hy have teachers heard of Bloom's taxonomy?

The vast majority of educational research fails to move even marginally beyond the walls of the ivory tower. Yet somehow the Taxonomy of Educational Objectives for the Cognitive Domain—informally known for its lead editor, Benjamin Bloom—entered the common knowledge base of working teachers and stuck there. Knowledge, comprehension, application, analysis, synthesis, evaluation—the levels of the taxonomy—tend to roll, rapid-fire, off the tongues of the initiated. Colorful pyramids depicting the taxonomy adorn classroom walls. Curriculum rubrics teem with references to it. And professional development seminars often begin, and end, with Bloom.

It may be an overstatement to call the taxonomy, as some have, "the basis for much of the curriculum making for the last half-century."[1] Nevertheless, such claims underscore the idea's visibility and staying power. Half a century after its creation, Bloom's taxonomy appears in teacher training classes, in-service programming, curriculum guides, and lesson plans across the nation—all this despite the fact that Bloom and colleagues never set out to create a tool for K–12 educators.

The ubiquity and endurance of Bloom's taxonomy is even more impressive given the diffuse nature of American education—a mosaic of organizations, institutions, and actors, with no clear central authority identifying key concepts or core philosophies. The taxonomy has been used differently, without question, by scholars, curriculum designers, teacher educators, and teachers. And even within each group there is great variation: some teachers, for instance, use it to plan their daily lessons, and others have never used it at all. But whatever the diversity of implementation, the idea that thinking can be divided into six hierarchical categories has become a well-worn truism. It is an idea that nearly everyone in American education is familiar with.

So what explains the tremendous success of Bloom's taxonomy in making the leap from the ivory tower to the schoolhouse? As this chapter reveals, the taxonomy was a unique and provocative idea. Yet that can be said for a great deal of scholarship that never travels beyond a narrow band of educational researchers. Unlike those ideas, however, the taxonomy possessed four crucial characteristics—characteristics that allowed it to exceed all initial expectations. To understand the success of the taxonomy, then, we need to trace the full arc of its development, considering not just how it acquired those characteristics but also the role they played in its eventual place in the lives and minds of K–12 teachers.

MAKING A TAXONOMY

Bloom's taxonomy was hardly his alone. While Benjamin Bloom—a testing expert and later a professor at the University of Chicago—was the undisputed leader of the group that published its framework of objectives in 1956, the effort engaged faculty and staff from over a dozen colleges and universities. Further, though the meetings that directly led to the creation of the taxonomy began in 1948, the roots of the idea actually stretched back a quarter-century earlier—to an effort to determine what, exactly, is worth knowing. And, while the taxonomy would ultimately have its greatest impact in K–12 schools, it was without question the distinct product of debates about the purpose of American higher education.

In 1929, Robert Maynard Hutchins assumed the presidency of the University of Chicago. In keeping with a sentiment among faculty that programs should be restructured to give "the student an opportunity . . . to assume full responsibility for his own education," Hutchins began a push for a reorganization that would emphasize general education.[2] Proposing a number of structural reforms that built on the conceptual framework established by former president Chauncey Boucher, Hutchins transformed undergraduate education at Chicago. In 1931, the university adopted the "New Plan of General Education," which established a core series of survey courses. The plan was to allow students control over their course selection while simultaneously mandating familiarity with a broad range of content. In so doing, the plan also eliminated grades for the new courses, favoring comprehensive subject exams designed to measure student achievement.[3]

The faculty, according to Bloom, believed that separating teaching from testing would foster more ideal student-teacher relationships. And, by setting degree requirements solely in terms of performance on comprehensive exams—not coursework or seat time—they sought to foster in students a sense of motivation and accountability, as well as to preserve the ideal of a well-rounded student in an age of creeping specialization. A Board of Examinations was created to administer and oversee the examination system.[4]

The question that fell to the newly created Board and its first director, L. L. Thurstone, was what such exams might look like. For the first several years, Thurstone and the Board focused on issues of objectivity, validity, and reliability of measurement. Yet the challenge of crowding an entire year's worth of material into a single test soon began to raise concerns about the nature of exam *content*. Having grown in length to an average of several hundred questions, each test took roughly six hours to complete. Additionally, some faculty members were concerned that if exams focused exclusively on factual information, the college would soon begin to produce graduates "who do nothing but read textbooks."[5] Consequently, many wondered if subject matter knowledge should be the primary outcome of instruction, and by extension, the primary focus of examination.[6]

With content knowledge virtually limitless, and instructors determined to teach students something more than how to train their memories, the examiners proposed an alternative. "Examinations should place emphasis on the student's ability to reason with the principles of his subject," they proposed in 1933, "rather than the ability merely to repeat factual material by rote memory."[7]

Debates about what should be taught and tested coincided with the hiring of Ralph Tyler as the new director of examinations. Tyler, who had directed the evaluation of the Progressive Education Association's Eight-Year Study—an experimental program designed to challenge traditional curricular practices—became university examiner in 1938, and brought with him a particular vision rooted in the belief that tests could be designed only once clear educational objectives were established. As Tyler later wrote in his classic 1949 treatise on curriculum design, "The real purpose of education is not to have the instructor perform certain activities but to bring about significant changes in the student's pattern of behavior." Consequently, he argued, any statement of teaching objectives "should be a statement of changes to take place in the student."[8] Work on identifying such aims was well under way at the University of Chicago by the time that Bloom, Tyler's doctoral student, became coexaminer in 1943.[9]

Members of the University of Chicago Board of Examinations were not alone in seeking to identify clear educational objectives. Distinct but related work, often under the banner of "general education," was being conducted at other colleges and universities, where advocates worked to defend a broad liberal arts education against curricular fragmentation and specialization—trends driven by public demand as well as by the rise of what Clark Kerr would later call the "multiversity."[10] As Alvin Eurich of Stanford University put it in 1939, "'general education' is a term that symbolizes a current groundswell in American colleges and universities."[11]

Yet, despite such a groundswell, there was little progress in terms of collectively identifying learning objectives that would reflect an ideal of well-rounded scholarship. How could general education be defended if its proponents could not commonly define it and articulate its benefit to students? In 1934, the Institute for Administrative Officers of Higher

Institutions met to work on *A New Definition of General Education*. Unable to formulate such a definition, the group changed the title of its proceedings to *General Education: Its Nature, Scope, and Essential Elements*.[12] Most schools, without zealous leaders like Hutchins driving them forward, simply gave up on an effort that was often as unpopular as it was difficult.[13]

Aware that others were interested in such work, Bloom sought to expand upon what he and Tyler were doing at Chicago by connecting with examiners from other schools.[14] Such efforts began informally: at the 1948 convention of the American Psychological Association (APA), Bloom and several colleagues from other institutions began discussing the possibility of creating a framework for facilitating communication among them.[15] Over the course of the next few years, Bloom and colleagues met periodically, with the aim of establishing a common language about learning goals and a basis for curricular decisions.[16] But eventually, at Bloom's urging, the group's aim became more ambitious: classifying educational goals and objectives, across institutions, for the cognitive, affective, and psychomotor domains.

Working from the ground up, the group gathered learning objectives in use at colleges and universities and distilled them into six primary categories. Together, they arranged their categories in order—from the simple to the complex. But it was Bloom alone who pushed the group to identify their end product as a *taxonomy*. The term had clear implications about the seemingly scientific, hierarchical, and universal nature of their work—and it squared with the ambitious vision that Bloom articulated at a 1949 conference: "A taxonomy of educational outcomes could do much to bring order out of chaos in the field of education. It could furnish the conceptual framework around which our descriptions of educational programs and experiences could be oriented. It could furnish a framework for the development of educational theories and research. It could furnish the scheme needed for training our teachers and for orienting them to the varied possibilities of education."[17]

The product was primarily intended for a relatively narrow audience—its architects, after all, were still referring to it as the "examiner's taxonomy."[18] Still, there was a sense that, if properly framed, the taxonomy might do more than just structure exam questions. And Bloom pushed the group to consider the full extent of their potential influence.

In 1951, the group presented a draft of their "Taxonomy of Educational Objectives" to the APA convention. Motivated by a positive reception, they shrewdly followed with a print run of one thousand copies of what they had begun referring to as "the Handbook," which they then distributed to their peers in higher education, as well as to curriculum professionals working in the K–12 world. Those receiving copies of the taxonomy included 162 members of the Testing, Measurement, and Evaluation division of the APA, 155 members of the National Society for the Study of Education, 87 directors of statewide testing programs and their staff, 62 members of the Association for Supervision and Curriculum Development (ASCD), and 36 Illinois curriculum workers.[19] Sent as a draft for comment, it produced few. But as Bloom's collaborator David Krathwohl recalled, the move "enlarged the base of individuals who were aware that the taxonomy existed so that when they or their colleagues needed it, they knew where to find it."[20] In short, it prompted discussion about the significance of a work that otherwise might have gone unnoticed.

In 1956 the Committee of College and University Examiners—now consisting of Benjamin Bloom, Max Engelhart, Edward Furst, Walker Hill, and David Krathwohl—published its final draft, edited by Bloom. The *Taxonomy of Educational Objectives, the Classification of Educational Goals, Handbook I: Cognitive Domain* was a thoroughly considered product. Beyond merely outlining the six categories of cognitive performance, the work explained the history of the project, the philosophy behind it, the research base underpinning it, the potential uses for it, and its invariable shortcomings.

The bulk of the text, which ran to roughly two hundred pages and was divided into two parts—"Introduction and Explanation" and "The Taxonomy and Illustrative Materials"—was dedicated to Part II. The section moved methodically through the categories of Knowledge, Comprehension, Application, Analysis, Synthesis, and Evaluation, introducing each term, dividing it into its constituent parts, explaining those parts, and outlining a manner of testing. And each section ended with a series of "illustrative test items."

The treatment given each category was extensive. Still, each could be summarized, as well as understood through example test questions. Knowledge, for instance, consisted of "those behaviors and test situations which emphasize the remembering, either by recognition or recall, of ideas, material, or phenomena."[21] A model question asked students what Jean Valjean was first sentenced to the galleys for stealing. Multiple-choice answers included:

1. the Bishop's candlesticks.
2. a loaf of bread.
3. a few sticks of wood.
4. a widow's cow.
5. the cloth from off the altar.
    Answer: a loaf of bread.

Next on the list was comprehension, described as "probably the largest general class of intellectual abilities and skills emphasized in schools and colleges."[22] Comprehension, as Bloom and colleagues described it, meant understanding "the literal message contained in a communication."[23] A sample test question asked students to read an excerpt written by René Descartes, to "state which of his explanations are still accepted as valid, and indicate which of his explanations are no longer accepted."[24]

Application—third on the list—required a "step beyond" comprehension.[25] Students faced with new problems would apply appropriate knowledge in order to solve them. Further, they would do so "without having to be prompted as to which abstraction is correct or without having to be shown how to use it in that situation."[26] A sample question asked students to apply their knowledge of atmosphere to explain why a sunbather would be more likely to suffer a severe sunburn in the middle of the day.[27]

The fuzziest category in the taxonomy was analysis. Analysis, according to Bloom and colleagues, "emphasizes the breakdown of the material into its constituent parts and detection of the relationships of the parts and of the way they are organized."[28] While noting that no clear line could be drawn "between analysis and comprehension at one end or between analysis and evaluation at the other," they identified it as the domain in which students distinguish fact from hypothesis, identify conclusions and evidence, and determine relevance and interrelation.[29] At this fourth taxonomic level, test questions asked students to identify assumptions, distinguish "logical conclusions" of arguments, and determine the function of particular passages. One particular question asked students to select "the best description of the article as a whole."[30]

Synthesis, the fifth level, was identified in the taxonomy as the "putting together of elements and parts so as to form a whole."[31] Through pattern making and structure building, students operating at the synthesis level would recombine parts of previous experience with new material into "a new and more or less well-integrated whole."[32] In a sample test item asking students to write a paper on the question of the future of private property in America, students were instructed that their work "must include a discussion of the moral bases and social effects of the kind of ownership which you favor or wish to attack . . . must relate your thesis to the arguments pro and con of the *passages* distributed before the examination which are relevant to your position . . . must show some *application* of your theoretical position to one or more examples of property rights drawn from your own experience, observation, or reading . . . [and] should be clear, interesting, and acceptable to the *audience* to which it is addressed." Acceptable work, as the authors noted, also needed to be "effectively organized and well written."[33]

The last stage—the highest level of the taxonomy—was evaluation. Students working at this level would make "judgments about the value, for some purpose, of ideas, works, solutions, methods, material, etc."[34] Listed last because it ostensibly required the use of other categories of cognitive behavior, evaluation meant appraising the accuracy, effectiveness, efficiency, or performance of a particular product. Model questions at the level of evaluation were lengthy, presenting scenarios like: "For items 6–11, assume that in doing research for a paper about the English language you find a statement by Otto Jespersen which contradicts some point of view on language which you have always accepted. Indicate which of the statements would be significant in determining the value of Jespersen's statement."[35] Another sample test question asked students to evaluate a sonnet in "an essay of from 250 to 500 words." Students were instructed to "employ such terms as will reveal your recognition of formal characteristics of the poem" and to make clear the "principles of evaluation" being used.[36]

Bloom did note that evaluation was "not necessarily the last step in thinking," and that it could often function as the "prelude to the acquisition of new knowledge, a new attempt at comprehension or application, or a new analysis and synthesis."[37] Still, the taxonomy sent a distinct message about the purpose of education. Students might begin by identifying Michael Drayton as the author of "Since There's No Help," moving on to describe the poem's meaning and distinguish it as a sonnet. Eventually, however, an ideal classroom would produce students who would argue for or against the beauty of the poem based on criteria like its theme, rhyme scheme, language, and use of imagery.

"A USEFUL TOOL FOR EDUCATIONAL RESEARCH WORKERS"

The *Taxonomy of Educational Objectives, Handbook I: Cognitive Domain* was not an immediate sensation. It was, however, widely reviewed in scholarly publications and quickly adopted into relevant education subfields. Gradually, educational researchers, test developers, and curriculum designers integrated the taxonomy into their work, as well—ensuring that it would have a life beyond that of an in-house publication at the University of Chicago. Thus, as the taxonomy entered into the institutional framework of schooling, it not only moved closer to teachers but also seemed to grow in significance.

To be clear, the taxonomy did have some early appeal to those interested in classroom practice. One of the first reviews of it, for instance, appeared in the journal *Improving College and University Teaching*.[38] Typical, however, was a 1957 review in the *Elementary School Journal* that focused on the taxonomy's implications for test design and examination. "The book should facilitate communication about objectives and about how to assess attainment of them," reviewer E. I. Sawin wrote, "particularly among examiners and others specializing in educational assessment." It should also, he observed, "provide a stimulus for more comprehensive development and evaluation of objectives."[39] It did not discuss the implications for classroom teaching.

Whatever its appeal to those working across various fields, the taxonomy was most easily absorbed by those in higher education and those working on questions of measurement and evaluation. In part, this was the result of the nature of the taxonomy—a relatively technical piece of scholarship produced by a group of college and university examiners. This was foreseen by Bloom and colleagues, who observed that they had hoped to create a "useful tool for educational research workers."[40] Additionally, it reflected systemic differences in capacity for absorbing new knowledge, as well as distinct incentive structures. As professional consumers and producers of research, scholars and experts had only to align the taxonomy with other research in their domain. They could quickly integrate it into existing frameworks, or, engaging it more directly, test it in various applications, compare it with other schemas, manipulate it, amend it, and appraise it. For professionals, being familiar with the taxonomy was a means of staying current in the field. And for those seeking to expand their research agendas or land a publication or two, it was something new to test, challenge, apply, or reinterpret.

In the decade after its release, scholars conducted dozens of research projects focusing on the taxonomy, most of which concerned testing and test design. Julian C. Stanley and Dale Bolton, for instance, wrote "A Review of 'Bloom's Taxonomy of Educational Objectives' and J. R. Gerberich's 'Specimen Objective Tests Items: A Guide to Achievement Test Construction'" in 1957—perhaps the earliest reference to the work as "Bloom's," and appearing just one year after the taxonomy's publication.[41] Other early applications in the realm of testing included publications by Leon Lessinger, by Robert W. McFall, and several by Russell P. Kropp and Howard W. Stoker.[42]

By the mid-1960s, scholars began to expand their studies of the taxonomy, which was adaptable for multiple uses. And most interestingly, many began to explore applications to the K–12 classroom. Some of these scholars were from the field of testing and evaluation, interested in teacher-designed tests and the ways that practitioners established pedagogical objectives.[43] But many were policy-oriented researchers, teacher educators, or curriculum specialists. Some sought to align the recommendations of national education committees with the cognitive objectives outlined in the taxonomy.[44] Others used it to categorize the kinds of questions teachers asked.[45] And some scholars took interest in the ways that it might be used to more effectively design lessons.[46] Whatever the angle they took, 118 research projects examining the taxonomy were conducted by 1970.[47]

Scholars in colleges and universities, mostly writing with and for each other, were hardly alone in exploring the practical uses to which the taxonomy might be put. Practitioners in the field of test design, whether in state departments of education, consulting firms, or private agencies, also saw in the taxonomy a means of advancing their work. As Bloom and colleagues commented in 1964, "The Taxonomy has been of value in classifying test material for exchange among test workers and as a basis for reviewing and criticizing standardized tests."[48] The observation was confirmed by a set of researchers who noted, "Since its publication, the Taxonomy has received increasing use by test and measurement and curriculum specialists."[49]

The taxonomy also began to make inroads among curriculum developers as they pursued more systematic and scientific approaches to their work in the 1960s.[50] The taxonomy, after all, was well covered by scholarly literature in the field and was easy to adapt to the work of K–12 curriculum design. Hence, the taxonomy soon became a "common referent" in the field.[51] The Biological Science Curriculum Study began to use the taxonomy for planning evaluations.[52] Several school districts in California, as well as the state department of education, began using the taxonomy to design lessons and academic programs.[53] In 1966, the Los Angeles City Schools published *The Art of Questioning in Reading*—an "instructional bulletin for workshop use to assist teachers in developing thought-provoking questions." Derived from the Taxonomy of Educational Objectives, the bulletin illustrated "the possible use of a taxonomy of questions in the classroom."[54] And just north in Oregon, the Portland Public School System developed an in-service training program for using the taxonomy to plan courses.[55]

All of these developments pushed the taxonomy in the direction of the classroom. Some scholars and professional groups even began to suggest that the taxonomy might be of direct use to K–12 teachers. Ambrose Clegg, for instance, believed that the taxonomy should be taught to students in teacher preparation programs as a part of their professional training.[56] Most documented uses of the taxonomy in teacher education programs in the 1960s, however, employed it as a means of analyzing the questions asked by teacher educators and novice teachers.[57] The ASCD Commission on Teacher Education, for instance, made early use of the taxonomy, but did so as a means of classifying the educational objectives of teacher training programs.[58]

Still, the taxonomy had several advantages that allowed it to continue expanding beyond its original use as an "examiner's" tool. Key among those advantages was its transportability. The taxonomy moved easily because it was easy to understand. It had scholarly legitimacy, certainly—a matter of critical importance—but it could also be clearly conveyed to K–12 test developers or curriculum designers. As one of Bloom's research assistants later reported back to him, the taxonomy was transported at the K–12 level through mechanisms like a "Pac-Man desk aid" for students, as well as through teachers' guides like the "Suggested Method for Introducing Bloom to Students—15 days, 15 minutes a day."[59] As a result, the taxonomy continued to establish footholds in closer proximity to K–12 teachers, growing in perceived significance as it inched closer to the classroom. By the 1970s and 80s, as one author noted, teachers would begin coming of age "not only familiar with and 'acceptant' of the general categories of the Taxonomy, but also persuaded that the Taxonomy's identified higher-order skills . . . are essential to education at all levels."[60]

But before we explore that part of the story, it is important to take a step back and examine the broad appeal of the taxonomy—an idea that somehow had the power to generate multiple constituencies without sparking opposition.

A PROGRESSIVE TRADITIONALISM

The work of Bloom and colleagues was highly specific to their particular needs as examiners in colleges and universities. And yet, the taxonomy also tapped into broader educational concerns that made it relevant for a much wider audience. It did so only implicitly, but that was to its advantage. Multiple, and even oppositional, constituencies could read their particular viewpoints into the taxonomy, and they could do so without being directly confronted by ideas hostile to their perspectives. This combination—of ideological openness and perceived substance—made the taxonomy philosophically compatible among a range of actors and allowed it to slowly take root. It won supporters, but more importantly, it rarely developed an opposition.

One audience for the taxonomy was among those who believed that the purpose of schooling was not to assist children in the acquisition of information, but rather to develop among them the ability to grow intellectually. Often self-identifying as "progressives," such educators did not read into the taxonomy something that was not there. On the contrary, the idea of growth was a core concern in the crafting of the taxonomy. As Bloom wrote: "Much emphasis must be placed in schools on the development of generalized ways of attacking problems and on knowledge which can be applied to a wide range of new situations. That is, we have the task of preparing individuals for problems that cannot be foreseen in advance, and about all that can be done under such conditions is to help the student acquire generalized intellectual abilities and skills which will serve him well in many new situations."[61]

It was hardly a paean to the work of progressives like John Dewey and George Counts. Still, it echoed the emphasis placed by pedagogical progressives on intellectual growth over the acquisition of mere facts.

Beyond tapping into a belief widely shared by progressive educators about the importance of intellectual growth, the taxonomy also seemed to offer a means of promoting that aim in education. The progressive message had major traction with educators, whom it cast not merely as labor implementing the curriculum, but as experts helping children develop. Consequently, even as the progressive movement ebbed in the 1950s, its basic tenets persisted as a powerful undercurrent, and the concept of student growth maintained a strong appeal for teachers.[62] Thus, though the Progressive Education Association folded in 1955, organizations like the National Education Association continued to assert that the central purpose of American education should be "the development of the ability to think."[63]

The problem, however, was that progressive pedagogy often failed to provide educators with the same degree of structure and direction that the formal curriculum had. As a result, pedagogical progressivism had trouble making a lasting penetration into the classroom.[64] As one author observed, "A half-century of educational literature suggests that the main emphasis in schools is teaching children *facts*, even though teachers and curriculum designers attest to the importance of teaching children *thinking*."[65] Studies from the 1960s found that roughly two-thirds of questions required students to recall facts, whereas only 20 percent required students to "think"—figures consistent with research from half a century earlier.[66]

The taxonomy appealed to teachers sympathetic to the progressive aim of development, and particularly to those frustrated by the paucity of clear instruction about how to promote that aim. A focus on a finite number of thinking skills made progressivism practical. Teachers could gear questions toward various levels of thought, create developmentally appropriate assignments, and lace their lesson plans with specific references to the taxonomy.

But what made the taxonomy particularly unique was that, unlike other progressive-tinged ideas, it was not a direct attack on the traditional curriculum. The taxonomy, after all, was not explicitly tied to any theory of learning. Consequently, while some interpreted it as an extension of progressivism, others saw nothing of the sort.

Progressivism had long faced opposition from scholars like William Bagley, Albert Lynd, and Arthur Bestor. As Elliot Eisner put it, such critics viewed the work of pedagogical progressives as "laissez-faire, mindless, and without purpose or direction."[67] But that had not always been the case. As Bestor wrote in *Educational Wastelands*, progressive education in the 1920s was in his estimation "definitely on the right track."[68] Where it went wrong, however, was in the effort to bypass "essential stages in the process of learning to use the mind," ignoring John Dewey's dictum that the child could not simply *grow*, but must be guided by the curriculum in a particular direction.[69]

The taxonomy, as Eisner argued, seemed to offer a "corrective for this state of educational affairs."[70] Those concerned with the evaporation of content in the school curriculum could look plainly at the first level of the taxonomy—knowledge—for conciliation. The level upon which all other acts of mind rested, its placement could be read as a clear signal of the importance of content. The taxonomy did seem to emphasize critical thinking skills over the mere acquisition of factual knowledge, but that was not what bothered curricular traditionalists. In fact, as Bestor wrote, "Liberal education is training in thinking . . . not the mere communication of facts."[71] Instead, what bothered them about progressivism was the move "against all reason and experience . . . to train [students] to perform the culminating acts of thought, while skipping all antecedent steps."[72] The taxonomy established those steps, and it did so with factual content at the base.

The taxonomy seemed to reconcile curricular traditionalists and pedagogical progressives. But equally important, it seemed to reconcile traditionalists with an increasingly powerful cadre of so-called administrative progressives.[73] Motivated by concerns with social utility and organizational efficiency, the administrative progressives posed a significant threat to the entire scope and sequence of the American curriculum. Occupying positions at universities, in school districts, and in departments of education, they sought to make the curriculum more varied in order to accommodate different kinds of students, many of whom they viewed as intellectually incapable. And worse, at least in the eyes of many traditionalists, the administrative progressives sought to make the curriculum practical and vocationally oriented.

As much as this shift toward the practical was the product of top-down reform, it was also the result of consumer demand for a practical education—a demand driven by expanding access and a tighter coupling between educational attainment and occupational status. As the authors of a 1938 report by the National Society for the Study of Education wrote, the movement toward "further specialization," was brought on by "a rather sudden shift" in which students began demanding more specialized training for the work force.[74] One post–World War II study, for instance, found that graduates focusing on general, rather than vocational, education were mostly dissatisfied with their programs of study, maintaining a perception that those with specialized training held an advantage, particularly in the business world.[75] These consumer desires were further exacerbated by increasing rates of knowledge production, which forced students to identify areas of specialization early enough in their academic careers to master increasingly complex fields.[76]

All of this, critics insisted, was leading to curricular incoherence at all levels of the education system. Wilford Aikin, in his history of the Eight-Year Study, wrote that by 1930 so many subjects and courses had been added to the high school curriculum that it "resembled a picture puzzle, without consistent plan or purpose."[77] Each student cobbled together the requisite pieces to graduate, but, as Aikin argued, "because neither he nor his teachers had definite, long-time purposes for his work, he had no clear road to follow or compass to guide him in finding his way through the tangled underbrush of the curriculum."[78]

Those who saw the taxonomy as a defense of traditional liberal education, as with their more progressively inclined counterparts, were not reading into the work something that was completely absent. The taxonomy suggested that particular aspects of the knowledge base were prone to change, and that the most practical education was in fact one that prepared students to continue learning. One need only look at the shift in knowledge about the atom, Bloom and colleagues suggested, for evidence that professionals in every field needed to continue learning in order to keep pace with their fields. Others supported this position, making the case that the best training for jobs, even in areas like science and medicine, was a liberal education with no element of vocationalism.[79]

Additionally, those familiar with its history knew that the taxonomy was a product of the general education movement—a movement that, according to one group of supporters, "originated as a reaction against overspecialization and compartmentalization."[80] More specifically, the taxonomy was created at the University of Chicago during the presidency of Robert Maynard Hutchins, who—along with faculty members Mortimer Adler, Scott Buchanan, and Richard McKeon—had pursued high-profile projects focused on the study of the so-called great books of the Western world, and who had made the case in 1936 that general education was "education for everybody, whether he goes on to the university or not."[81] Thus, although the taxonomy was agnostic on the matter of general education, its place of origin carried with it a particular implication.

The consequence of all this was that whatever their positions on the question of what should be taught, those looking to find a particular philosophical or ideological compatibility in the taxonomy could often find it. This was, in part, the result of hopeful readings of the work. But it was also the product of the taxonomy's design, which made it seem extraordinarily evenhanded. As its authors noted, "Neutrality with respect to educational principles and philosophies was to be achieved by constructing a system which, insofar as it was possible, would permit the inclusion of objectives from all educational orientations."[82] Their aim, after all, was to create a "larger synthetic theory of learning" that could be used by all comers, and such an aim could not be achieved if the taxonomy described only the objectives associated with particular ideological orientations.[83]

The result was an idea with broad philosophical appeal. The taxonomy addressed a range of concerns about the curriculum, but it did so without taking sides—reconciling competing visions in a manner that made no enemies among self-identified progressives or curricular traditionalists.

SORTING AND EQUALIZING

Tapping into various perspectives about what should be taught, the taxonomy sidestepped the fault lines separating curricular traditionalists, pedagogical progressives, and administrative progressives. No less significant, however, was the taxonomy's ability to speak to different ideas about *who* should be taught. As the tension between the selective and equalizing forces of education came to a head in post-war America, the shape-shifting powers of the taxonomy once more allowed it to achieve philosophical compatibility among groups with oppositional aims.

The connection between education and social status has deep historical roots. Given limited participation, however, the use of schooling to promote social mobility did not begin to emerge until the latter half of the nineteenth century. The creation of publicly funded high schools meant that, whatever their origins, students could expect occupational and pecuniary rewards commensurate with their educational attainment.[84] Still, enrollments remained limited and highly skewed toward students of middle- and upper-class backgrounds.

In the first several decades of the twentieth century, that began to change. Students were not only enrolling at greater rates in high school, but also graduating in increasingly larger numbers. Whereas only 17 percent of seventeen-year-olds were enrolled in school in 1920, that figure skyrocketed to 60 percent by 1950.[85] To some, expanding enrollments meant further realization of the school's potential as a great equalizer— a meritocratic solution to the problem of socioeconomic inequity. But the vision of education as an equalizing force did not displace that of education as a tool for selection. Instead, it created a deep tension—a tension that the taxonomy would deftly negotiate—about the purpose of education.

As high school enrollments expanded, more privileged consumers scrambled to acquire a distinct set of credentials, perpetuating the selective function of schooling. At the same time, administrative progressives exacerbated this effect by championing the creation of separate tracks as a means of "democratizing" the high school. In light of the "entrance of large numbers of pupils of widely varying capabilities, aptitudes, social heredity, and destinies in life," they proposed to serve students differently according to their different needs, preparing some for college and others for the world of work.[86] As W. W. Charters proposed, classroom objectives for the non-college-bound, who might aspire to positions such as store clerk, would include noncognitive skills like "friendliness," the "spirit of 'follow-up,'" and "copying skill."[87] And by the late 1940s, those who maintained that "some pupils are slow in learning what other pupils learn rapidly" could take pride in the fact that the non-college-preparatory tracks were serving the largest percentage of students.[88]

Many, however, opposed what they saw as discriminatory and inequitable practices. Disparities in social capital among students, paired with well-worn prejudices about the intellectual abilities of minorities and working people, ensured that tracking reflected socioeconomic status more than it did interest or innate ability. Two studies from the 1940s, for instance, found that students from higher social classes were, for the most part, in college preparatory tracks, and that general and vocational tracks were composed primarily of students from lower-class backgrounds.[89] Not surprisingly, the practice of tracking students struck some as resoundingly unfair, and particularly problematic given the growing connection between educational attainment and employment.[90] It was bad enough to be competing in the educational marketplace against more privileged students, but worse still to be channeled into curricular tracks that would further narrow educational opportunity.

Yet stratification maintained proponents. After all, students did differ in their classroom performance, and often markedly so. Further, for those benefiting from it, the tracking system seemed highly reasonable, based on ostensibly objective measures, and dividing up the advantages of education according to ostensibly meritocratic achievement.

The fault lines in this debate were clear, at least for policy elites, who tended to take strong positions either for or against tracking. But reality as it played out in classrooms was much more complicated, and many teachers found themselves maintaining seemingly contradictory beliefs about sorting and equalizing. Thus, just as teachers saw much of merit in the traditional curriculum while also seeking to facilitate the progressive aim of student growth, many saw policies like tracking as simultaneously useful and problematic. As a pedagogical tool, it had significant appeal; as a social tool, however, it contradicted much of what teachers held dear.

The taxonomy, though, was philosophically compatible with teacher sentiment. By transforming thinking from a *means* of knowledge acquisition to the *end* goal of the educational pursuit, it suggested that all students were endowed with relatively equal potential. Whoever they were, the taxonomy implied, the end goal of higher-order thinking was the same for all learners. As Bloom's wife, Sophie, put it, "Ben was convinced, backed by significant research evidence, that *what any person can learn, all can learn.*"[91] And as former Bloom student Thomas Guskey wrote, "Bloom believed that all students could be helped to reach a high criterion of learning if both the instructional methods and time were varied to better match students' individual learning needs."[92]

At the same time, however, the taxonomy allowed for the acknowledgment of differences in present ability. Some students, teachers could see, were able to perform at higher levels on the taxonomic hierarchy of objectives. While all students might *someday* develop equal critical thinking skills, they were currently in different stages of that journey. The message of the taxonomy, then, was that differences among students should be neither ignored nor reified, and that equity could be pursued within a highly stratified system.

Policy divides further deepened during the late 1950s and early 1960s—a period characterized by the struggle for equity as much as by peaking educational stratification. In this context, teaching all students to "think critically," no matter their differences, was viewed as a way of bridging the divide. Consequently, the taxonomy won significant traction among educators working in complex environments. A 1966 publication of the Los Angeles City Schools Division of Instructional Services, for instance, observed that "virtually every set of educational objectives includes the development of critical thinking."[93] And as M. Frances Klein wrote in 1972, "There is a general consensus among educators that a primary aim of schooling today is the development of the rational powers of the individual—the ability to think."[94]

The sorting function in American education—insofar as it produced a meritocratically defensible set of winners, as well as a number of efficient returns to the national economy—was more deeply rooted than many equity advocates cared to recognize. And a strong coalition of parents and policy makers were both ideologically and politically positioned to protect the interests of the nation's "best and brightest" or "gifted and talented" students. Yet the vision of education as an equalizing force continued to grow over the course of the century, acquiring its own set of well-positioned constituents. The taxonomy implied that the work done by slower learners was different in degree than that done by their more advanced peers. But it also implied that their work was similar in *kind* and that, in time, they could realize the aim of critical thinking. In other words, it affirmed that all children could become critical thinkers, while acknowledging the existing disparities between them. Consequently, different groups could see in the taxonomy what they wanted, promoting its adoption in a wide range of settings. Further, its universally acceptable message made it less likely to be rejected, dismissed, or excised.

Perhaps most importantly, the taxonomy matched the lived reality of those involved with schools. Educators and parents experienced, on a daily basis, the fact that all students *are* different—acquiring knowledge at different rates, wrestling with concepts of distinct levels of complexity, succeeding, and failing. And yet, adults in and around schools were also witness to breakthroughs among slower learners, powerful insights by the non-college-bound, and the occasionally transformational power of the educative process. Whether or not the taxonomy was *right*, it did offer a reasonable and uncontroversial way of explaining the world of learning.

In short, the taxonomy was a shape-shifter. It seemed to address major questions about the process of schooling without proposing a theory to be refuted. As a consequence, it was philosophically compatible among different—and sometimes ideologically opposed—groups, some of whom worked as teachers and many of whom worked in other positions. Yet despite all this inherent complexity, the taxonomy was, at its core, quite simple. Made up of six hierarchical categories, beginning with knowledge and ending with evaluation, it could be easily described, represented, and transported.

A LIFE IN CLASSROOMS

The taxonomy did not move directly into K–12 classrooms. Instead, it took hold in other places first—mentioned in curriculum guides, textbooks, strategic plans, and pedagogy courses. Eventually, however, a system of multiple exposures arose, and classroom teachers could not help but be touched in some way by the idea.

One source of exposure was through scholars who had worked on or with the taxonomy—scholars who continued to exert an influence on their fields of research, their doctoral advisees, and their students. Bloom, for instance, trained scores of future researchers during his tenure at the University of Chicago, as did his collaborator David Krathwohl, who went on to become dean of Syracuse University's School of Education.

Many other scholars whose research endorsed the taxonomy were also teacher educators—at private schools like Cornell and Columbia, top-tier public universities like UCLA and the University of Texas, and regional institutions like Florida State University and Wayne State. Consequently, those exposed to the taxonomy during their undergraduate or graduate studies took their familiarity with it not only into the ivory tower, but also into practical work in schools. Clifford B. Elliott, for instance, wrote his master's thesis about the use of the taxonomy among secondary school teachers, and carried that knowledge with him to his position as principal of Hamilton Local School in Columbus, Ohio.[95] And Stuart R. Johnson completed his doctoral dissertation on the taxonomy in 1966, and subsequently accepted a post as program administrator for the University of California's teacher education program.[96] Thus, teacher educators—many of whom would remain in their positions for decades—were well positioned to expose future educators, as well as school administrators, to the taxonomy.

Many scholars interested in the taxonomy were also the authors of teacher training textbooks, who included the idea in works targeting elementary and secondary school teachers. Such references were not common in the early 1970s, yet given the imitative nature of the genre they quickly spread.[97] Some of those textbooks merely listed the taxonomy as one of many approaches to identifying curricular aims. Others, however, made much stronger cases for the centrality of the taxonomy. As one 1977 pedagogy textbook put it: "Bloom's *Taxonomy* is the most widely used cognitive classification system in education."[98] Mentions of the *Taxonomy* would become both more frequent and more positive. And eventually, the taxonomy was included in the Praxis exam required for licensure in many states.[99]

After they left school and entered their own classrooms, teachers were once again likely to encounter Bloom. Some of these exposures were district-specific. In 1964, for instance, the San Diego County Department of Education produced a test bank designed around the conceptual framework of the taxonomy and utilizing its language.[100] Other curriculum-related endorsements of the taxonomy took the form of workshops like the Leadership Training Project—an effort documented in a 1965 issue of the *Journal of Secondary Education*—that brought together high school curriculum specialists to work with the taxonomy and use it to design objectives.[101] And still other adoptions of the taxonomy were statewide. California's Project Talent, for instance, used it as a cornerstone for curriculum development, and in the early 1970s the Florida Department of Education commissioned exam questions that used Bloom's taxonomy.[102]

Whatever the particular nature of teachers' exposure to the idea in training courses, the taxonomy was one of few concepts echoed in practice through curriculum guides and professional development workshops. Bloom was aware of this, and wrote in his personal papers that the taxonomy benefitted from what he called "overlaps." In-service training, he observed, "spills over into [teacher education], and vice versa and also into [objectives], [curriculum construction], [and the] classroom."[103] And whatever such repetition did for deepening teacher knowledge of the idea, it sent a clear message about the importance of the taxonomy as a piece of research. Thus, the idea's transportability not only helped it spread, but also raised its perceived significance in the eyes of teachers.

Of course, had the taxonomy been highly complex or demanding for educators, no number of exposures would have been sufficient to locate it in practice. The beauty of the taxonomy, though, was that it paired an ostensibly scientific theory of learning—one that scholars and practitioners of various stripes referenced without provoking disagreement about its validity—with a seemingly straightforward means of implementation. After all, whatever its intricacies and complexities, the taxonomy at its most basic was quite simple. It consisted of six categories—not sixteen, or sixty—that teachers could easily memorize and employ. And although there is no evidence that Bloom and colleagues read George Miller's influential paper "The Magical Number Seven, Plus or Minus Two"—a piece in which Miller made the case that working memory is taxed by more than a range of five to nine items—their work was perfectly in line with his findings.[104] They did include twenty subcategories in their outline of cognitive objectives. But the main ideas, as Lauren Sosniak wrote in 1994, "were small in number" and "painted in broad strokes."[105] And as Bloom noted in his personal papers, there were "virtually no references to the subcategories" in applications of the taxonomy—something Bloom attributed to the "KISS [Keep It Simple, Stupid] principle."[106] In other words, the small number of main categories meant that while test developers wrestled with the taxonomy in its full complexity, others could quickly understand its basic tenets.

The language of the taxonomy was similarly simple and straightforward, employing commonsense terms that practitioners could interact comfortably with. As Bloom collaborator David Krathwohl noted, "The design of the framework with the distinctions and vocabulary of teachers in mind added considerably to the ease with which the Taxonomy could be understood."[107] This, together with the austerity of its categories, gave the taxonomy the appearance of being easy to understand. It was, as one teacher training textbook called it, "sensible."[108] As such, the taxonomy often stood out from other ideas that teachers encountered in preservice or in-service training.

Much of what made the taxonomy easy to implement, at least in some form, was crafted intentionally. Bloom and colleagues, though they envisioned their work being used chiefly among university examiners, sought to establish something that could be used in any context. One chief aim for them, then, was that their model be universally applicable. Unlike particular approaches to teaching distinct subjects, the taxonomy was independent of discipline. "Whether one is teaching English or mathematics or science, the core process is identical," wrote Robert R. Newton in 1979.[109]

In some sense, the taxonomy's indifference to academic discipline—whether history or math or biology—was by the mid-1960s already out of step with trends in educational psychology. When the taxonomy was first published, influential behaviorists like B. F. Skinner defined the field with arguments about the universality of learning. Any intellectual domain, Skinner argued, could be approached in the same way.[110] But the so-called cognitive revolution—marked by the 1959 Woods Hole Conference and Jerome Bruner's publication of *The Process of Education*—began to alter the way educational psychologists thought about learning. Domain specificity, Bruner and others argued, was highly influential in the development of intellectual ability, and simply could not be ignored. Not everyone in the field agreed; Robert Gagné, for instance, continued to assert that there was "no sound rational basis for such entities as 'mathematics learning,' 'science learning,' 'language learning,' or 'history learning,' except as divisions of time devoted to these subjects during a school day or term."[111] But projects funded by the National Science Foundation, the National Defense Education Act, and a slate of other government programs indicated that the tide had turned.

The shift away from behaviorism and toward cognitivism, however, affected scholars and reformers more than it did K–12 educators. For school leaders looking to help teachers grow professionally, the taxonomy had a distinct appeal: not because they sided with scholars like Gagné over those like Bruner, but because the taxonomy was a one-stop shop. In a single training, all teachers in a school could be introduced to a tool with a variety of perceived upsides, not the least of which was its promotion of curricular unity. "Rather than working toward separate and disconnected goals," Robert Newton explained, "teachers of the disciplines can see themselves as working toward a common purpose which at the same time permeates and transcends each discipline."[112] During a period of intense battles over the curriculum and increasing concern that education was without a sound theoretical foundation, this had particular resonance.[113] As Bloom himself recalled, the taxonomy "met a previously unmet need for basic, fundamental planning in education."[114] As a consequence of this seeming universality, the taxonomy appeared occupationally realistic, and that once more raised its perceived significance in the eyes of educators—even if the idea was sometimes challenged by scholars.

Other aspects of the taxonomy's pragmatic appeal, and particularly the ease of appearing to adopt it without changing practice, were less intentional. Because it was originally created by and for university examiners, it focused exclusively on outcomes rather than on a means for producing them. It did not "impose a set of teaching procedures," as Bloom recalled, nor did it outline objectives "so detailed and restrictive that a single teaching method is implied."[115] As one teacher observed, "They wished to develop a classification system that would provide a common format for curricular development and evaluation and yet not necessitate the standardization of curricula."[116]

The result was that teachers could continue what they had always done, making minor adjustments to the taxonomy, their practice, or both. It was treated as what David Tyack and Larry Cuban have called an "add-on" that could be, as Robert Newton put it, "superimposed on the existing curriculum."[117] Thus, without having to overhaul their occupational practices, educators could align themselves with status-bearing research that seemed consistent with their values and concerns.

In some ways, this was unquestionably positive—allowing educators to make use of the idea without unrealistically expecting them to overhaul their practices. Still, given the seeming ease of implementation, many teachers engaged with the taxonomy only shallowly. As one teacher wrote in a blog posting: "I have heard the phrase [Bloom's taxonomy] quite a bit and I even went to the trouble to look up what it was all about and now use the phrase myself. However, the only times I use it are when I need something; it seems to carry a prestige with [its] use that gets more attention than simply using the word 'application.'"[118] Rather than using the taxonomy as a tool for developing classroom goals, many teachers simply applied its language to the work they were already doing.

Other teachers who did strive to use the taxonomy in their classrooms were often limited by relatively superficial understandings of it. Without clear guidance about how the concept might be best used, some never moved beyond the simple language of the taxonomy's six chief categories. As a result, many believed that they merely needed to ask six different kinds of questions in order to reap the taxonomy's full benefits—moving their students from the acquisition of basic content knowledge inexorably toward the development of critical thinking skills.

This view was not held by teachers alone. And as interpreters made the case that the taxonomy was a kind of panacea, it became easier for teachers to believe that teaching critical thinking involved little work beyond tweaking existing lessons. "The thinking of the teacher does not need to be significantly altered, and no fundamental shifts in educational philosophy are required," wrote Richard Paul in a 1985 issue of *Educational Leadership*. "The Taxonomy and the ability to generate a full variety of question types are all that an intelligent teacher really needs to teach critical thinking skills."[119] As Robert Kloss put it: "If an introduction to Benjamin Bloom's taxonomy does not magically allow one to create an instantly 'more beautiful' question, it does at least help the instructor formulate pretty ones."[120]

Bloom and colleagues did not believe that merely asking students to apply, analyze, synthesize, or evaluate would produce the acts of mind identified in the taxonomy. Rather, the hierarchy of the objectives was intended as a means of classifying behaviors by complexity, in keeping with the hypothesis that "problems requiring analysis and synthesis," for instance, "are more difficult than problems requiring comprehension."[121] The taxonomy in use, however—at least among some teachers—seemed to convey a different message. Frequently represented by boosters as a sectional pyramid (see figure 1.1), with knowledge at the bottom and analysis at the top, the interpreted taxonomy implied not only directionality, but also a natural progression.

The acts of mind identified by the taxonomy, then, were frequently translated as a sequence through which to move students. Once they had acquired knowledge, they would begin to comprehend; once they had achieved comprehension, they could apply; and, eventually, once all intermediate steps were completed, they could be asked to evaluate. In other words, one had only to begin with the easiest task—deciding which facts to review—and then progress up the hierarchy by asking new kinds of questions.

Still, even if teachers shallowly understood the taxonomy or had unreasonable faith in its power to foster critical thinking skills among students,

FIGURE 1.1

Taxonomy of Educational Objectives for the Cognitive Domain

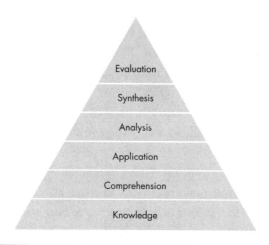

it was often a valuable addition to the classroom. Teachers employing the taxonomy used it to think in new ways about lesson planning, reflect on their classroom goals, and gauge the degree to which all students were being challenged. Even at the most basic level of understanding, the taxonomy sent a clear message about the importance of helping students learn to think, while also identifying some of the forms that such thinking might take. For many, that was enough to make the tool useful. As one teacher wrote in a blog entry, "In my opinion, this will help me to design an appropriate lesson considering all the different types of learning objectives."[122] And in response to a question about the usefulness of the taxonomy in the classroom, another teacher reflected, "It lets you know how in depth your lesson plans and lectures should be." It also, she added, "helps you understand what you can expect of your students at each level."[123]

The taxonomy gained traction in K–12 classrooms because teachers were repeatedly exposed to it, because they believed it made sense with regard to how it addressed issues of student ability, and because they saw it as relatively straightforward to implement. Consequently, it entered the common knowledge base and steadily spread across both space and time.

For many teachers this was positive; they felt that the taxonomy was a useful tool for helping them grow as educators. Still, the crucial characteristics that allowed the taxonomy to enter practice did not ensure that it did so perfectly. The idea's highly transportable core, for instance, was often mistaken for the sum total of its value and meaning. And the ease with which it could be added to existing practice—and which made it occupationally realistic—often brought about only superficial kinds of adoption. Thus, even as the taxonomy became a signature concept in education, it would remain known and used with varying degrees of thoughtfulness and intensity.

CYCLES OF LEGITIMACY

The taxonomy's general and nonideological focus on critical thinking, along with its simple and straightforward structure, gave it a broad appeal. And although advocacy for it was not always fierce, no great opposition movement arose against it. Further, the concept was easy to adopt, if often only superficially.

That alone, however, would not have been enough to give the taxonomy staying power in the world of American education. In fact, as time passed, one might reasonably have expected it to join the flotsam and jetsam of other ideas dragged from the ivory tower into the schools and eventually abandoned. Yet the taxonomy took root and persisted.

One element that gave the taxonomy staying power was the fact that it was difficult to disprove. A number of research studies did examine whether the taxonomy was, in fact, hierarchical, and several found that its various "levels" interacted with each other in a manner much more complex than presented by Bloom and colleagues.[124] Mostly, however, the taxonomy maintained scholarly legitimacy. More critical research, confined to small-circulation academic journals, hardly made a ripple in the sea of taxonomy-related research.

Another edge for the taxonomy was the fact that it had something of a timeless feel to it. Its authors, after all, had not made claims about the abilities of particular kinds of children or about the relative value of specific curricular content—the sorts of claims that might identify the taxonomy as the product of a particular historical moment. Instead, it classified seemingly objective and enduring thinking skills.

Further, there was the fact that the taxonomy was easy to store in documents like curriculum frameworks, assessment rubrics, and posters of taxonomic pyramids. As David Krathwohl observed in 1994, the "institutionalization" of the taxonomy in various forms was a major part of its durability.[125]

Finally, there was the fact that the taxonomy, once well accepted, became a touchstone for those looking to shore up their authority. This is perhaps clearest in the case of teacher education textbooks. As Amelia Kreitzer and George Madaus noted in 1994, the taxonomy "receives treatment in virtually every textbook in general education and in measurement for prospective teachers."[126] After all, including the taxonomy came with little cost beyond that of ink and paper, and held the potential upside of validating the text in the eyes of adopters. Leaving it out, on the other hand, had the potential to limit adoptions in courses where instructors made the taxonomy a central topic. An array of other teacher-oriented materials used in licensure programs also referenced the taxonomy as a means of establishing credibility. Notable among them is the bestselling *Understanding by Design*, by Grant Wiggins and Jay McTighe, which extensively quotes Bloom; its six "facets of understanding" even call to mind the six levels of the taxonomy.[127]

The taxonomy was also used by teachers and administrators who, working at the local level, sought to ground their work in its authority. When it came time for them to engage in lesson study or revise district curricula, for instance, the taxonomy was a common referent. And by citing the taxonomy in artifacts like evaluation rubrics or schoolwide goals, educators only furthered the idea's legitimacy—amplifying its significance in the eyes of other teachers.

As a result of such processes, the taxonomy was absorbed into the institutional framework of American schooling, and the concept became a part of the natural order of K–12 education. In fact, even those who seemingly reject the taxonomy tend to be familiar with it—expressing citation fatigue rather than ignorance of it or skepticism about its quality. As one Georgia elementary school teacher summed up her experience with the taxonomy: "I have heard of Bloom's ever since I started [teaching] ten years ago . . . We all know what it means . . . [but] do we really need to throw the term around?"[128] More commonly, though, teachers tended to accept and respect the concept. As Bloom's research assistant, Barbara Davis, concluded in a 1988 memo to him: "Teachers KNOW that materials keyed to [the taxonomy] are thought to be better."[129]

Perhaps the strongest evidence of the widespread acceptance of the taxonomy is the limited impact of the update to it done by David Krathwohl and former Bloom advisee Lorin Anderson.[130] Their work, which they called a "revision of Bloom's taxonomy," was characterized by verbs rather than nouns (see figure 1.2). It replaced "knowledge" with "remember" and removed "comprehension" in favor of "understand." Perhaps most significantly, it substituted "create" for "synthesis" and moved it to the top of the hierarchy above evaluation (now "evaluate").

FIGURE 1.2

Taxonomy of Educational Objectives for the Cognitive Domain, as revised by Krathwohl and Anderson

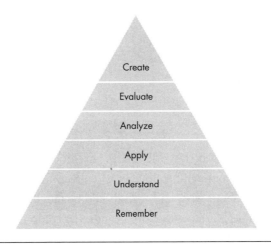

The revision of the taxonomy might have caused a stir, raising questions about the validity of work that educators had been doing for decades. Instead, curriculum guides and standards documents in states like North Carolina simply swapped out the old for the new. And in some cases, states even continued using the original taxonomy, either alongside the revised version, or without bothering to make the update. Delaware's Framework for Curriculum Design, for instance, highlighted both the original taxonomy and Anderson and Krathwohl's revision.[131] The New Jersey World Languages Curriculum Framework included a guide for designing lessons using the original taxonomy—a guide that the state borrowed from Nebraska.[132] And in South Dakota, the Department of Education revised its curricular standards by integrating the levels of the original taxonomic hierarchy.[133]

Adaptable for the uses of different kinds of actors working in different roles and regions, seemingly easy to implement, and defined by a simple and recognizable core, the taxonomy became a standard form in American education. Once that was the case, it became one of a handful of classic ideas—one of very few scholarly concepts to make the arduous journey from the world of research into the knowledge base of teachers. And in that pantheon, the taxonomy became a hallmark concept with the power to bestow its legitimacy on its users. Consequently, it went from being widespread to being ever-present. As Beverly Joyce Love concluded in her study of the inclusion of the taxonomy in state curriculum documents, most states now use the language of knowledge, comprehension, application, analysis, synthesis, and evaluation in their standards, even if they do so only as an act of ceremony.[134]

CONCLUSION

In the wake of World War II, the Taxonomy of Educational Objectives created by Benjamin Bloom and colleagues was a seemingly perfect fit. It addressed questions about what and who should be taught as the tug-of-war over those issues began to peak, deftly negotiating complicated ideological terrain. And it did so without imposing a particular set of principles or procedures, meaning that educators could use it as they saw fit.

If it had merely been philosophically compatible and occupationally realistic, however, the taxonomy would hardly have gained a foothold in practice. But it also had high levels of perceived significance. The work had a scholarly basis, making its first impact in the bookish domain of testing and measurement and originating from a prestigious research university. Further, it addressed—in a singular way—a topic of deep interest: the objectives of education.

In a sense, then, the taxonomy was the best of many worlds. It was serious scholarship that took up an issue of seeming importance. But it could be interpreted in a way that made it easy for people with different beliefs, and who occupied different positions, to accept. And while it was seemingly scientific, it was also easy to understand and simple enough to describe to a colleague down the hall, making it highly transportable.

The taxonomy was hardly an instant hit. Despite its distinct flexibility, it took years for the idea to enter practice, even with Bloom and colleagues perceptively working to proliferate their work. As Bloom observed, the concept was first applied to testing and only "later moved to general curricula and classroom [application]."[135] In part, that was a product of design—Bloom and his workgroup had not set out to affect K–12 education; their concerns were squarely with evaluation and measurement at the college level. Equally, however, the measured pace at which it entered K–12 classrooms was a product of a highly decentralized system. Yet the taxonomy was in many ways built to last, and it was able to slowly enter classrooms via a wide array of conduits.

With something to offer a broad range of audiences, the taxonomy gained support without provoking opposition, allowing it to grow and take root. The more widely it spread, the more legitimacy it garnered. In turn, the more legitimacy it gained, the better it was able to penetrate the multiple spheres of American education. The taxonomy became a known entity—something perhaps more important than empirical verifiability— and was integrated into education research, covered in teacher training courses, written into textbooks, and incorporated into curriculum standards. Within a generation, its perceived significance in the eyes of educators was unparalleled.

Once translated into the structural framework of American education, the taxonomy became institutionalized, which made it even more transportable. And all the while it remained both philosophically compatible and occupationally realistic.

Of course, to say that the taxonomy has entered the knowledge base of classroom teachers is not to say that it has done so in a uniformly robust and positive way. Frequently, it has been reduced to a shallow form. In such cases, the taxonomy functions less like a practical instrument than it does like window dressing.

Critics might further make the case that the taxonomy has reinforced the status quo in schools. The ease of overlaying the taxonomy onto practice, in tandem with the prestige of adopting a benchmarked concept, has exempted many educators from closer examination of their work, either self-directed or otherwise. A 1985 report for the California Department of Education, for instance, found among teachers a "tendency to teach facts in isolation from the thinking skills"—the aim being to provide students with knowledge and then expect them to think about it.[136] Such practices maintain the division between factual information and critical habits of mind, even while ostensibly targeting the former as a means of promoting the latter. The result, as several scholars have found, is that the tasks assigned to students tend to be at the lowest level of the taxonomy.[137]

Yet whatever the challenges and unintended consequences, the taxonomy has stimulated thought and discussion among teachers over the course of many decades—a rarity for a piece of educational research. It has given teachers a common vocabulary for talking about educational objectives, served as a framework for considering the arc of student development, changed the way that many teachers think about lesson design, and oriented many teachers away from rote memorization and toward the development of thought. And though the nature of teaching practice has often complicated efforts to use the taxonomy, it has nevertheless crossed a great divide and shaped the way many educators reflect on their work. As one teacher blogged, "Bloom's taxonomy made me think . . . [and] although there isn't time this year to make a change, I've already discussed with my colleagues the changes we'll make in our year-long curriculum next year."[138]

Without question, the taxonomy has had an uneven life in practice. But to focus exclusively on its limitations is to ignore a broader, and perhaps more important, truth: in a fragmented system devoid of a true research-to-practice pathway, Bloom's taxonomy left the ivory tower, entered the knowledge base of K–12 teachers, and took root. It crossed the great divide.

CHAPTER TWO

Theory of Many Uses
Howard Gardner's Multiple Intelligences

L ike Bloom's taxonomy, Howard Gardner's theory of multiple intelligences is a hallmark concept in American education. As likely to be
referenced by teachers as by educational psychologists, the theory's penetration into K–12 classrooms has made Gardner a star. And though it
has achieved greater traction in some schools than in others, the degree
to which teachers recognize Gardner's work has fueled the dreams of researchers striving for relevance.

This is not to say that Gardner's theory has been without critics. No
piece of scholarship as visible as multiple intelligences can persist without
rousing some degree of opposition. Still, even its detractors can agree that
the theory of multiple intelligences has been a success in one important respect: bridging the divide between the worlds of research and practice. So
what explains its impressive leap from the ivory tower to the schoolhouse?

In a sea of possibilities, the theory of multiple intelligences stood apart
for a number of reasons. First, it was authored by a Harvard professor and
MacArthur "genius" who ran his own center on cognition and learning.
And while many of his colleagues were content to publish in scholarly
journals, Gardner worked diligently to make his research as visible as possible to practitioners. Equally, if not more important, however, was the fact
that the theory appeared to square with fundamental teacher beliefs and
concerns. At a time when K–12 educators were increasingly sensitive to

interventions led by outsiders in top-down fashion, multiple intelligences appeared to side with teachers and to reflect the world as they saw it.

In terms of classroom use, Gardner's theory had an additional set of advantages. It was seemingly intuitive and relatively abstract, allowing busy practitioners to quickly understand the core of the concept and put it into some kind of use. As one group of supporters put it, the theory "is popular because it is compatible with the . . . approaches already in place in many schools."[1] And the idea was easy to transport—conveyed through a set of seven (later nine) self-explanatory labels for various kinds of learners. As a result, the theory successfully bridged the worlds of research and classroom practice.

Its entrance into practice was not perfect. Specifically, although some applications of multiple intelligences are more or less faithful to the theory as articulated by Gardner, others bear only a passing resemblance—using the language of multiple intelligences, but in loosely interpreted applications. And while Gardner himself has rejected particular readings of the theory, he has done so with little impact on teaching practice. Hence, the history of the theory of multiple intelligences highlights not only the crucial nature of particular characteristics for moving research into practice, but also some of their insufficiencies for doing so in a consistently productive manner.

Whatever the complications around its entrance into the world of K–12 education, however, the theory of multiple intelligences continues to shape the way that teachers think and talk about cognition and student ability. It is a highly visible example of educational research entering the world of practice. And it promises to teach us a great deal—not just about how an idea can move from the ivory tower into the schoolhouse, but also about the kinds of supports that might facilitate a more consistently productive transmission of research into practice.

"OF INTEREST CHIEFLY TO THOSE TRAINED IN MY DISCIPLINE"

In 1983, the year the National Commission on Excellence in Education published the report *A Nation at Risk*, Howard Gardner published *Frames of Mind: The Theory of Multiple Intelligences*. His intention was, within the field of cognitive-developmental psychology, to challenge the idea that all human thought ultimately developed toward the ideal of scientific thinking. As Gardner would later recall, "I believed that my work would be of interest chiefly to those trained in my discipline, and particularly those who studied intelligence from a Piagetian perspective."[2]

By the time *Frames of Mind* was published, Gardner had already been directing Project Zero at Harvard University's Graduate School of Education for more than a decade. Originally created in 1967 for the purpose of studying learning in the arts—about which "zero" research had been done—Project Zero gradually expanded to include learning across all disciplines, and Gardner was named codirector in 1972.

The work that led directly to the development of the theory of multiple intelligences began in 1979, when the Bernard Van Leer Foundation sponsored a study on "the nature and realization of human potential."[3] Seeking to better understand the concept of intelligence, Gardner conducted a "subjective factor analysis" in which he drew on neurobiology, developmental psychology, psychometrics, biographies, and cross-cultural research. Consequently, he looked not only at research on "normal" and "gifted" individuals, but also at studies of brain-damaged patients, idiot savants, experts in different lines of work, and individuals from diverse cultures.[4]

In writing *Frames of Mind*—the first in a series to be issued under the aegis of the Project on Human Potential—Gardner had a particular set of aims. His first two goals were relatively specific to the cognitive-developmental domain. On the one hand, he intended to "expand the purviews of cognitive and developmental psychology" to include the biological roots of cognition and cultural variations in perceptions of cognitive competence.[5] On the other hand, he sought to help create a method of identifying an intellectual profile for children as a means of identifying students with particular talents and enhancing their "educational opportunities and options."[6] Gardner's second two goals related to practical applications of the theory. Among educationally oriented anthropologists, he wished that his work might inspire studies of the relationship between intelligence and cultural settings. And among policy makers, he expressed hope that *Frames of Mind* would broaden understandings of what intelligence is and what it looks like. His focus was not on K–12 instruction.

Whatever Gardner's contribution in *Frames of Mind*, the book's central claim—that intelligence is not a unitary concept that can be captured by a single number—was hardly novel. As Gardner wrote, "The idea of multiple intelligences is an old one, and I can scarcely claim any great originality for attempting to revive it once more."[7] The theory of multiple intelligences, he freely admitted, was an updated version of the nineteenth-century concept of faculty psychology, which posited that all students possessed different strengths that could be nurtured. Other researchers working long before Gardner—scholars like L. L. Thurstone and J. P. Guilford—had "argued that intelligence was better conceived of as a set of possibly independent factors."[8] In short, multiple intelligences was not a radical new concept.

The genius of *Frames of Mind* was its simplicity and linguistic clarity. Whereas Guilford's framework for intelligence consisted of up to 150 different factors, Gardner focused his analysis on seven intelligences: logical-mathematical, spatial, linguistic, bodily-kinesthetic, musical, interpersonal, and intrapersonal. Further, Gardner used straightforward terminology, accessible language, and evocative examples. He told stories about a Puluwat youth from the Caroline Islands whose particular intelligence manifested in learning the culturally prized practice of sailing, about an Iranian teenager with the ability to memorize the entire Koran, and about a young Parisian learning to program a computer. All of them, according to Gardner, possessed innate intellectual gifts, and he made a strong case for expanding traditional views about intelligence. And, as Gardner later put it, "One of my strengths is that I can take questions, even questions which are relatively esoteric, and describe them in plain English."[9]

Despite his interest in affecting conceptions about intelligence and its interaction with culture, Gardner explored practical applications of multiple intelligences only briefly in *Frames of Mind*. Educators seeking to find a particular message they might apply in the classroom had to do the heavy lifting themselves. Still, Gardner did offer bits of teaching-related applications, like the suggestion that "the intelligences can function both as subject matters in themselves and as the preferred means for inculcating

Amazon.com Vendor Return -- OVERSTOCK

SINGLE-PACKAGE SHIPMENT

Qty.	Item	ASIN	UPC/EAN
1	School Libraries and Student Learning: A Guide for School Leaders	1612506367	9781612506368
3	From the Ivory Tower to the Schoolhouse: How Scholarship Becomes Common Knowledge in Education	1612506690	9781612506692
1	"It's Being Done": Academic Success in Unexpected Schools	1891792393	9781891792397

Vendor Return
Shipment ID: 15404513360551
VRET ID: VRET1304703738531
Process Date: October 28, 2018
IOG: Amazon.com

Shipped From:
1700 SPARROWS POINT BLVD
Sparrows Point, MD 21219-1046
United States

Shipping Address
Harvard Education Publishing Group
c/o PSSC
46 Development Rd
Fitchburg, Massachusetts 01420

SMmAQzC7t

Remit To:
Amazon.com
PO Box 80367
Seattle, WA 98108-80367
USA

diverse subject matter."[10] In other words, students could access content by using their different strengths.

Lest educators think they might teach children to read by having them practice sailing, however, Gardner made clear that "whether the actual process of reading involves, in significant measure, intelligences other than linguistic ones is problematic."[11] Thus, while learning to sail should be seen as an act of intellectual growth, it could not be expected to have more than a limited impact on a student's ability to read, write, or cipher. Further, he concluded that the promotion of particular kinds of intelligence "must be considered in the light of goals pursued by the wider society." Sometimes, he continued, "individuals with gifts in certain directions must nonetheless be guided along other, less favored paths, simply because the needs of the culture are particularly urgent in that realm at that time."[12]

In keeping with the evenhanded and reserved approach he took in *Frames of Mind*, Gardner made only modest efforts to promote multiple intelligences. Nevertheless, the theory soon found adherents well beyond the world of cognitive-developmental psychology. And Gardner, for his part, would eventually become a master of public relations.

EARLY ADOPTION IN INDEPENDENT SCHOOLS

At the leading edge of those enlisting Gardner's research in the world of practice were administrators at independent schools. Working within the particular context of American education in the mid-1980s, such leaders pursued the theory as a means of buffering their reputations and distinguishing themselves from competitors—practices long commonplace among private schools, and particularly the elite nonparochial schools among them.

Early after the publication of *Frames of Mind*, Gardner was invited to address the annual meeting of the National Association of Independent Schools—a "customary talk of fifty minutes," as he later put it, "followed by a small number of easily anticipated questions." Gardner expected a small crowd. What he found, instead, was an audience that "grew steadily in size until it spilled into the hallways on both sides of the room." After the session concluded, he was mobbed by teachers, trustees, and headmasters who, as Gardner put it, were "reluctant to allow [him] to slip back into anonymity."[13] The overwhelming enthusiasm surprised Gardner, who was unsure what to make of it, but who would nevertheless prove himself a willing and able partner in promoting multiple intelligences.

Perhaps the clearest allure of the theory for private school leaders was the fact that it seemed to support progressive educational ideals. Practices like learning by doing, the project method, student-directed activity, and portfolio assessment had long been cherished in boutique independent schools. But whereas progressivism had once dominated public discourse, its trajectory in the second half of the twentieth century had largely been one of decline—and particularly so during the back-to-basics push of the 1970s and the early years of the standards and accountability movement in the 1980s. As Gardner observed, school reformers were increasingly united "in their dissatisfaction with 'progressive' ideas in American education . . . and [in] their impatience with approaches that cherish the individuality of each student, teacher, and school building."[14] A cherished worldview seemed under attack.

More troubling to private school leaders than a philosophically unfavorable policy climate, however, was the idea that their autonomy might be challenged. In the wake of *A Nation at Risk*, many began to express concern that the surge of standards- and accountability-oriented school reforms would lead to increased regulation—something they had long opposed. "There are a great deal more state efforts to mandate curriculum, and that's very troubling," observed Robert L. Smith, executive director of the Council for American Private Education, in 1983. "The freedom of each school to develop its own program is generic to their whole mission."[15] And, as Stephen Hinrichs, executive director of the New York State Association of Independent Schools, noted in a 1985 interview, "it is important to maintain educational diversity . . . different kids need different schools."[16] These ideals, strongly held by private school leaders, were also prized by teachers in such schools—teachers who asserted more curricular independence than their public school counterparts and who had grown accustomed to the progressive climates of their schools.

In this context, Gardner's theory was a small piece of good fortune. Specifically, what multiple intelligences provided for independent schools was an up-to-date and ostensibly scientific basis for the progressive mission. Such schools had long made the case that in order to educate the whole child, teachers needed to meet the unique needs of each particular student.[17] They pursued practices like "individual goal setting," honoring "student differences," and planning "for the wide range of diverse needs."[18] Consequently, the chief initial appeal of multiple intelligences, at least to administrators, was that it sanctioned such practices, and that it did so bearing the imprimatur of Harvard University. As one school leader put it, *Frames of Mind* "really pulled together and gave some legitimacy to the ideas that we had been trying to implement."[19]

Teachers at independent schools, insofar as they subscribed to the progressive vision, also saw multiple intelligences as a useful addition. Like administrators, they were drawn to the idea's seeming authority. Whatever cachet pedagogical progressives like John Dewey and George Counts continued to carry, Gardner was a MacArthur "genius grant" winner whose work could be found on bookstore shelves.[20] As Larry Cuban later observed, the theory gave "scientific legitimacy to include all children as learners" and granted "strong credibility to those teachers who take the next steps to individualize their classroom practices."[21] But perhaps more importantly, Gardner's theory was occupationally realistic. It did not, for instance, require an overhaul of the curriculum already in use. It did not demand changes to classroom authority. And its use was not contingent upon the implementation of a new daily schedule. Instead, it fit with the structure and rhythms of school life as it already existed.

Multiple intelligences also presented a unique opportunity for independent schools to market themselves as champions of a "well-rounded" education—something that appealed not only to parents with children at such schools, but also to teachers. The mid-1980s was a time of increasing policy talk about the necessity of reforming American education in light of the threat posed by globalization, and public schools were dragged through the mud for failing to prepare American students to compete with their foreign competitors.[22] Independent schools, however, worked to position themselves as above the fray—a move that would not only secure their reputations, but also safeguard the autonomy and professional status of their teachers.

One way that independent schools responded to the increasingly potent standards and accountability movement was by promoting themselves as defenders of the arts. After all, while many Americans supported plans for higher standards and clear measures of achievement in public education, many were concerned about the narrowing effects such efforts would have on the curriculum.[23] The nascent standards movement, whatever its potential for increasing achievement, stirred fears that subjects like art and music would be jettisoned in favor of more instruction in subjects like English and math. Such concerns, of course, were not limited to private school educators. A 1983 conference, for instance, drew public school teachers from seven states to discuss "Arts in Education: An Action Agenda for the '80s." Worried that the arts were seen as a "frill" and should be treated differently than more "academic" subjects, speakers "urged that arts educators develop a new 'language' that both they and the public can use when advocating the arts in education."[24]

The debate about curriculum during the early years of the standards movement went beyond the arts, though—raising fundamental questions about the purpose of schooling. While some argued that schools needed to focus on so-called "academic" subjects as a means of promoting rigor, others made the case that schools should include a wider range of subjects as a means of educating the whole child.[25] This, independent school leaders and teachers were able to argue, was a false choice. Private schools, in the progressive tradition, had long done both—promoting rigor while also taking a more holistic approach to educating students. That fact, they argued, separated them from their public school peers. Thus, while Gardner wrote in 1990 that schools were not prepared to develop the full "range of human intelligences," private school teachers and administrators could make the case that *they* actually had the resources to do it—and in fact, that they had been doing it for quite some time.[26] That was something teachers in such schools were proud of, even if they were doing it only for a small cross-section of American students.

Parents, particularly those paying private school tuition, were also interested in ensuring a rigorous and well-rounded educational experience for their children. Generally concerned with recognizing the uniqueness of each child and supporting all of a child's varied interests, they believed that a standardized approach to schooling undermined messages being sent at home. For teachers at schools catering to such parents, adopting the theory of multiple intelligences presented a perfect opportunity—a chance to raise their professional standing by adopting seemingly significant and philosophically compatible research. Gardner's theory, after all, seemed to demand that rather than uniformly implementing a standardized curriculum, teachers should praise students for their interests, encourage them to follow their passions, and respect their differences. As one pair of multiple intelligences authors wrote in 1991, educating students effectively meant "schooling for a lifetime, not for a test."[27] Such rhetoric had strong traction with parents, and established among teachers a distinct theoretical base upon which to establish their claims on professional expertise.

Many middle-class parents wanted the particular strengths of their children recognized for more pragmatic and less philosophical reasons. As the college admissions process became increasingly competitive in the 1980s and 1990s, it raised the stakes around grades and other perceptions of talent. Many parents refused to believe that their children were B or C students and therefore would be denied admission to top colleges. Many private schools, in turn, used multiple intelligences as a way of responding to such concerns. As Thomas Hoerr of the New City School put it, "MI theory teaches us that all kids are smart," and that all could succeed.[28] Additionally, inasmuch as other talents also mattered in college admissions, multiple intelligences provided a distinct justification for nurturing those gifts. Musicians, athletes, and student leaders were the kind of well-rounded students that many colleges and universities were looking for.

Finally, Gardner's theory was philosophically attractive to teachers because it seemed to support practices that made for a pleasant classroom environment. Rather than demanding that all students meet particular standards of achievement, teachers in multiple intelligences classrooms could praise children for at least seven different kinds of clearly identified "intelligences." Schools, multiple intelligences supporters believed, could be happier and more humane places if students were recognized for their strengths rather than for their weaknesses. And multiple intelligences came in the form of a relatively straightforward framework that could be super-imposed on what teachers were already doing in their classrooms.

The fact that Gardner's theory first caught on in the world of private schools makes a great deal of sense. Such schools—particularly the elite, nonparochial schools among them—are characterized by the highest degree of curricular freedom and are highly sensitive to the distinct concerns of tuition-paying parents. And at a time of increasingly vigorous policy talk antithetical to much of what made such schools unique, teachers and administrators saw multiple intelligences as a kind of validation, as well as a potentially useful tool for talking about their goals.

The theory of multiple intelligences, however, was not confined to the world of independent schools. After all, much of what gave multiple intelligences traction in practice was unrelated to the specific concerns of private school educators. Gardner's clear language and straightforward categories made the concept easily transportable. Its organization and open-endedness made it seemingly easy to merge with existing occupational practices. It appeared both highly credible and singularly significant. And it squared with teacher philosophies about the nature of learning and the measurement of success. Consequently, public school teachers were receptive to multiple intelligences as well—and they became increasingly so as the emerging standards and accountability movement raised unsettling questions about curricular autonomy and the professional status of those working in K–12 public schools.

IN THE PUBLIC SPHERE: SIDESTEPPING BLAME AND ADJUSTING TO NEW REALITIES

By the late twentieth century, the notion that all children can learn had become firmly established as a cherished truism in American education. Only a few generations earlier, perspectives on intelligence were strongly influenced by jaundiced thinking about race, class, and gender. Over time, though, Americans had evolved their positions—largely in response to developments in social science research and shifts in political currents.[29]

Still, despite the apparent consensus about student ability, teachers and policy makers took distinct perspectives on the matter. Experience taught teachers that students brought their own particular sets of intellectual strengths and weaknesses into the classroom, and that no amount of teaching could produce uniform results. Some students excelled in solving math problems or in reading; others did not. But life in classrooms had also taught teachers to appreciate a wider range of student strengths—not all of which showed up on exams. Some students, for instance, were adept at asking questions or stood out in class discussions. Some were effective leaders and worked well with others. Some were driven and motivated. Some were talented artists or musicians. And some were simply pleasant to be around.

Policy makers, on the other hand, had rejected the simplistic prejudice of the early twentieth century—that only *some* children could learn—in favor of an evenhanded overgeneralization about student potential. All children, they began to argue, should be achieving at a benchmark level of proficiency that could be objectively evaluated. For them, the phrase "all children can learn" suggested that low student achievement must, by definition, reflect a kind of teacher failure.

The standards and accountability movement of the 1980s brought this tension to a head, as policy makers worked to establish a core body of essential knowledge that students would then be tested on. To classroom teachers, the use of a single test to measure achievement for all students seemed to contradict the complex reality they experienced in classrooms each day. Yet the powerful rhetoric of the standards movement was making it increasingly difficult to take a stand against testing—at least without appearing to doubt either the competence of teachers or the ability of all students to learn. In this context, the theory of multiple intelligences seemed particularly attuned to the worldview of classroom teachers.

Teachers, it seems, would have felt uneasy about the standards and accountability movement whether or not multiple intelligences had entered the sphere of K–12 schooling. Yet the theory seemingly possessed scientific credibility and provided teachers with straightforward concepts and clear language to use in resisting what they viewed as a misguided and top-down policy move. It gave them a way of talking about intelligence, provided the backing of a Harvard professor, and even seemed to imply some direct and easy-to-implement classroom applications. Hence, even though Gardner did not envision his work as the basis for school reform—or for the rejection of reform efforts—he soon found himself involved in a major policy debate.

Whatever his original intentions may have been, Gardner did not sit idly by and hope that teachers would see his work as relevant to their interests. Instead, he quite intentionally framed multiple intelligences as a challenge to traditional forms of testing, and became increasingly outspoken as the standards and accountability movement gained momentum in the late 1980s and early 1990s. Writing in 1989, Gardner argued that "MI theory grows out of a conviction that standardized tests, with their almost exclusive stress on linguistic and logical skills, are limited."[30] A year later, he was even bolder: "MI theory challenges the viability of standardized, machine-scored, multiple-choice assessments, which by their very nature appraise students' knowledge through the filter of the linguistic and logical-mathematical intelligences."[31] And by the mid-1990s, Gardner had found the voice that would make him a star. Writing in *Multiple Intelligences: The Theory into Practice*—his follow-up to *Frames of Mind*—Gardner accused policy makers of "calling for 'uniform' schools" and criticized them for favoring "the same curriculum for all students, the same methods of teaching, and the same 'standardized' methods of assessment." State-level technocrats, he argued, had no interest whatsoever in "individual differences."[32] That same year, an *Educational Policy* survey found that 77 percent of teachers agreed with the statement that "tests are bad and not worth the time and money spent on them."[33] Gardner had his finger on the pulse of teacher sentiment.

Teachers did not merely take issue with standardized tests on philosophical grounds. Teacher professionalism was the result of decades of struggle, frequently through collective bargaining, to build systems and structures acknowledging their expertise and authority. The creation of teacher credentialing, the establishment of tenure practices, and significant increases in pay were all long-fought battles to endow the occupation with the trappings of a recognized profession. Curricular standards and accountability testing, however, threatened to reverse much of this progress. Instead of deciding for themselves what content should be emphasized, what skills developed, and what assessments given, teachers faced the possibility of having all of those choices made for them at the state level. Further, unless the standards were quite low, a large cross-section of the American student body would fail accountability tests. And teachers stood to shoulder the blame for those failures, which would in turn bring about more finger pointing, deeper cuts to teacher autonomy, and even decreased job security.[34]

By the 1990s, it had become clear that teachers were not going to slow the forward march of the standards and accountability movement. Beyond abstract national discussions, George H. W. Bush and Bill Clinton both took steps toward establishing content standards.[35] And by the close of the decade, nearly all states had developed curriculum standards for K–12 education. Thus, well before 2002 when the Elementary and Secondary Education Act was reauthorized as No Child Left Behind, the standards movement had already become a force impossible to keep outside the classroom. Accordingly, teachers were faced with the reality of implementing standardized content and preparing their students for state-mandated tests. For antitest advocates, it appeared to be a dismal scenario. As school leader Thomas Hoerr asked, "How much fun can it be to read from a script all day? What's the message to us about our competencies when everything is set out and predetermined by a faraway publisher?"[36]

Such rhetoric perhaps overstated the degree to which the standards movement would undermine teacher autonomy, but the movement did threaten to alter the teaching profession in unwelcomed ways. Yet Gardner's theory could be useful even if curricular standards and accountability tests were instituted. Teacher satisfaction and "feeling like a professional," wrote Hoerr, "comes from knowing that you've made a difference in a child's life . . . from knowing that you brought your curricular expertise, knowledge of pedagogy, and understanding of child development together to reach your students." And, he argued, "MI allows teachers to do just that."[37]

This interpretation of multiple intelligences positioned teachers as experts in tailoring curricula—even *standardized* curricula—to student needs. By using the theory to customize instruction, teachers could maintain a kind of professional control and autonomy of their classrooms. As Gardner wrote in a foreword to a 2004 book, "If educators are professionals, and if education is a discipline rather than a set of fads, then educators must insist on working in ways that they know engage students' minds and lead to deeper understanding, no matter how countercyclical these approaches may seem."[38] By adopting multiple intelligences, many teachers believed, they could maintain their claims on professionalism through the judgments they made about student strengths, as well as through innovative and resourceful lesson planning designed to maximize learning.

Multiple intelligences was a theory with different uses for educators. It could challenge the validity of tests, open up standardized curricula, and defend cherished beliefs about teacher professionalism and student ability. But whatever the use, it was a theory philosophically compatible among public school teachers. And it was highly transportable—seemingly easy to understand from the names of its "intelligences" alone. The ironic downside of this, of course, was that it could also be used as a bulwark against real deliberation or debate. As Gardner himself wrote, "It is possible to wave the MI flag without having to think, change, or grow."[39] Though likely not a majority, that was certainly true for some.

Yet what many teachers wished for was not to fend off change, but rather to usher in the particular changes that they viewed as valuable. Specifically, they wanted answers for what to do in the classroom to improve student achievement. And, as an industry of professional development providers and entrepreneurial consultants worked to meet demand with supply, multiple intelligences would take on that function as well—an easy-to-implement means of producing tangible results.

MULTIPLE INTELLIGENCES
AND PROFESSIONAL DEVELOPMENT

The theory of multiple intelligences was a grassroots phenomenon with a clear appeal for a wide range of educators responding to various threats, pressures, and forces in the late twentieth and early twenty-first century. But it was also supported by a fast-growing network of consultants, content providers, and other for-profit entities rushing to fill the market void left wide open by Howard Gardner, specifically with regard to classroom applications of his theory. Altering multiple intelligences in their own ways, these entrepreneurial third parties capitalized on the fact that multiple intelligences was occupationally realistic in its orientation and easy to transport across contexts. And in translating it for immediate practitioner use, they turned multiple intelligences from a phenomenon into a blockbuster. Along the way, a theory with several uses quickly became a theory of many uses.

Frames of Mind and *Multiple Intelligences: The Theory in Practice* sold hundreds of thousands of copies—major successes in the world of education publishing. But neither book gave explicit instructions for how the theory of multiple intelligences should be introduced at the school-site level. "Scattered notes," Gardner wrote in *Frames of Mind*, were as far as he was prepared to go "in trying to draw some educational and policy implications."[40] Yet Gardner's reluctance to outline classroom applications of the theory did not hinder its growth. In fact, it may have helped.

While Gardner may have felt uncomfortable peddling multiple intelligences as a panacea for K–12 instruction, others had no such scruples. In fact, working in an unfettered and decentralized marketplace of ideas unregulated by the state or by standards of scholarly review, enterprising third parties had every incentive to adapt multiple intelligences for classroom use and sell it as aggressively as possible. Not surprisingly, then, when specialty publishing houses discovered multiple intelligences in the 1980s and 1990s, they took an idea with great potential appeal and tweaked it to amplify its inherent strengths. In so doing, they made it a bestseller.

The most prolific of these houses was SkyLight Publications of Illinois, which published David Lazear's *Eight Ways of Teaching: The Artistry of Teaching with Multiple Intelligences* in 1991 and *Multiple Intelligence Approaches to Assessment* in 1994.[41] In 1993 it published Carolyn Chapman's *If the Shoe Fits: Developing Multiple Intelligences in the Classroom*, as well as her following books—*Multiple Assessments for Multiple Intelligences* and *Multiple Intelligences Centers and Projects*.[42] SkyLight also published a host of other multiple intelligences–related works, including Sally Berman's *A Multiple Intelligences Road to a Quality Classroom*, Anna T. O'Connor and Sheila Callahan-Young's *Seven Windows to a Child's World*, James Bellanca's *Active Learning Handbook for the Multiple Intelligences Classroom*, Robin Fogarty's *Problem-Based Learning and Other Curriculum Models for the Multiple Intelligences Classroom*, and Fogarty and Bellanca's *Multiple Intelligences: A Collection*.[43] By 1996 there were already fifty books on using multiple intelligences in the classroom.[44] Today, there are hundreds.

Entrepreneurial consultants, in many cases authors of books on using multiple intelligences in the classroom, soon began offering workshops and materials to support professional development around the theory. Robin Fogarty, for instance, started Robin Fogarty and Associates, and began consulting for state departments of education across the United States, as well as for ministries of education in countries like Singapore, Russia, and New Zealand.[45] Similarly, after authoring works on multiple intelligences applications, Carolyn Chapman went on to start Creative Learning Connection, Inc.—a Georgia-based consulting firm offering workshops, courses, keynote addresses, and printed materials. Another entrepreneurial proponent of Gardner's theory—Spencer Kagan, author of *Multiple Intelligences: The Complete MI Book*—started Kagan Publishing and Professional Development. And Dee Dickinson, coauthor of *Teaching and Learning Through Multiple Intelligences* with Bruce and Linda Campbell, started New Horizons for Learning.[46] New Horizons soon began to focus on the theory, and by 1990 it had sponsored eight international conferences on multiple intelligences applications. It has since become a major destination for those interested in resources on the subject.

Other entrepreneurs have joined in by creating multiple intelligences diagnostics, curricula, and assessments. Harvey Silver, Richard Strong, and Matthew Perini, for instance, developed the "Multiple Intelligences Indicator," while Keith Rogers of Brigham Young University developed the "Rogers Indicator of Multiple Intelligences." Walter McKenzie developed the "Multiple Intelligences Inventory," and C. Branton Shearer developed the "Multiple Intelligences Developmental Assessment Scale"—a "Swiss Army knife of self-assessments that guides people to a deeper appreciation for their intellectual and creative lives."[47] Multiple intelligences curricula for particular courses include Edna Kovacs's *Writing with Multiple Intelligences: Creating Opportunities for Teachers, Writers, and Therapists*; Peter Smagorinsky's *Expressions: Multiple Intelligences in the English Class*; Hope Martin's *Multiple Intelligences in the Mathematics Classroom*; and Sandy Tasker's *Science Solutions* books on using multiple intelligences in the science classroom. Without question, these products have enriched their authors. Yet it is important to remember that multiple intelligences consultants and entrepreneurs also played an important role in making the idea more occupationally realistic for classroom teachers, as well as in raising the profile of Gardner's work. And even if their readings of multiple intelligences were sometimes problematic or overly simplistic, they were key players in moving the theory into practice.

Among the most successful of the multiple intelligences consultants and entrepreneurs has been Thomas Armstrong. Author of five books on the theory, including *Multiple Intelligences in the Classroom* and *Seven Kinds of Smart: Identifying and Developing Your Multiple Intelligences*, Armstrong entered the multiple intelligences marketplace early and published often.[48] And, like other providers of multiple intelligences–related professional development, he quickly translated his publication success into speaking engagements with schools, districts, and state offices of education. In recent years, Armstrong has counted among his clients the departments of education in Arizona, Georgia, Kentucky, North Carolina, North Dakota, and South Carolina, as well as more than eighty school districts including Baltimore, Chicago, Denver, San Diego, San Francisco, New York City, and Los Angeles.[49]

Much of Armstrong's success might be attributed to effective marketing. Yet he also has a highly valued product: a straightforward message that is easy to digest in an afternoon and seemingly effortless to implement. Both of those factors are a result of how Gardner framed the theory. But Armstrong has pushed those characteristics much further—selling multiple intelligences as a road-ready panacea for ensuring success among students of all abilities. As Armstrong wrote in *Educational Leadership* in 1994, "The master code of this learning style model is simple: for whatever you wish to teach, link your instructional objective to words, numbers or logic, pictures, music, the body, social interaction, and/or personal experience." Such practices, he concluded, provided a "blueprint for ensuring [student] success in school and in life."[50] Such claims were a distinct departure from Gardner's own work.

Despite Gardner's stardom, then, devising applications for multiple intelligences in the classroom quickly developed into a bottom-up process driven by a wide range of providers. Those enterprising third parties might have promoted other ideas instead of multiple intelligences. In fact, for many of them, multiple intelligences products represented only a fraction of trainings and merchandise sales. Yet the theory had a simple enough core—a handful of discrete intelligences—that it could be described in a single seminar. Additionally, it had the benefit of being authored by a scholar at a prestigious university, who was also willing to pen forewords or provide dust-jacket blurbs. Further, as Gardner operated at some remove from practical work on multiple intelligences, it was an idea that could be adapted to make it even more appealing to classroom educators concerned with applications—translated into a simple curricular add-on. As Gardner put it in an interview, "When you're doing professional development, you're trying to sell a product . . . [you need] something that can be picked up pretty quickly . . . and you want to have some easy victories."[51] For providers looking to land one-shot professional development workshops at K–12 schools, multiple intelligences was an easy pitch.[52]

School district central offices, for their part, did not possess the capacity to provide alternative trainings to those offered by third-party providers.

In fact, whatever shortcomings they were previously characterized by, districts were further limited by downsizing in the 1980s and 1990s.[53] Yet, as Judith Warren Little has written, despite their decreased capacity, schools and districts remained "inclined to do *something* in the name of professional development (before the fiscal year ends, the state program expires, or the school board demands results)." Turning to a decentralized network of third-party providers, they have relied on a traditional menu of training options: "workshop series, special courses, or in-service days devoted to transmitting some specific set of ideas, practices, or materials to teachers."[54]

The result of this shift has been a bigger, if not necessarily better, marketplace of choices for consumers of professional development. Competing with one another for often lucrative contracts, third-party providers have a strong incentive to entertain their clientele without asking too much in return, and to develop a message general enough that it can be adapted in multiple settings. Thus, despite research indicating that effective professional development is time-intensive, context-specific, and content-rich, a great deal of training relies on traditional methods of delivery and is strongly shaped by consumer desire.[55] As Dennis Sparks and Stephanie Hirsh have suggested, such training is often evaluated only in terms of the "happiness quotient" measuring participant satisfaction and their "off-the-cuff assessment regarding its usefulness."[56] The result is often what Edward Joyner has called a disconnected "smorgasbord of staff development workshops" with little long-term resonance.[57] Whatever its inherent advantages in making the move from research to practice, then, multiple intelligences was still affected by the problematic nature of professional development—frequently entering classrooms only shallowly, or in some manner distorted.

Gardner did, eventually, get into the act himself, in part because he began to see so many interpretations of the theory that he "found repugnant."[58] First, he signed on with the Multiple Intelligences Institute, which offers curriculum, professional development, a school management system, and accreditation.[59] Soon, however, Gardner backed out of that arrangement, which he saw as too entrepreneurially oriented. He has since launched his own venture—MI Oasis. Still, Gardner's new project is one of literally hundreds of resources on the Web, and not among the most visible. This, in some ways, is to be expected, given the increasingly prominent role that intermediaries have played in providing teacher professional development services. In any case, the idea has been dramatically shaped by those whose professional and personal interests compelled them to liberally interpret multiple intelligences; Gardner has long since ceased to control the idea.

"ADAPTED AND INTERPRETED"

Not surprisingly, given the free-market approach to providing multiple intelligences–related professional development and the absence of a central authority, The theory has been repeatedly modified. As one multiple intelligences intermediary put it, the idea was "adapted and interpreted" to show K–12 teachers "the value of the concept and its applicability to uses in the classroom."[60]

Such assistance in moving multiple intelligences into the knowledge base of teachers was, without a doubt, instrumental. Enterprising intermediaries understood quite clearly what would succeed among teachers and were highly motivated to sell books and seminars. Consequently, they adjusted Gardner's theory to ensure maximal popularity.

One case in point is the argument in favor of alternative forms of evaluation. Gardner, for his part, did little but challenge the validity of the kinds of standardized tests used to measure student achievement. But third-party intermediaries went a step further, proposing a broader range of evaluative methods—student portfolios, independent projects, student journals, and other creative tasks—that would capture a fuller range of student ability.[61] Thomas Armstrong, for example, advocated for "authentic assessments" that, rather than reducing "children's rich and complex lives to a collection of scores, percentiles, or grades," would give teachers a "felt sense" of a "child's unique experience as a learner."[62] Such proposals certainly were unlikely to overturn federally mandated state accountability procedures. Nevertheless, they gave teachers something concrete to advocate for in place of machine-scored multiple-choice tests.

Other interpretations—like the notion that multiple intelligences can serve as a framework for differentiating instruction—have been more problematic in practice and less in keeping with Gardner's research. Such readings have echoed the basic notion at the core of multiple intelligences that students are smart in different ways. Yet many of these practical applications have stretched the theory beyond sensibility and usefulness. Armstrong, for instance, suggests that in the language arts classroom, children rating high in the "naturalist" intelligence might use twigs and leaves to spell words, and that for children with a high degree of "bodily-kinesthetic" intelligence, a teacher might associate movement with spelling.[63] Thus, by fusing the theory of multiple intelligences with the concept of "learning styles," Armstrong and others have sold teachers on the idea that there are particular "multiple intelligences strategies" that might be used to teach the same content to different kinds of learners.[64] Such messages have been so pervasive, in fact, that many pedagogy textbooks now include the theory of multiple intelligences in a chapter alongside material on learning styles.[65]

Gardner and others have been explicit about the fact that the theory is not equivalent to the concept of learning styles.[66] Each intelligence is aligned with certain kinds of content. Consequently, the intelligences, as defined by Gardner, are not conduits for teaching content from outside their particular domains. Music, for instance, though it might be included in the history curriculum as a way of engaging students and making the past more real, cannot be used to teach students to think historically. And while an instructor might use a metaphor in one medium for teaching in another, Gardner was sure to note in *Multiple Intelligences: The Theory into Practice* that "at some point, the learner must translate back into the [original] domain."[67]

Again, though, it is important to note the essential role that intermediaries played in moving multiple intelligences from the ivory tower into the classroom. As school curricula narrowed at the turn of the century, multiple intelligences somewhat unrealistically suggested that the whole range of student abilities should become a part of what was taught and tested. And that was simply not going to happen. To make it fit better with the world that teachers actually inhabited—a world in which music and art classes were being dropped in favor of longer blocks of instruction in math and reading—enterprising third parties made the case that some intelligences could be used for teaching the content of other intelligences.

Whatever their contributions, though, entrepreneurial interpreters of multiple intelligences have prepared some reckless and nonsensical interpretations of the idea, many of which have resonated. Singing, for instance, is frequently mentioned as a means of teaching content traditionally associated with the "logical-mathematical" intelligence. Among available materials from Kagan Publishing are songs for learning history, including one about Christopher Columbus set to the tune of "The Itsy Bitsy Spider." Thomas Armstrong recommends teaching John Locke's concept of Natural Law by having half of the class chant "'natural law, natural law, natural law, natural law . . .' while the other half repeats: 'life, li-ber-ty, happ-i-ness, life, li-ber-ty, happ-i-ness'"[68] And another multiple intelligences advocate praised the teaching of multiplication through "the African American tradition of 'ham bone,' a chant accompanied by rhythmic knee slapping." By slapping their knees, she reported, children "who had trouble remembering their math facts were able to recall the multiplication tables quite easily."[69] None of these practices are particularly faithful to the theory as articulated by Gardner. And Gardner has said so. As he observed in a 1995 *Phi Delta Kappan* article, singing may simply function as a mnemonic device for students, hardly engaging any musical intelligence, and not authentically engaging other forms of intelligence in question.[70] Further, as others have observed, using song to generate student interest and help children learn material by rote has long been common in elementary classrooms. Thus, rather than being a multiple intelligences–specific practice, it is a traditional one.[71]

Gardner has often redirected educators back to his work and occasionally raised questions about popular revisions of the theory. According to him, "There is no point in assuming that every topic can be effectively approached in at least seven ways, and it is a waste of effort and time to attempt to do this." As he recalled in the mid-1990s, children in ostensibly multiple intelligences–oriented classrooms are sometimes "encouraged simply to move their arms or to run around, on the assumption that exercising one's body represents in itself some kind of MI statement." Exercise, he noted, is not a bad thing. "But random muscular movements have nothing to do with the cultivation of the mind . . . or even of the body!"[72] Referring to lesson plans designed at Thomas Hoerr's New City School, for instance, Gardner responded that "the only answer I can give is this: I would certainly not want to be in a school where a lot of time was spent doing these things."[73] In a foreword to Mindy Kornhaber's book *Multiple Intelligences: Best Ideas from Research and Practice*, Gardner wondered if adapters had "even read the original publications."[74]

Still, Gardner is well aware of his reliance on intermediaries, who in many cases made the theory of multiple intelligences more philosophically compatible or occupationally realistic than it otherwise might have been, and often did so without unreasonably distorting it. Consequently, he has endorsed the work of even his more liberal interpreters. He wrote the preface for Thomas Armstrong's *Multiple Intelligences in the Classroom*, observing that Armstrong had "always stood out . . . because of the accuracy of his accounts."[75] And he wrote the foreword for Robin Fogarty and Judy Stoer's *Integrating Curricula with Multiple Intelligences*, praising the authors for their "ample examples of how to approach authentic curricular goals and assessment needs within an MI framework."[76] In his most telling foreword, though—for *Multiple Intelligences in the Elementary Classroom*—Gardner followed his praise for the authors with an acknowledgment of their autonomy. "No longer is there a single or a 'right' way to use MI," he wrote. "Rather, educators are encouraged to become familiar with a range of approaches and choose the one that makes most sense in light of their own goals and contexts."[77] Gardner, in other words, recognized that he was not in control, and that perhaps he never had been.

Such reinterpretations, it seems, are a product of the transportability problem in education. Without reliable conduits for moving scholarship into practice, and without robust systems of support for such movement, ideas tend to travel only in their simplest forms—as outlines or catchphrases or images like the pyramid representing Bloom's taxonomy—that are easily passed along and quickly understood. Multiple intelligences had a simple and durable core, but was otherwise open and flexible. In some ways, that was important to its fit with teacher philosophy and occupational practice—making it possible to adapt the idea to teacher needs and concerns, as well as to local context. But in other ways, the simplicity of the form that traveled—a list of several seemingly self-explanatory intelligences—led directly to wayward understandings.

Adaptation and reinterpretation, as particular examples bear out, have not always been problematic. Many educators have used Gardner's theory exactly as it was intended—as a basis for discussion about intelligence and the way it is ordinarily perceived and measured. Others who reinterpreted the theory did so in a manner that brought energy and vitality to their classrooms. As teachers at one school found, the existence of various intelligences among students mandated that teachers serve a wider range of responsibilities, and they accordingly developed site-specific solutions.[78]

Still, many reinterpretations have been questionable, revealing a clear downside to highly transportable concepts. Without support for ideas once they enter the classroom, it seems, they can continue to transform in unexpected ways. And while this may make them more popular among teachers, it may ultimately drain an idea of its power. Though it is certainly important that ideas gain enough traction and popularity with teachers to get a foot in the schoolhouse door, it is also important that those ideas challenge teachers, help them grow, and drive their practice in a consistently positive direction.

CONCLUSION

Howard Gardner's theory of multiple intelligences has been a blockbuster in American education—what one set of backers called "contemporary education's most popular idea."[79] A search of the federal government's Education Resources Information Center (ERIC), for instance, returns over twelve hundred articles on "multiple intelligences"—twice as many results as a search for "Bloom's taxonomy," and a few hundred more than a search for "progressive education," though not nearly as many as for "state standards." It is extensively, and positively, covered in textbooks for aspiring teachers.[80] Those curious about multiple intelligences conduct hundreds of thousands of Internet searches for it each year.[81] And there are at least six schools in the United States named for Howard Gardner.[82] Despite its critics, the idea has taken hold in schools large and small, public and private, across disciplines, and at all grade levels.

Multiple intelligences, somewhat surprisingly, did not bridge the worlds of theory and practice because it was demonstrably right, or because it had been shown to promote school improvement. Instead, it made the long leap into practice because it possessed characteristics that most pieces of educational scholarship did not. To put it another way, the theory was simply a better fit for a challenging environment than most other ideas.

One chief reason why educators in public and private schools took note of Gardner's work was because it seemed so harmonious with their views. Unlike so much educational research, multiple intelligences seemed particularly attuned to the perspectives and concerns of teachers and school administrators—a philosophically compatible piece of scholarship in contentious times. Multiple intelligences, in short, read less like the product of the ivory tower, and more like the product of a K–12 insider—something Gardner quite intentionally cultivated. Additionally, Gardner bore several important status symbols—as a Harvard professor, a MacArthur genius, and one of few educational researchers whose work could be found at the corner bookstore.

Multiple intelligences also had an edge over other pieces of educational research because it was easy to transport. Almost anyone who had read Gardner's work or heard him speak could describe the idea of multiple intelligences to a peer—a key advantage in a field marked by little centralized authority and in which most teachers rely on their colleagues for professional guidance. The intelligences were small enough in number that one might remember them all, but large enough to indicate complexity. And they were named in a manner that captured the core of each intelligence in a single word.

The entrance of multiple intelligences into the knowledge base of teachers was also the consequence of tremendous support from third parties who helped make the idea occupationally realistic. Some educators, certainly, were able to intuit applications for the theory in their classrooms. But many more teachers were able to see a use for the idea only once it was championed by professional development providers. Motivated mostly by profit, and crafting interpretations of uneven quality, these intermediaries offered thousands of multiple intelligences seminars and created dozens of workbooks. In so doing, they played a significant role in winning Gardner a place in K–12 schools.

Work by educational scholars like Larry Cuban and David Cohen suggests that the language of reform is more readily adopted than its substance.[83] Yet in the case of Gardner's theory, it seems that adoption of multiple intelligences language may have led to substantive kinds of actions. After all, teachers drawn to the theory of multiple intelligences can immediately begin using it to shape lesson plans and assessment. In fact, without much coaching or support, without authorization from administrators, and without even having read anything by Gardner himself, teachers have used multiple intelligences to support a wide range of classroom practices.

The result of this, some critics have argued, has impeded reform efforts and undermined educational rigor for students of all abilities. According to Maureen Stout, author of *The Feel-Good Curriculum*, multiple intelligences is merely a new guise for the self-esteem movement in American education. In her eyes, the theory taught teachers to praise students for their various qualities, even if those students were unable to competently read or write. Consequently, she argued, "All of us are beginning to lose our respect for the authority of reason in our society."[84] Others have leveled similar criticisms. As Alan Wolfe wrote in 1993, "MI theory has its limits, not because it is impractical, but because our schools, which are increasingly teaching less and doing other things more, will jump on any theory that lets them avoid the one kind of intelligence that insists there are some answers that are most definitely right and others that are most definitely wrong."[85]

Still, for every critic of multiple intelligences, there are dozens of educators who feel that Gardner's work has helped them in developing their practice. And scholars like Mindy Kornhaber have published results indicating that schools systematically using the theory can show substantial growth in standardized test scores, student behavior, and parental participation.[86]

Without question, the theory of multiple intelligences has been implemented in a wide range of ways, with different degrees of faithfulness, and varying levels of commitment. As Gardner put it, the theory is frequently "understood superficially."[87] And some teachers, it is clear, have used multiple intelligences to avoid difficult discussions and plow ahead with pedagogically questionable approaches.

But multiple intelligences may also have played a key role in helping teachers develop as reflective professionals. It has prompted new kinds of discussions in some schools, caused many teachers to reevaluate the degree to which they are engaging all of their students, and provided some common vocabulary for those opposed to the narrowing of educational aims.

Ultimately, whatever the limits of teacher knowledge about multiple intelligences, the idea is recognized by K–12 educators in a way that most research is not. Multiple intelligences did often enter practice problematically. But dubious interpretations of the theory were not preconditions for its passage into classrooms. Instead, they were *side effects* of that move. Given this, it is not impossible to imagine a world in which an idea like multiple intelligences, supported by thoughtful policies and practices, might make a more thoroughly and uniformly productive entrance into classrooms.

CHAPTER THREE

"Wholehearted Purposeful Activity"
The Project Method

Like Bloom's taxonomy or Howard Gardner's theory of multiple intelligences, the project method is an extraordinary example of educational scholarship that moved from the ivory tower into the schoolhouse. Yet unlike those two ideas, the project method is a concept without a history, at least in the eyes of educators. While "projects" are a familiar presence in K–12 classrooms, educators tend to see them as timeless components of the teacher toolkit rather than as a particular methodology. And even many of those who *do* recognize projects as the product of educational scholarship know only of the idea's most recent incarnation: project-based learning.

At first blush, then, this might seem to indicate that the project method has won less of a foothold in practice than the taxonomy or multiple intelligences. But in fact the opposite is true. The project method is *so* well accepted that modern educators simply view it as property of the educational commons. And the success of repackaged versions of the method—as project-based learning or problem-based learning—only further illustrate the enduring power of the idea.

First detailed by Columbia University professor William Heard Kilpatrick in a 1918 essay, the project method quickly entered the world of practice—used as a means of actively engaging students in the process of

learning. And, despite the fact that its designer and chief proponent retired in 1937, the idea continues to stream through K–12 education and
the knowledge base of teachers as a kind of pedagogical inheritance. From
coast to coast and across grade levels, students each day conceive of and
complete tasks of their own design, engaging in what Kilpatrick called
"wholehearted purposeful activity." Even in an age of standardized curricula and high-stakes accountability tests, "projects" remain central in thousands of classrooms.

Like Bloom's taxonomy and multiple intelligences, the project method
had high-status academic origins, seemed to address core educator concerns, and tapped into dominant sentiments among teachers looking to
formalize their practices without compromising their beliefs. Like those
other ideas, its most basic form demands little overhaul in the structure or
culture of the occupation. And, insofar as the project method is explained
by its name, it is similarly transportable.

But the project method is different from those other cases in two re-
gards. First, though Kilpatrick's name is often unrecognized today, he became a much larger star than either Bloom or Gardner, and the project
method was a much more immediate sensation than either the taxonomy
or multiple intelligences. Hence, an examination of the method promises
to further illuminate the means by which research can enter practice, and
particularly to reveal how a scholarly idea can gain such sudden and stun-
ning perceived significance.

Second, at nearly a century old, the project method has a history
nearly twice as long as the taxonomy and four times as long as multiple
intelligences. Thus, having persisted across several generations, the project method promises not only to deepen our understanding of how ideas
move across *space*, but also to reveal how they move across *time*. After all,
even as Kilpatrick's star faded and knowledge of the idea's scholarly origins
diminished, the use of projects in K–12 classrooms endured.

This chapter looks at the history of the project method, from its development at Columbia University's Teachers College early in the twentieth
century through the present. In so doing, it examines the historical context
in which the method was developed, its alignment with the progressive

movement in education, and the work of its champions to build their brand. Finally, the chapter tracks the project method into the schoolhouse, looking at how teachers adopted it into practice and passed the idea both down the hallway and across the generations.

A NEW(ISH) METHOD

William Heard Kilpatrick joined the faculty at Columbia University's Teachers College in 1911 and, like many ambitious new professors, quickly began looking for a way to make his mark. Already in his mid-forties, he sought—as he noted in his diary—to achieve "power and influence" and to be remembered as an "original thinker," not merely an "acceptable teacher."[1] But unlike many scholars in the field, Kilpatrick saw the route to power and influence extending well beyond the walls of the university. He set his sights not on gaining status among fellow academics, but rather on building his reputation among several hundred thousand K–12 teachers.

Kilpatrick's strategy for raising his profile among teachers was, in his words, "to think of a small + popular book" that would "appeal constructively + so sell better."[2] That was not exactly the plan that he executed. Instead of a book, it was an article—"The Project Method," which ran in a 1918 issue of *Teachers College Record*. And, rather than selling it, Kilpatrick and his allies at Teachers College would give it away for free. Still, such thinking reveals that, from the outset of his career, Kilpatrick possessed not only the ambition to reach beyond the ivory tower, but also a sense of the distinct moves required for achieving such an aim.

The article, by all standards of educational scholarship, was a smash hit. The print run of the journal quickly sold out, leading the Teachers College Bureau of Publications—at Kilpatrick's behest—to distribute sixty thousand reprints.[3] And Kilpatrick, who was promoted to full professor, immediately won the recognition for original thinking that he so desired. As Mendel Everett Branom wrote one year later, Kilpatrick had produced "a radical departure from the commonly held viewpoint."[4] And in the years that followed, the project method was widely hailed as a highly original concept and evidence of Kilpatrick's genius.

While Kilpatrick's expression of the project method was in many ways original, projects had actually been used in various educational programs long before the twentieth century. In fact, a flexible definition of the word *project* would classify many forms of apprenticeship—an ancient educational practice—under the banner of the so-called project method.

More formal uses of projects in schoolwork were also documented long before Kilpatrick burst onto the scene. In the early eighteenth century, for instance, students at the Académie Royale d'Architecture in Paris were asked to complete final projects as evidence of their competence. Applying principles of composition and construction learned in lectures and tutorials, students built models rather than completing papers or sitting for oral exams.[5]

The first American scholars and researchers to discuss the use of projects in the curriculum were those concerned with vocational education. In the late 1890s, Charles R. Richards, professor of manual training at Teachers College, proclaimed that the aim of career-oriented education should be "to arouse the highest degree of purposeful self-activity through a direct appeal to the life and healthy interests of the pupil."[6] In an example project, fourth-grade students built a Greek temple out of clay, casting their best pieces in plaster to create a complete class model.

Richards was not alone in outlining such a program for K–12 classes. David Snedden, a leader in the push for vocational education and curricular tracking, also discussed the potential usefulness of projects, as did reformers like Franklin Bobbitt and W. W. Charters. Yet these turn-of-the-century discussions of classroom projects did not lead to widespread implementation. As Snedden wrote in 1916, "The project as a pedagogic unit of organization in practical arts and in vocational education had found a place, if not always a welcome."[7] Projects remained a minor act well outside of the spotlight.

Kilpatrick's model was different for several reasons. First, he was interested in general, rather than vocational, education. A student of math, physics, and philosophy, Kilpatrick was a firm believer in the "avid pursuit of truth" and saw great value in the traditional disciplines.[8] Second, Kilpatrick's reputation depended on the success of the project method far more so than did the reputations of highly influential administrative progressives like Snedden or Bobbitt. Accordingly, he presented projects not merely as activities, but as the very core of the reformed K–12 classroom. And finally, because Kilpatrick framed projects as an approach grounded in a broad range of educational science, he was able to make a much stronger case for their importance and value. Tying seemingly unrelated scholarship together in a single concept, he was able to position the project method as both timeless and cutting-edge—a move crucial to the idea's perceived significance among educators.

"SCIENCE" OF ALL SORTS

Kilpatrick's influence and the success of the project method have frequently been attributed to the rise of pedagogical progressivism.[9] But while Kilpatrick eventually became a celebrity in the movement, he was a relatively minor figure before the appearance of his groundbreaking article. Further, the project method drew on a wider range of research than that generated by pedagogical progressives. After all, Kilpatrick's aim was to establish as much authority for his method as possible, not merely to align himself with John Dewey and the progressives. The project method, he repeatedly wrote in his piece in *Teachers College Record*, was not merely an invention; it was, he argued, firmly rooted in the "laws of learning" established by a wide range of scholars. As Kilpatrick put it, his aim was to unify "a number of important related aspects of the educative process" into "one concept."[10]

Of clear influence to Kilpatrick were the child-centered teachings of Europeans like Johann Pestalozzi and Friedrich Froebel. As Kilpatrick wrote in 1916, "More than any other of his time Froebel respected the individuality of the child," and noted that "for him the child's natural interests are proper and worthy of all fostering." Pestalozzi, he added, stood "next to Froebel" among defenders of childhood.[11]

Kilpatrick's interest in these thinkers was genuine, and their work resonated with his personal experiences as an elementary school teacher and principal. As he would later tell biographer Samuel Tenenbaum, he worked diligently to help students understand that he "was not judging them." Rather, he was "really and wholeheartedly trying to help them."[12] Still, whatever Kilpatrick's personal feelings about figures like Pestalozzi and Froebel, tapping into European romanticism was a deft move. Though the dominance of European thinkers in education was more characteristic of the nineteenth century than the twentieth, romantic thinking about children remained a powerful undercurrent among twentieth-century educators.

At the same time, Kilpatrick was deeply affected by contemporary pedagogical progressives, and especially by his Columbia University colleague John Dewey. Of particular influence with regard to the project method was Dewey's dictum that interest and effort were linked—an idea that Kilpatrick soon began to refer to as "the Dewey analysis."[13] As Dewey wrote, for the pupil to truly learn, he must have a "continuous activity in which he is interested for its own sake."[14] Such notions would form the theoretical groundwork for many of Kilpatrick's thoughts about education.[15] And tying himself to Dewey would also locate Kilpatrick at the vanguard of pedagogical thought. Thus, despite the fact that Kilpatrick found Dewey's lectures dull and often confusing—he criticized him for failing to "prepare the ground, so that a newcomer can follow him"—Kilpatrick continued to quite consciously reference Dewey and position himself as an interpreter of the famous philosopher.[16]

Finally, Kilpatrick was drawn to the work of psychologists, and particularly to that of William James and Edward Thorndike. Referencing James's maxim on the importance of a connection between the student's life and the material being studied, Kilpatrick was able to draw on the most influential psychologist of the old guard. And referencing Thorndike's assertion that learning happened through discrete and observable steps, he was able to draw on the scientific authority of a new generation. As Kilpatrick later wrote in a letter to Abraham Flexner, "What is done in the prosecution of this wholehearted purposeful activity will, by Thorndike's laws of readiness, exercise, and effect, be learned in the degree it is accepted as helping the activity towards its goal."[17]

Projects, thus, would ostensibly utilize the laws of learning as then established, and do so at a period when the effort to establish a "science of education" was on the rise.[18] Such efforts were not lost on Kilpatrick's audience. As one of the era's leading educationists, Henry Suzzalo, wrote in 1920, "'Project teaching' is the more inclusive swing of a current movement which is trying to organize education on a practical psychological basis."[19] Further, for those attuned to other methodological approaches—like those of Dewey or the European romantics—the project method seemed to square with that literature as well.

By situating the project method in this manner, Kilpatrick sent a clear signal about the scholarly merit of his proposal. Straddling a turning point in educational science, he tied his method to leading theoretical and empirical research, as well as to popular ideas—many of them European in origin—that had entered the mainstream. By doing so, Kilpatrick deftly substantiated his claim on legitimacy. Further, he positioned such work in the context of developments in demography, industry, science, social life, and international relations.[20]

He was, without question, interpreting scholarship quite liberally. As Ellen Lagemann has argued, all that supported the project method were "random, anecdotal data; quotes taken from essentially incompatible educational theories (including those of Dewey and Thorndike); and Kilpatrick's personal energy, charisma, and persuasiveness."[21] But to working educators, the project method might have seemed on the cutting edge—or, if not on the cutting edge, at least in line with recognizable standards of scholarship.

Still, whatever the flaws of the project method, Kilpatrick was no fool. More interested in connecting with teachers than with scholars, he quite intentionally played fast and loose with research. He was having it, in a sense, both ways. As a result, he soaked up the scientific authority of other scholars while simultaneously creating a simple, synthetized concept that teachers could easily draw on for classroom use.

INFLUENCING AND EVANGELIZING

Kilpatrick recognized the necessity of establishing scholarly legitimacy for his idea. But he also realized that the project method would not simply migrate into practice on its own merits. Rather, he understood the importance of promoting the idea and used every advantage at his disposal to make the project method more visible.

One such advantage was his position at Teachers College. In the first decades of the twentieth century, Teachers College was the unrivaled citadel of educational "science." It had twenty full professors, six associate professors, thirty-nine instructors, seven lecturers, and five part-time faculty from other departments. By contrast, the faculties of Princeton, Johns Hopkins, Penn, Yale, and Harvard had a combined total of four professors of education.[22] Such a position gave Kilpatrick significant visibility in the field. And it exposed him to far more students than he might have taught at a smaller institution. As he wrote in his diary in 1931: "In the country at large, I am increasingly well known . . . My teaching gives me in the aggregate my greatest power."[23] By one estimate, he reached thirty-four thousand students between 1909 and 1937.[24]

Other Teachers College faculty members, certainly, had these same advantages. Yet unlike some of his colleagues whose research helped establish the project method's so-called laws of learning, Kilpatrick himself did not seem to possess a clear research agenda. Consequently, the project method was not one of many products in an ambitious and ongoing program. Instead, it was a cornerstone around which to build a legacy, and Kilpatrick used every avenue available to him.

Kilpatrick also took advantage of his position to carefully cultivate enthusiasm for his idea. A 1920 annotated bibliography in *Teachers College Record*, for instance, listed dozens of articles on the project method for seemingly no reason other than to promote Kilpatrick's idea. As author John P. Herring wrote, "The purpose of this bibliography is to spread such knowledge of the project method as now exists." Yet the apparent impetus for the article seems to have been Kilpatrick himself, whom the author thanked for "suggesting that the bibliography be made, for beginning the collection of titles, and for criticizing the annotations."[25]

Kilpatrick also took more formal steps to foster support for the project method. Immediately upon publication of his article, he organized a project method "propaganda club"—"an informal relatively secret organization," as he referred to it in his diary.[26] The language Kilpatrick used in describing the club was, no doubt, somewhat satirical. Nevertheless, it clarified the resolve with which Kilpatrick approached the task of introducing his idea into K–12 schools and his awareness that, in order to accomplish such an aim, he would need help.

Among the members of the propaganda club was James Hosic—Kilpatrick's former doctoral student and, eventually, his chief ally. Hosic had written his dissertation about practical school implementations of the project method and after graduation joined the Teachers College faculty. When Kilpatrick's informal propaganda club took on a more formal moniker—the National Conference on Educational Method—Hosic assumed leadership of it, as well as of the group's in-house publication: the *Journal of Educational Method*. The aim of the journal, as Hosic wrote in its first issue, was to present the project method "as a serious and consistent point of view, likely to have far-reaching effects in bringing about a reorganization of the curriculum."[27] And Hosic, as editor, went about this by soliciting articles that depicted the method as modern, research-based, and rapidly spreading across the nation's schools.

A former school supervisor, Hosic targeted the journal to superintendents, principals, and other administrators. Accordingly, much of its content consisted of practical suggestions for implementation, replete with examples of exemplary programs and lists of additional resources to draw on. Hosic himself was a frequent contributor, and offered nuanced counsel to those introducing the project method into their schools and districts. As he wrote in the journal's seventh issue:

> It would seem to be advisable to call a meeting of the teachers as early in the year as possible, at which time a general discussion of the school work should be taken up. The "project method" should not be thrust forward at once, as to do so might produce a contrary "set" on the part of some which might be very difficult to overcome. Time is not pressing. It would be preferable to proceed slowly and keep going, than to proceed rapidly until some unforeseen difficulty were met upon which the whole project might be wrecked. Rather

draw out criticisms of the present condition of the school work and methods and thereby produce a condition of healthy dissatisfaction. From this proceed to select work which has been observed where the teacher, without calling it "project," has used the "project method" and achieved noticeable results. Bring these before the teaching group and attempt to draw out the question "Why?" The teachers now being interested, the supervisor can begin to talk "project method," definitely connecting the term with the work already accomplished. He will find that the teachers have all done some of this kind of work and are on familiar ground, from which they will enter willingly into an interesting discussion, thereby producing a common bond. This may require several meetings.[28]

Hosic, it is clear, was not merely a proselytizer, but a perceptive and shrewd observer of school culture and the sensibilities of teachers. It is hard to imagine more astute advice given his aim and the context within which he was operating.

Hosic was just as active outside of the journal's offices. In 1921 and 1922, for instance, he taught extramural courses on "The Project Method Applied to Education" in Yonkers, New York; Haverhill and Brockton, Massachusetts; and Hackensack, New Jersey. He spoke on "The Project Method Applied to the Course of Study in English" at the Educational Association of Western Pennsylvania. And he proselytized at a meeting of the Teachers College Club of Pittsburgh.[29]

Kilpatrick was equally busy. For the first three years of its existence, most issues of the journal included lead articles by Kilpatrick, who also continued writing for other publications. He also churned out several books, including an extremely successful textbook that a 1927 Harvard study found to be the third most used work in education classes, behind texts by Alexander Inglis and John Dewey.[30]

Kilpatrick also placed a strong emphasis on the project method in his teaching, as his course syllabi indicate.[31] He even asked students taking the final exam for his Foundations of Method course in 1918 to outline how teachers might "transmit to others the results of the 'project' experiences"—a savvy move given the administrative roles so many Teachers College students went on to assume after graduation.[32]

And perhaps most influentially, Kilpatrick went evangelizing outside of Teachers College. Like Hosic, he led workshops and professional development seminars at school districts from coast to coast for decades. In 1921, he led a one-week seminar with the Milwaukee Teachers Association (MTA) in which he instructed teachers almost exclusively in the use of the project method.[33] A year later, the MTA announced that it had used his ideas to lead the charge for a "renaissance in the educational system."[34] He conducted similar professional development workshops in places like Nebraska, Iowa, Ohio, and Minnesota, where in 1924 he headlined for three nights at the Orpheum Theater in St. Paul.[35] Nearly three decades later, Kilpatrick was still at it, working with Pasadena, California, Superintendent Willard E. Goslin in the late 1940s. During Kilpatrick's visit, seven hundred of the city's thirteen hundred regular certified instructors attended voluntary workshops. And, as he had encouraged Milwaukee teachers to do, Kilpatrick challenged Pasadena teachers to continue their experimentation with the method through peer groups after his departure.[36]

When pitching the project method to teachers, Kilpatrick displayed keen perceptiveness of audience and focused primarily on how teachers could keep students focused and engaged in the classroom. Maintaining student interest, as Kilpatrick understood, had long been a problem for teachers. As his former teacher Charles DeGarmo had written in *Interest and Education*, "The learning of a grammar lesson or the translation of a Latin sentence may seem as remote from real life as self-denial now is from heaven hereafter."[37] And things had only gotten more difficult in the first decades of the twentieth century. As Kilpatrick liked to point out, the historical record revealed the case of old-fashioned schools in which it took dozens of beatings a day to maintain order.[38] Yet modern teachers, faced with an audience of students compelled to attend, were expected to educate without corporal punishment.

Whether responding to a real or imagined problem, school reform rhetoric would be dominated for several decades by the question of what to do for the student attending school under what Kilpatrick termed "dire compulsion."[39] The project method, as he framed it, was a corrective for this state of affairs because it would give students a sense of ownership and endow their work with a feeling of relevance.[40] Specifically, it would transform an antiquated curriculum—designed for a minority of students attending school by choice—into a modern curriculum suited for a majority population attending by compulsion and who, as Kilpatrick later put it, "in former years would have dropped out."[41] As Kilpatrick asked in a 1917 speech in Des Moines, Iowa: "Do our children hate school and school activities? Or do they leave us ready and anxious to continue along the lines of our teaching?"[42]

The project method, pitched as an idea with the power to restore student interest, had a strong appeal among teachers and was highly compatible with dominant educator philosophies. As Mendel Branom wrote in 1919, "Every teacher has had moments of enthusiastic activity on the part of every pupil in dealing with some situation. All problems of discipline were gone. The situation engrossed their every attention. What a joy it was to teach under such conditions!"[43] Kilpatrick understood the appeal of a classroom characterized by full student engagement. Thus, the message behind his method was that classroom complications would dissolve upon the introduction of projects, giving way to a harmonious scene of engaged and inquisitive students.

THE "VITALIZERS"

The project method had astute and passionate advocates in Kilpatrick and Hosic, who raised its perceived significance and underscored its philosophical compatibility. But the idea was also championed by an army of administrators, teacher educators, and professional development providers who themselves had something to gain from it. Aware of the project method's advantages—its scholarly legitimacy, its potential appeal to teachers, and its seeming simplicity among them—such intermediaries used the idea to advance their own interests. And in so doing, they played a key role in amplifying the perceived significance and philosophical compatibility of the project method.

Many promoters of the project method were former students of Kilpatrick's. Given the prestige of their degrees, Teachers College graduates in the first decades of the twentieth century fanned out across the nation, assuming positions of leadership in schools and districts. Many were doctoral students—each year the school enrolled hundreds, compared with dozens at their largest competitors. As Elmer Ellsworth Brown observed in 1923, the school had "come to be preeminently not a college for teachers, but a college for the teachers of teachers."[44] But even a master's degree from Teachers College, which according to a bulletin from the Milwaukee Teachers' Association was "the Mecca of all students of education," was sufficient cause for distinction.[45]

As Teachers College graduates assumed positions in schools and districts, they were often expected to bring with them modern pedagogical methods. And not surprisingly, they frequently turned to the project method. In 1916, for instance—two years before publication of "The Project Method"—an article in the *Minneapolis Morning Tribune* reported that a new administrator would bring to the city "some of the ideas that are now in practice in the established schools in the East . . . [among them] Columbia University." She promised to "vitalize and motivate the work" of Minneapolis students by "putting into practice some of the more modern ideas of the best methods of education."[46] Expected to help the city modernize its practice, she articulated a plan to place particular emphasis on the project method, to which she had been exposed in her studies.[47]

Other professors of education also became promoters of the method. At a time when conducting original research was less important than being a *part* of a broader movement, many tried to attach themselves to the biggest idea of the day. As a consequence, a flurry of project method–related works proliferated across the 1920s, with most titles applying it to English, math, science, history, and other subjects.[48] Some young scholars did so as a way of establishing themselves. Mason Crum, for instance, studied at the University of South Carolina, completed his dissertation on *The Project Method in Religious Education*, found a publisher for it, and soon after joined the faculty at Duke University. Others, who had already achieved positions of influence, may have seen project method–related scholarship as a means of selling books. Samuel Chester Parker of the University of Chicago, for instance, wrote several textbooks in which he discussed the project method. Whatever their experience, it seemed, there were scholars who saw a great benefit in joining sides with Kilpatrick.

Not everyone simply hopped on the project method bandwagon. In 1921, Teachers College hosted a symposium—"Dangers and Difficulties of the Project Method and How to Overcome Them"—and while participants were generally sympathetic toward their colleague, some, like William C. Bagley, were clearly not convinced by the method or comfortable with its implications. That same year, the National Society for the Study of Education attacked the method as flawed and portrayed Kilpatrick as overstating his claim.[49] And in 1922, professor of education W. W. Charters warned of the project's many limitations, referring to the "history of American education" as "a chronicle of fads." He urged that educators adopting the project method also engage in "a systematic study of subjects, by drills, and by exercises."[50]

Still, the project method continued to gather momentum. Extensively covered in pedagogy classes and in journal articles, it quickly became a staple of teacher professional development. At a 1921 meeting of the New Jersey Organization of Teachers of Colored Children, keynote speaker Carter Woodson—editor of the *Journal of Negro History*, and former dean of the College of Arts and Sciences at Howard University—was followed by a "demonstration of the project method in geography by Miss Mary Washington."[51] Nearly three hundred miles south, a Virginia Teachers Association meeting focused on "modern pedagogies" included a presentation on "Problem and Project Method in Teaching Geography."[52] Six years later, the annual meeting of the Child Study Association included an exhibition on the project method—"part of the association's effort to stimulate a high quality of work among public school teachers," according to the *New York Times*.[53] And at the 1931 National Education Association conference, a twenty-three-minute film made by Kilpatrick ran continuously for attendees until 3 a.m.[54]

School districts also got in on the act. In 1921, the Detroit Public Schools made a movie demonstrating that handwriting could be taught via the method. A few years later, Milwaukee's superintendent made the case that schools should use the project method rather than "Fordizing" children—a reference to the assembly-line manufacture of automobiles. "Today," he argued, "we are heaping endless amounts of things to know upon the boy and giving him nothing to do."[55] And in Cleveland, the superintendent of the city's schools wrote that pupils engaged in the project method were "far more likely to be alert, interested, and active than those who study by the traditional fact-cramming method." As he observed, "All this and much more is but part of the spirit of scientific research which from the day of Francis Bacon has been creating a new world."[56] Thus, while Kilpatrick and Hosic did a great deal of work to appeal to educators, they were hardly facing an uphill battle.

Why were so many willing to become promoters of the project method? Rather than acting out of altruism or fervent belief, most were acting, at least to some degree, out of self-interest. School districts were looking to modernize their practices and saw the project method as a scientific and practicable idea. And teachers and administrators, for their part, stood to gain in professional status by making claims on specialized knowledge.[57] And professors of education were often working not just to win tenure or to sell books, but to justify their newly created positions in colleges and universities by tying themselves to the most legitimate scholarship in the field. In short, these actors had something to gain by linking themselves with important scholarship in the field, and the project method was perceived as extraordinarily significant.

Soon, the idea was being pitched by entrepreneurs and educationists as a panacea for virtually every educational ill. Kilpatrick later described the phenomenon as a "get-rich-quick scheme," but in the 1920s it made him one of the biggest stars in American education.[58] Still, while seemingly universal praise for the project method raised its profile dramatically, it may have accelerated a shift away from it. By the 1930s, idea peddlers moved on in search of new opportunities, and references to the project method dropped dramatically (see figure 3.1).

The shift away from textual references to the project method, however, should not be mistaken for a rejection of it in practice. Instead, such

FIGURE 3.1
Textual references to "Project Method," 1900–2000[a]

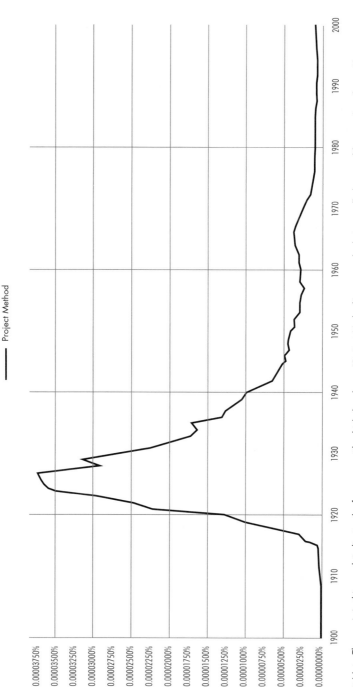

Project Method

[a] *Note:* The y-axis in this graph indicates the frequency with which the phrase "Project Method" appeared relative to all phrases of five words or fewer. The phrase "project method" actually appears twice as frequently as "Project Method," but because the percent values tell us less than does the shape of the curve, either graph will suffice.

a decline can be attributed to the nature of educational research and the motivation behind particular lines of inquiry. Once the project method had been adequately "covered"—through various applications and reconsiderations of the idea—there were fewer incentives for scholars and intermediaries to write about the idea, or at least less low-hanging fruit to be plucked.

Yet while the project method was becoming less topical for scholars, administrators, and third parties, it continued to move through K–12 schools. Easy to use and highly transportable, the idea spread widely and became a standard part of the teacher toolkit.

WHAT THE "PRACTICAL PEOPLE" CAN AGREE TO

Whatever the scholarly bona fides of the project method, its influence would have been minimal had it imposed undue burdens on teachers to implement. The beauty of the method, however, was that it seemed so easy to put into use. In fact, its very name seemed to explain its purpose. And, although Kilpatrick eventually decided that it had been "a mistake to marry [his] program to the term," which he came to view as "provocative and ambiguous," the highly transportable name of the project method would instruct generations of teachers.[59]

Kilpatrick's achievement of simplicity and practicality was particularly impressive when contrasted against the work of other seemingly like-minded scholars from the period. John Dewey, as Herbert Kliebard has written, made the case that science does not tell us what to do; instead, "it offers us the opportunity to reexamine our practices in the light of certain findings."[60] That would have been sufficient had teachers been blessed with the time and the structural support to reexamine their work. In lieu of that, however, many teachers wondered how to *be* progressive. As Larry Cuban has documented, many more teachers ended up talking progressively than actually instructing progressively—in part, no doubt, because they lacked clear direction.[61] But the project method *did* tell teachers what to do, presenting them with a fairly straightforward plan for implementing "laws of learning."

The weakness of the method was that it asked *so much* of teachers, seemingly demanding that they overhaul their entire approach to curriculum design and classroom instruction. Yet the method had a strength that made up for this: its extraordinary flexibility. Insofar as its highly transportable name described its core premise—that students should be encouraged to conceive of and complete projects of their own design—the method was quite clear. Otherwise, however, it was difficult to pin down, and that proved to be a crucial asset in gaining traction with a wide array of teachers working in highly diverse settings. That they should teach with projects was obvious. But fundamental questions—like what a project is—were effectively left to them to decide. As a result, teachers took advantage of the idea's ambiguity to transform the project method into a curricular "add-on."[62]

As a mere add-on, of course, the project method would hardly realize a vision of total curricular revolution—a source of frustration to Kilpatrick. Yet while Kilpatrick may not have imagined or necessarily endorsed this kind of adaptation, it played a key role in making the idea occupationally realistic. Kilpatrick's proposed overhaul of the official curriculum through student-directed projects, after all, threatened to erode traditional school schedules, courses, and lessons. Such a shift would undermine the disciplines as subject areas, and by extension, teachers of art, chemistry, foreign languages, or other specialized subjects. And perhaps more importantly, it would challenge the traditional authority and professionalism of teachers, stripping them of virtually all claims on subject-matter expertise.[63]

Reinterpreted, the project method asked teachers only to add new kinds of activities to the existing curriculum. This stripped the idea of much of its tranformative power, but it also made the project method more practical. In large part, that was due to pressure exerted by administrators who, though they wished to appear progressive and therefore in line with the reform ethos of the period, were also constrained by tradition. Consequently, as Kilpatrick told his biographer, many "insisted that teachers adopt the project method," while mandating "that the teachers teach the same subject matter prescribed by the curriculum."[64] Other administrators simply adopted the project method thoughtlessly and shallowly, leading to a similar outcome, if for different reasons.

Other times, project-oriented curricula were haphazardly or shallowly introduced. As Samuel Tenenbaum noted in 1939, many school leaders had pursued the project method via "mass procedures and mass attacks."[65] The result, as W. W. Charters put it, was that the idea was warped as it passed "from school to school across the land." There was no longer, according to Charters, a "common definition by which to describe its varying forms as it appears in practice."[66] Schools and districts, lacking the ability to provide adequate support for teacher professional development, struggled to help educators address the complex issues associated with adopting the project method.[67] In short, as David Levine has argued, supporters of the method failed to devise "an approach for forging new collegial relations and structures within school systems."[68]

This left many teachers to glean an understanding of the method from very basic definitions of it. But as a Milwaukee assistant superintendent observed, the basic definition of the project method did not "assist the teacher to distinguish between projects suitable for school use and those that are not." As he saw it, projects could include "any wholehearted activity from swatting an annoying fly to winning the Great War." He wanted to know "*what projects* shall be undertaken and *under what conditions*."[69] After all, as Daniel R. Hodgdon observed in 1923, "every known idea and method under the sun has been called a project."[70]

Still, inconsistency or superficiality in implementation, problematic though it may have been, was a necessary tradeoff if the project method was going to gain traction in K–12 classrooms. An inherently idealistic proposal, the project method failed to recognize deep structural and cultural constraints like teacher time limits or the power of curricular tradition. As it turned out, however, the idea was malleable enough that educators could craft it into something that might actually get used. And what resulted was a form that would endure.

For his part, Kilpatrick eventually realized the importance of occupational realism and began endorsing new interpretations of his idea. By 1925, he had expanded his definition of the project method to include what he called the "learning project," which described a traditional approach to curriculum. Learning a scientific principle or an element of language would count as a "project" according to this new rubric. And by 1927, Kilpatrick had adapted the method even further. In "School Method from the Project Point of View," he accepted curricula and lesson plans, provided that they did not unnecessarily restrict the students' scope for action. Teachers could even motivate students "artificially," make the subject matter "interesting," and carry out tests if needed.[71] By the 1930s he was writing of "teacher-guided, student-pursued activities" when discussing his favored approach to learning.[72] He was, it appears, willing to adjust the method in order to gain traction in practice, even if it would seemingly undermine his broader goals of student empowerment and curricular relevance.

Kilpatrick, ultimately, was a pragmatist who recognized the constraints of reality and adapted accordingly. That does not mean that he did so gladly. In 1936, he confided in his diary: "I feel that I am compromising sadly in order to get half-leaf that the practical people can agree to."[73] But unlike John Dewey, who, according to scholar David K. Cohen, paid little attention to such "teacherly work," Kilpatrick cared most about creating something that would actually be *used*.[74]

Less than a decade after the project method's original appearance in *Teachers College Record*, a more practical, more usable, and more teacher-centered version was born. Projects, as amended, would supplement the traditional curriculum. And though they would occasionally demand large blocks of unplanned and unscripted time, they would be sandwiched in between standard episodes of classroom life.

Eventually, this version of the project method would become so commonplace that it could hardly be recognized as a specific method. Yet it did not recede into the background immediately. In fact, thirty years after Kilpatrick's article, some were still blaming the project method for the perceived shortcomings of public schools. As one critic complained, "Academically, the children of this present generation are, it seems to me, the most ill-equipped that the public schools have ever produced." And, as he saw it, the explanation was simple: teachers were spending less time on "cramming basic facts into [the student's] thick skull" and instead allowing students to learn "through activity, through the project method."[75] Thus, whatever people's particular feelings about it, it can be said with some degree of certainty that the project method remained salient for several decades after its creation.

MISSION ACCOMPLISHED?

Between 1920 and 1930, during the peak of references to the method, dozens of scholarly books and journal articles appeared with titles like "The Project Method in Geography," "The Project Method in Composition," "The Project Method in Biblical Instruction," and "The Project Method in Advanced Inorganic Chemistry." It was nothing short of a sensation.

Wildly popular though it was, however, the method and its founder gradually receded from the limelight. Kilpatrick retired in 1937, the nation went to war in Europe and Asia, the post-war era ushered in a host of new educational concerns, and the progressive movement of which Kilpatrick had been a leading figure diminished in influence. By mid-century, scholarly attention had moved on to other ideas and other lines of research. In 1965, Kilpatrick died.

Projects, however, persisted, because they had won a foothold in the knowledge base of classroom teachers. Mostly, teachers used the method on an ad hoc basis. They developed their own favorite projects and integrated them into existing practice. But they did so without any consistency across grade level, subject area, or region. The idea moved through an inhospitable environment. It did so, however, on the strength of its own internal characteristics.

In some cases, though, the use of projects reached a tipping point. Even without formal support for moving the idea into practice, some conditions were favorable enough that the method became not an *exception* to the rule, but the *rule itself*. The mission project in California is one such case, and it provides a clear window into how the method changed over time.

It is not clear when, exactly, teachers in California first began asking fourth graders to build replicas of Spanish colonial missions. Likely, teachers were doing their own versions of it before World War II. But the first printed references to mission projects come from the 1960s and make clear that teachers still believed in the power of the project method. In Northern California, for instance, one class wrote letters to various missions, asking for information about the history of each building. As the Placerville *Mountain Democrat* put it, teachers hoped that students would develop "research and writing skills through taking notes from audio-visual material and books" and were pleased that the project had generated so much enthusiasm among students.[76] Five hundred miles south, in San Dimas, California, another teacher had her class make a model of the nearest mission in order "to make the unit more meaningful and interesting [to] all the students."[77]

The project method gained traction with a wide range of teachers because it was perceived as significant, it addressed teacher concerns about student interest, it was easy to add to the existing curriculum, and it was easy to understand. But it spread with particular intensity among fourth-grade teachers in California. Why?

First, all California students study the state's history in fourth grade—a year that teachers might be particularly likely to try to engage students through activity—and the Spanish colonial period is a major part of that history. Second, because two dozen missions dot the state, every school is within relative proximity of its own "local" mission. And third, given the simplicity of colonial mission design—mud bricks and clay tiles—they are fairly easy to reproduce. As a result, students across California were increasingly expected to learn about Spanish colonial architecture, religion, and exchange with native peoples through the construction of model missions.

Perhaps most interestingly, the mission project spread not just across the state, but also across generations of California teachers. In 1991, for instance—nearly thirty years after first discussing the project method—the *Mountain Democrat* was still covering student-produced missions. As the paper reported, students at Camino School had been given "a choice of projects" including a diorama, a model, a mural, or a play, and were excitedly completing their work.[78] By the late 1990s, according to the *Sonoma County Independent*, "literally millions of [missions]—hundreds of thousands per year—[had] been obediently built."[79] And students continued assembling them. As a parent blogged a generation later: "If you grew up in California or have had children in California public schools, you know about the fourth-grade mission project. At our children's school, every fourth grader had to build a model of one of the twenty-one California missions."[80] Over half a century, Californians built enough replica missions to wrap around the earth.

The endurance of the project method across generations should not be taken as an indicator that teachers in the state saw themselves as disciples of William Kilpatrick. In fact, by the twentieth century many may not have associated their classroom mission projects with any formal theory about education. Instead, they may have simply been reproducing the practices of teachers before them, drawing on what scholars refer to as the "apprenticeship of observation."[81] With few structured and systematic opportunities to discuss pedagogical practice with mentor teachers, scholars, or knowledgeable administrators, teachers often fall back on their experiences as students for guidance. They teach much as they were taught, often repeating what they recall from classes they enjoyed. All teachers were once students, and many remember little from fourth grade beyond a classic assignment like the mission project.

The apprenticeship of observation is problematic for a number of reasons, but primarily because students are hardly prepared to reflect on teacher practice. Children are not trained to identify what is successful or unsuccessful, to see the rationale behind a particular action or the preparation that went into it, or to think beyond what is enjoyable in order to ask questions about educational value. Even if they were trained in such a manner, and even if they were cognitively capable of such activities, students would remain driven by a host of concerns distinct to their particular position in the classroom.

The result is that projects—California mission replicas included—are often an exercise in formalism. Having absorbed knowledge of the method through the apprenticeship of observation, many teachers see it as both standard and legitimate, yet have not reflected on the usefulness of projects for promoting learning. As one set of scholars wrote in 1991, teacher "knowledge of the concepts and the process skills addressed by a project may not be sufficient to enable them to distill the concepts the project addresses, identify possible links between the central ideas in the project and other concepts in the subject area covered in the curriculum, or recognize ways other disciplines can be incorporated into projects."[82] Projects, in other words, need to be carefully cultivated as pedagogical tools. Frequently, however, they are not.

Some teachers clearly see mission replicas as a means of engaging students in deeper historical inquiry. Often having students work in groups to complete a single model, they assign roles, require research, and ask students to reflect on the nature of their particular task—practices that promote critical thinking and the acquisition of historical knowledge. Even critics agree that such thoughtfully designed projects can be used as a means toward a serious educational end. "Model building is fine," UCLA professor Greg Sarris observed, "as long as you use it as an entrance into your students' minds."[83]

But many teachers simply put students through the motions—a phenomenon that has seemed to bother students less than their parents, who are often tasked with completing the missions late at night while their children sleep. "When my boys were younger," one parent wrote online, "the 'mission project' was an exercise in parent 'creativity.'"[84] As another griped in response, "The kids learn nothing with these projects."[85] And a third commiserated, "I wrote a polite but firm note to the teacher that I would be happy to help [my child] investigate a mission, but I wasn't willing for her to put in countless hours on a project from which she would learn nothing."[86]

Yet while parents are often skeptics, most do not question classroom practice, and particularly one as widespread as the project method, which many of them experienced as students. One parent, for instance, blogged that she failed to see "how building a model helps the kids understand the missions any better," but concluded that questioning the practice "would be vaguely heretical." "None of the other moms I talk to are sure what the point of the project is, either," she wrote, "but we're all resigned to the idea that the mission model is like death and taxes—annoying, but unavoidable."[87] Whatever the reason for their existence, projects were simply a part of life in K–12 classrooms.

Given this state of affairs, many have simply looked for the most pain-less way to complete the mission replica. And savvy entrepreneurs have capitalized on the opportunity. Consequently, in addition to selling the Styrofoam board, popsicle sticks, and glue so often used in the construction of replica missions, California arts and crafts stores now also stock easy-to-construct mission kits like those sold by PaperModels, Inc. The models, according to the manufacturer, are "very easy to build," and are specifically designed for "fourth-grade mission school projects."[88]

Obviously, such products deeply undermine any educational aspects of the mission project, but many parents are simply more concerned with getting the work done. As one parent wrote in a testimonial: "The model worked great. My son got an A."[89] The project method, thus, lived on, though not always as Kilpatrick had imagined.

A PROJECT BY ANY OTHER NAME

Between 1950 and 2000, a generation of project method advocates retired from the academy, new scholars acted in accordance with professional incentives that encouraged work on newer ideas, and an explosion in the amount of educational research made it unlikely that any idea would ever achieve the kind of visibility that Kilpatrick's had in the 1920s. As a result, the project method appeared relatively rarely in scholarship during the second half of the century, and did so most often in retrospectives like "Student Assessment: The Project Method Revisited" and "The Project Method in Agricultural Education: Then and Now."

Still, the method remained a part of the common knowledge base of teachers, and it lived on through assignments like the California mission project and its East Coast counterpart, the Native American "longhouse" project. Insofar as that was the case, and insofar as Kilpatrick and his article, "The Project Method," continued to fade from memory, a market grew for rebranded or updated versions of the idea. After all, teachers continued to use the method, and continued to be interested in improving their practices. Scholars, however, had long since moved on from the project method as a topic of study. As a result, third-party providers filled the gap, promoting ideas like project-based learning—an updated and rebranded version of Kilpatrick's idea.

Third-party providers were not the first to revive interest in the project method. Educational researchers in the 1980s investigated the use of projects to structure the curriculum, and referred to it in a whole host of titular iterations—using *project* or *problem* with or without a hyphen or the word *learning* attached. Naming, however, was not their primary concern. Such scholars were seeking to understand how projects were used in the classroom, as well as how they might be better structured to promote the aim of learning. As one set of authors noted, "Projects were developed and disseminated without sufficient appreciation for the complex nature of student motivation and knowledge required to engage in cognitively difficult work."[90] Consequently, researchers sought to improve what was by then a common teacher practice by making use of "considerable advances in our knowledge about motivation, learning, teachers, and classrooms."[91]

Still, few scholars paid sustained attention to the idea. And by failing to use consistent nomenclature they further fragmented the research base—at least for busy K–12 teachers. Perhaps most importantly, though, most scholars were content to raise questions about projects without going so far as to produce clear and concrete recommendations about classroom implementation. As one group of scholars concluded, "Although research and theory have provided answers to many important questions related to implementing project-based education, we need to know a great deal more about how to sustain student motivation and thought in projects."[92] Such calls for "additional research"—common in the world of academia— would hardly have felt significant and inspiring to teachers.

Outside of the academy, though, others were willing to commit to building a project-based learning brand. Chief among them has been the Buck Institute for Education, a California-based nonprofit organization that works exclusively on project-based learning. When it was founded with philanthropic money, the organization had a general mission around education and worked on a number of different issues. But leaders at Buck quickly realized the potential in project-based learning and worked to establish the organization as the central resource for training teachers in the use of projects.

In addition to tightening its focus, Buck has extended its reach by partnering with groups like the Coalition for Essential Schools, the Stanford School Redesign Network, and the George Lucas Educational Foundation. All have helped raise Buck's profile, as well as to frame project-based learning as a grassroots movement driven by working teachers. Edutopia, for instance—a project underwritten by filmmaker George Lucas—has billed project-based learning as "filled with active and engaged learning" in which students develop deep knowledge, confidence, and self-direction.[93] Such partnerships have also made project-based learning more occupationally realistic and transportable. Buck, for instance, works directly with the Ohio and West Virginia departments of education, which have adapted project-based learning to their particular needs and made resources directly available to teachers. Additionally, Buck conducts one hundred workshops a year, consulting to school districts, states, charter networks, and school redesign organizations. And under the aegis of the Institute, John Thomas wrote the *Project Based Learning Handbook for Middle and High School Teachers*, which has sold forty thousand copies to date.[94]

As a result of such promotional efforts, project-based learning has become a popular topic for education reformers interested in questions of curriculum. It has been incorporated into school redesign models like Expeditionary Learning and Envision Schools. It is a focus of school district professional development seminars. And in West Virginia, it has been framed as a core component of the state's educational improvement plan, legitimizing it even further in the eyes of educators. As one teacher put it, learning about project-based learning "was a pivotal moment in [her] career." Seeking to share her epiphany, she began training other teachers on "project-based methods" and posting lesson plans on Teach21, West Virginia's online curriculum resource for educators.[95]

Buck, of course, is not alone. Sensing that there was money to be made in project-based learning, Houghton Mifflin—the world's largest K–12 publisher—moved in the late 1990s to create an online "project-based learning space" for purchasers of Houghton Mifflin texts. Much of the site squared with the conclusions drawn by scholars, as well as with the work of the Buck Institute. It advised, for instance, that support is necessary to productively implement project-based learning and noted that "focus on teacher knowledge and classroom environment is essential."[96] Still, given Houghton Mifflin's profit motive, it is difficult to imagine sustained focus on project-based learning unless it can produce economic returns.

CONCLUSION

Nearly one hundred years after William Heard Kilpatrick published "The Project Method," the idea continues to course through the language and practice of American educators. This is not to say that K–12 teachers pore over reprints of the 1918 article, laboring to create curricular programs in line with Kilpatrick's vision. For most, Kilpatrick's name would produce only the faintest recognition. Instead, the means by which his idea lives on is muddier, more complex, and less direct. It has been passed along among teachers as a kind of folk wisdom. It has moved across generations through the apprenticeship of observation. And it has been adopted by enterprising and energetic third parties, renamed and rebranded most recently as project-based learning.

Over time, Kilpatrick's method became a standard practice in K–12 classrooms, and the use of projects became an ordinary part of the educator's toolkit. Not unlike Bloom's taxonomy or Gardner's theory of multiple intelligences, the project method moved from the ivory tower into the common knowledge base of classroom teachers and settled firmly into place. Yet unlike those other ideas, the project method eventually morphed into a generic and seemingly timeless piece of common knowledge. It became so well accepted that it hardly warranted mention.

In the early twentieth century, though, Kilpatrick was very much at the center of the project method's movement into practice, and particularly with regard to the idea's perceived significance. Sure, Kilpatrick taught at the nation's premier teacher education institution. But more importantly, he was a well-connected self-promoter who wielded his influence in every manner available to him. Drawing on both scientific and philosophical scholarship, Kilpatrick framed projects as a means of maintaining student interest. He billed his idea not as merely a new tool for addressing a core teacher concern, but as the solution to the problem.

Paired with a philosophically compatible message steeped in romanticism, Kilpatrick's seemingly significant idea made an immediate impact in the plural worlds of American education. Still, it was only over the next decade that the idea developed the crucial characteristic of occupational realism, which came only as Kilpatrick relinquished some control over what, exactly, "wholehearted purposeful activity" might look like. Adapted by working teachers, the project method may have been stripped of some of its transformative potential, but it became more occupationally realistic in the process. Eventually it became a curricular add-on, fully compatible with teacher-centered instruction.

Once the project method entered classrooms, its greatest asset—transportability—ensured it a long life in teacher practice. Bloom's taxonomy and multiple intelligences generally possessed the same crucial characteristics. They were perceived as significant and philosophically compatible. They could seemingly be implemented with ease by teachers. And they were transportable in the sense that they could be broadly outlined in a single conversation. Yet each could be used in a manner not entirely transparent to students. The project method, by contrast, required conspicuously different kinds of activities that were quite obvious when in use. Consequently, new generations of teachers assumed their posts having completed numerous projects across their K–12 experiences.

Do students actually learn from projects? That is hard to say. When used effectively, projects can accomplish much of what Kilpatrick originally promised, moving the student to look "upon his school activity with joy and confidence," to see the teacher as "a friend and comrade, and to see "himself on the side of the school and other social agencies."[97] And recent efforts around project-based learning have fostered critical awareness among teachers and provided more support for thoughtfully approaching the use of projects in the classroom. Still, projects often produce fewer benefits than their advocates would care to admit. As the author of a 1996 study wrote, they do seem to generate "much interest." But whether or not they lead "to the acquisition of important learning is unclear."[98]

Such critical appraisals raise serious questions about a widespread practice. But they should also be considered in context. After all, projects rarely displace hugely valuable content, riveting pedagogy, or more worthwhile forms of assessment. In fact, concerns about the degree to which students are actually learning might be voiced about *any* aspect of instruction. Certainly teachers could use projects more effectively in the classroom; however, they could also lecture more skillfully, organize more stimulating class discussions, or devise better tests. Thus, rather than fussing over whether students always learn from projects, we might better concern ourselves with the question of how to ensure that, when they are used, projects more consistently promote the core aims of education.

CHAPTER FOUR

Lessons of Last Resort

Direct Instruction

In a number of ways, Direct Instruction is unlike other pieces of scholarship to move from the ivory tower into K–12 classrooms. Its lead developer, Siegfried Engelmann, is not celebrated like Howard Gardner or Benjamin Bloom; in fact, even many of those who employ Direct Instruction in the classroom would be unfamiliar with Engelmann's name. Unlike the project method, Direct Instruction is rarely taught in teacher education programs or referenced in pedagogy textbooks; if mentioned, it is often presented in a negative light. And unlike all three ideas considered earlier in this book—ideas with a wide reach across all types of schools—Direct Instruction is rarely implemented in private or suburban schools and is primarily the domain of elementary education.

But perhaps what most distinguishes Direct Instruction from those other exemplary cases is the fact that educators are often averse to it. They routinely criticize the program for dumbing down the work of teaching, for promoting a cultural deficit model, for treating children like machines, and for emphasizing an overly narrow view of the process of education. And to look at Direct Instruction materials is to understand why. Lesson 53 of *Corrective Reading* Level C, for instance, instructs teachers to conclude a demonstration by telling students to "Say the rule the argument breaks." If students respond, "Just because you know about a part doesn't mean you know about the whole thing," the teacher is to praise them by exclaiming: "Great job saying that rule!"[1]

Whatever the criticisms of Direct Instruction, however, it has remained a known and used concept for nearly half a century. It has become, to the chagrin of many educators, a common program in American schools, and it has been used in the instruction of over a million children. A search for "Direct Instruction" in the Education Resources Information Center returns nearly two thousand hits—roughly twice as many as a search for "John Dewey" produces; leaders of Direct Instruction schools have been invited to testify before Congress; Direct Instruction texts continue to make money for their primary publisher, McGraw-Hill; and Engelmann's book *Teach Your Child to Read in 100 Easy Lessons* has spent the better part of the last decade in the top one hundred titles on Amazon.com's "Parenting and Family" section.[2]

The staying power of Direct Instruction, despite the criticisms of it, is largely due to the fact that Direct Instruction schools generally produce measurable gains in student achievement. In dozens of research studies, Direct Instruction has been shown to raise scores, and although standardized tests are limited in what they measure, they continue to carry great weight among policy makers, parents, and educators. Consequently, however much it may rub many teachers the wrong way, the program continues to be perceived as significant. And in high-need contexts where teachers and administrators are often desperate for solutions—in high-poverty schools, special education classrooms, remediation programs, and the like—the program has also managed to achieve a surprising level of philosophical compatibility. In fact, even the American Federation of Teachers has endorsed the use of Direct Instruction in work with at-risk students.[3]

Another factor in Direct Instruction's staying power is the fact that it is a prepackaged curriculum that can be adopted on a schoolwide basis. For many teachers, of course, the scripted nature of the program is an unacceptable affront to their autonomy and status as professionals. Yet the occupationally realistic and transportable nature of the program has allowed it to take hold quickly and penetrate deeply in a particular cross-section of schools. Currently, Direct Instruction programs are used in over ten thousand schools throughout the world, five hundred of which use Direct Instruction on a systematic basis for all classroom instruction.[4]

Despite contestation over the model, then, many educators continue to know and use Direct Instruction; many even *like* it. Thus, while the program has not gained a foothold in all kinds of K–12 classrooms, it has unquestionably made the leap from the ivory tower into the schoolhouse and penetrated the common knowledge base of a wide cross-section of working teachers—a phenomenon that this chapter seeks to explain. Exploring half a century of battles over Direct Instruction, it tells the story of how an idea continued to find its way into schools despite its seeming incongruity with trends in educational psychology, school politics, and the professional interests of teachers. And, ultimately, this chapter seeks to explain just how it is that some teachers began to see Direct Instruction in an entirely new light.

PROJECT FOLLOW THROUGH

In 1963, Siegfried Engelmann joined Carl Bereiter's University of Illinois research team. Bereiter, an educational psychologist, was exploring intellectual development in young children and, after seeing a film of Engelmann teaching math, invited him to join the research project.[5] Engelmann quickly gained a host of responsibilities, and from 1964 to 1966 he worked at the Institute for Research on Exceptional Children, directing two U.S. Office of Education projects. One of those, the so-called Bereiter-Engelmann Program, focused on economically disadvantaged children between four and six years old. Hence, the project had traction with policy makers drawn to programs—the most well known of which remains Head Start—that sought to improve educational outcomes for the disadvantaged by beginning work at an early age.[6]

In the Bereiter-Engelmann model preschool, children were given two hours a day of teacher-directed verbal instruction based on the assumption that such teaching was the most effective way of producing the "necessary learning in the limited time available."[7] Crafted in response to what Engelmann and Bereiter called "verbal bombardment"—their characterization of traditional and unsystematic classroom instruction—its aim was, in their words, to "identify what you want [students] to learn and teach it directly."[8]

The program was also motivated by thinking characteristic of the 1960s—that all children, regardless of socioeconomic status, could learn. "Man's capacity to learn is not fixed in any ordinary sense," Engelmann wrote in 1966. *"It is not fixed in terms of the responses it will produce; it is not fixed in terms of absolute level of knowledge it will achieve."*[9] The key was to create an instructional sequence that would realize that capacity in all children.

The model that emerged was based on behavioral principles and proceeded in a highly particular order. It utilized repetition, signaling, and rewards, and was based on the premise that any learning objective could—and should—be broken down into its component parts. In teaching reading, for instance, instructors would begin with phonics rather than whole words, and drill students on those sounds until students were proficient in recognizing them. It was fast-paced and involved frequent assessment and immediate correction. And finally, in order to ensure that the instructional sequence took place as designed, Engelmann developed scripts that teachers would use with students.

Bereiter left Illinois in 1967 for the Ontario Institute for Studies in Education—a setback for Direct Instruction, but not enough to deter Engelmann from continuing with the project. To continue receiving Carnegie Foundation funding, however, Engelmann needed to find a codirector with a faculty rank. To his good fortune, psychology professor Wes Becker—a behaviorist struggling with a phonics demonstration program—saw a partnership as mutually beneficial.

In 1967, Becker and Engelmann, whose new title at the university was Senior Educational Specialist for the Institute on Exceptional Children and Bureau of Educational Research, jointly submitted a proposal for Project Follow Through—a federal effort designed to build on the gains made by Head Start. Proposed as a $120 million project by President Lyndon Johnson, it was eventually scaled back to a $15 million design experiment in which various educational models would be tested in participating communities. Still, Follow Through represented an opportunity to reach an audience wider than most researchers could have dreamed. Over 75,000 low-income children in 170 communities were eventually involved in the project, and Direct Instruction was selected as one of 20 program sponsors for the experiment.

In Project Follow Through, instructional models were to be selected by parent committees in school districts with high numbers of economically disadvantaged students. Participating districts had no influence in choosing among the providers. For their participation, though, districts would receive significant financial compensation: $750 per student beyond the normal level of funding.

The models themselves were organized into several groups: "Cognitive/Conceptual Skills Models," like the University of Florida's Florida Parent Education Model, the University of Arizona's Tucson Early Education Model, and the High Scope Foundation's Cognitively Oriented curriculum; "Affective Skills Models" like the Bank Street College Model, the Open Education Model, and Far West Laboratory's Responsive Education Model; and "Basic Skills Models" like Direct Instruction and the University of Kansas's Behavior Analysis Model.

Parents, who in participating districts would be asked to select a model from the Follow Through menu, were given descriptions of each program to help guide their decision making. In the Direct Instruction synopsis, parents were told that students would be given placement tests and assigned to differentiated classrooms. As Engelmann and Becker later noted, "We grouped children homogeneously for instruction so that all children were on the same step of the instructional sequence."[10] Teachers, working with aides, would then present scripted lessons and use specific behavior management techniques and practices, with the explicit goal of moving through as many lessons as possible. Students would be tested every two weeks; if they showed mastery on the lessons, the class could move on. Supervisors would oversee the entire process, relying on forms that instructed them to look for management, organization, following format, correcting students, pacing, signaling students, and the grouping of students.[11]

In terms of what would be covered in the curriculum, the aim articulated was to help low-income and minority students "catch up" with their more privileged peers. As Engelmann recalled: "We designed the programs for the kind of kids we were working with—at-risk, inner-city kids. The individual programs targeted the skill deficiencies of these kids. For instance, they couldn't rhyme, so we taught rhyming and related it to orthographic changes in words that rhyme. In language, they could not reliably follow directions, so following directions was a major track in the language program. We revised and created supplements for the programs whenever we discovered that specific problems persisted."[12]

Some parents and outside observers were immediately put off by the Direct Instruction model. Others, however, saw great potential in it. As African American commentator Biloine Young wrote in *Phi Delta Kappan* in 1968: "The . . . approach seems particularly clearsighted and free from many of the obscure postulates that have clouded our thinking about why so many slum children fail in school. It has the kind of simple logic that makes educators wonder why they didn't think of it before."[13]

Many parents clearly agreed: twenty-two participant communities chose the Direct Instruction model, and it was adopted in roughly seventy schools. As a consequence, the Direct Instruction team struggled to keep pace with demand. Developing curricular materials on the fly, mimeographing close to a million sheets of paper each week, and trying to manage a faithful implementation of the model presented significant challenges. Yet each week, new scripts were ready to be delivered to participating schools.

Despite this seeming success, however, Direct Instruction was hardly a sensation. The education faculty at the University of Illinois sent a clear message to Engelmann, for instance, by refusing to offer him a staff position. And although Becker and Engelmann trained students in Direct Instruction methods for work with Follow Through, Direct Instruction was not included in the school's teacher education curriculum. "They'd have died before they let us in there," Engelmann later recalled.[14] As a result, Becker and Engelmann offered their $1.5 million grant program to other universities. After being unanimously voted down by the Temple

University faculty, they accepted an offer from the University of Oregon. In 1970, they arrived in Eugene with one graduate student—Douglas Carnine—in tow.

A SHIFTING MENTAL LANDSCAPE

Although Direct Instruction squared with several major trends of the time—a concern with poverty schools, a scientifically oriented search for solutions, and a concern with early-childhood education—it was out of line in other respects, and particularly with regard to developments in the field of educational psychology.

The first decades of the twentieth century had been dominated by behaviorists like Edward Thorndike. Popular with administrative progressives, Thorndike sought to make school curricula more rational and stressed the importance of learning through consequences, or as he called it, the *law of effect*. Other psychologists, like B. F. Skinner, further developed behaviorism, adding greater scientific credibility to the increasingly well-defined idea that behavior is shaped by the environment, reinforced by rewards, and discouraged through punishment.

But by the 1960s, behaviorism was under attack. On one front it was being assaulted by constructivists, who proposed that students are active agents in assembling knowledge and organizing reality, rather than merely absorbing it. Inspired by the research of Swiss psychologist Jean Piaget, whose work was being translated into English in the late 1950s and early 1960s, many educators and scholars quickly took up the language of constructivism and the view of learning described by it.[15] At the same time, the so-called cognitive revolution was shaping both educational psychology and broader conversations about student learning. Jerome Bruner, for instance, suggested that intellectual ability developed in stages and that learning was not a matter of committing results to memory. Instead, he argued, it was about participating "in the process that makes possible the establishment of knowledge."[16] Developmental stages, prior learning, context, and the inner worlds of students seemed to matter quite a bit more than behaviorists acknowledged.

In practice, this shift led to the rise of "inquiry" models, "experiential learning," and "developmentally appropriate" teaching.[17] Engelmann and his team, however, remained committed to behaviorism. A 1971 textbook by Engelmann, Becker, and Don R. Thomas, for instance, dedicated the first section of the work—236 pages—to "Behavior Modification."[18] The model for such an approach was that of stimulus-response, with the fundamental assumption being that "the teaching of *any* task involves tying some stimulus event(s) to some response events through reinforcement."[19]

Self-identifying progressive educators saw the work of constructivists and cognitivists as compatible with their own beliefs about children and learning. But behaviorism had always rubbed progressives the wrong way, and Direct Instruction had a distinctly behaviorist bent. Thus, as Engelmann speculated, if the selection process in Project Follow Through had been left up to professional educators rather than parents, "*none* would have selected our model." Direct Instruction, he added, "was the antithesis of everything they did . . . in terms of what was taught, how it was taught, what the schedule was."[20] As Engelmann recalls, an educator stood up during a presentation of the Direct Instruction model to potential Follow Through participants in New York and shouted: "Nowhere in his presentation did I hear about how to *learn by doing and do by doing!*"[21]

Others were even harsher in expressing their disdain for behaviorism. A 1970 review of the Direct Instruction model, for instance, noted that "like Pavlov's dog, the child has learned a rule, and an answer is given to the question, which Bereiter [and Engelmann take] to be educationally crucial, of how the rule 'gets into' the child."[22] Such an approach, claimed reviewer Brian S. Cittenden, was ineffective for teaching morality, or poetry, or other "skills which cannot be classified as 'behavior according to a rule.'"[23] Further, he argued, it failed to teach children "to raise relevant intermediate questions about something they wish to know or do."[24] In short, it was portrayed as dehumanizing.

Some of the language in Direct Instruction scripts seemed to support this critical view. "Start with a set of simple commands, such as 'Stand up' and 'Sit down,'" a 1969 Direct Instruction text read. "If the child does not

stand up on command, forcefully stand him up. From time to time re-
mind him, 'When I say 'stand up,' you stand up.' If he manages to make
the other members of the group laugh, ignore their responses. If he turns
his head away or tries to communicate with other members of the group,
forcefully turn his head back. Do not repeat commands . . . Let the child
know that you will continue with this punishment until he behaves."[25]
Such practices were not representative of Direct Instruction as a whole,
yet they provided fodder for opponents inclined to view behaviorist approaches in a negative light.

Whatever the psychological effects on children, behaviorist teaching techniques were also being challenged on the basis that they did not
promote learning. Studies in the mid-1970s, for instance, found that although students in behaviorist curricular programs scored highly on
criterion-referenced tests, they often misunderstood deeper concepts and
struggled to transfer knowledge to different problems.[26] In addition, research on efforts to create more academic environments in early-childhood
education found that students were less well adjusted socially and emo-
tionally and less cognitively advanced.[27]

Little of this scholarship, however, affected the way that Engelmann
and Becker—or for that matter, Bereiter, though he was no longer connected with the program—viewed educational processes. To them, what
mattered most was not the development of particular habits of mind,
but rather, tangible improvements in basic competencies. They continued to make the case that "instruction is a set of procedures for producing a change in behavior toward a pre-stated objective."[28] As Engelmann
later put it, "To get the desired result . . . it's just silly to ignore behavioral principles."[29] Thus, as the tide turned, their approach was increasingly
viewed for what it was *not*; namely, it did not promote the key elements of
inquiry-oriented learning: open-ended questions, exploration of student
ideas, student-initiated discourse, or choice of activities.[30]

The scale of Direct Instruction was still small, with fewer than a hundred schools participating via Project Follow Through. Yet, given the nature of Follow Through—a multimillion-dollar, pseudo-experimental, and

eventually quite controversial federal effort to improve educational outcomes—the visibility of Direct Instruction was magnified. With greater visibility came more widespread adoption, but also greater resistance.

CHANGING NOTIONS OF JUSTICE

The attack on behaviorism, while significant, was confined primarily to communities of scholars and researchers. What mattered more to a wider audience was that the particular behaviorist approach modeled in Direct Instruction did not square with a new vision of social justice emerging in the late 1960s and early 1970s. That new vision was no longer founded on the idea of intervention and remediation, which typified Direct Instruction. Instead, it was about autonomy, respect, and cultural recognition.

Education research in the 1960s was strongly oriented toward assisting the traditionally underserved. Particularly, such research focused on identifying what low-income and minority students were missing, and then working to fill in the gaps. As one teacher observed in 1962, "Teaching these children requires the utmost planning. You cannot play it by ear. You must know which questions you are going to ask each level of student in the class."[31] In such a world, Direct Instruction was a perfect fit. As Bereiter and Engelmann wrote in 1966, underserved students "must progress at a faster than normal rate if they are to catch up."[32]

But that approach sparked a line of resistance among those who came to deride it as a "deficit model." Children of color and from low-income neighborhoods, these critics argued, were not *lacking* in anything that their more privileged peers had. Instead, they were participants in an alternative culture—a culture that educators should tap into in order to motivate them and build on their prior knowledge. As Jonathan Kozol wrote in 1967, "The real trouble with perpetrating such colorless materials upon very colorful children was not only that the weak culture they purveyed was out of kilter with the one the children already had, but that it also was mediocre by comparison."[33]

In the eyes of progressive educators, the problem of the "deficit model" was not merely that culturally irrelevant materials failed to tap into student interest. The greater crime was that materials designed to address deficits never actually created strengths. Students could memorize vocabulary and perform phonics lessons, Kozol wrote in *Death at an Early Age*, but in overseeing such lessons, a teacher "had effectively taught them to be good liars and in fact had equipped them with a set of tools to keep themselves at as far as possible a distance from the truth."[34] Such arguments resonated with a broad audience, both inside and outside of the academy. Kozol, for instance, would go on to sell millions of books and be referenced roughly two thousand times in journals counted by the Social Sciences Citation Index.

There was also the question of racism. The deficit model, scholars like William Labov began to argue, was the product of a white worldview incapable of understanding culturally specific difference.[35] In his work on Direct Instruction, Engelmann had written about various deficits, including those in reading and in verbal language.[36] Yet he did not believe these to be cultural in nature. As he and Bereiter wrote, the deficits in question were in areas traditionally taught in school.[37] "It's not a deficiency in the *language*," Engelmann said in an interview, "it's a deficiency in the *skills the kids have*."[38] Nevertheless, the racial issue presented a challenge, and it hardly helped that Engelmann and his entire project team were white.

Even Kozol believed that some basics, like reading, had to be taught. As he wrote in 1972, many young white people came into "Free Schools" to teach and were "incredibly dogmatic and, ironically, 'manipulative' in their determination to *coerce* the parents of poor children to accept their notions about noncoercive education."[39] In his teaching, Kozol recalled, he used the "square, sequential, rather rigorous, old-fashioned phonics method, but [tied] it in with a lot of intense and good discussions about the struggles and the needs and longings that the kids in question lived with in their homes and in their neighborhoods."[40] Other radical education programs either succeeded by striking such a balance, or—as was the case with Bill Ayers's school in Ann Arbor, Michigan—failed because "no one learned to read there."[41]

Popular rhetoric in the world of education, however, was less nuanced. As Bereiter wrote in 1967, opposition to Direct Instruction was "tied to a number of widely held convictions about not 'forcing' young children, about the importance of play and free exploration, the primacy of social or nonverbal learning, and so on."[42] Coupled with the sentiment that middle-class white values should not be used to evaluate low-income and minority students, the discourse of the period was increasingly hostile to Direct Instruction.[43]

Such a shift was particularly frustrating for Engelmann, Bereiter, Becker, and colleagues, who continued to work for what they perceived as social justice. As Engelmann and Bereiter wrote in 1966: "To claim, as [Kenneth] Clark does, that cultural deprivation is a myth is to ignore the overwhelming evidence that disadvantaged children are already well below average in academic abilities at the time they enter school."[44] The notion "that in order to produce a well-rounded child, one must have a well-rounded program," they asserted, "reveals an ignorance of the fact that a world exists outside the schoolroom door."[45]

Even more troubling for Direct Instruction advocates was that they were cast as agents working against a goal that they believed themselves to be working *toward*. Yet this should not have been surprising. When Engelmann and Bereiter, for instance, argued that "the disadvantaged child masters a language that is adequate for maintaining social relationships . . . but he does not learn how to use language . . . for carrying on verbal reasoning," they made themselves an easy mark.[46] The more nuanced point that Engelmann and colleagues were making, of course, was that "there are standards of knowledge and ability which are consistently held to be valuable in the schools," and that failure to master such content and skills would ultimately have consequences.[47] Their message fell on deaf ears, however, and Engelmann and colleagues—self-identified political liberals—were accused of perpetuating oppression in schools.

Beyond the language used to describe the model, Direct Instruction provoked opposition because it sought to provide students with different kinds of educational experiences. That raised concerns, and understandably so given the policy context of inequitable and segregated schooling. Public funding for southern black schools in 1954, for instance, was only 60 percent of that for southern white schools.[48] Even fifteen years after the

Brown decision, 63 percent of black students and 78 percent of white students attended schools that were more than 90 percent segregated.[49] And achievement, by any measure, continued to differ markedly in predominantly white and predominantly minority schools. Thus, even into the twenty-first century, many critics of Direct Instruction continued to ask the question: "How many wealthy districts use these programs?"[50]

Engelmann maintained that the program would work for anyone. Yet "some people," he later observed, "have the mistaken notion that these are programs that work only with low performers."[51] Still, middle- and upper-class schools did not, and never would, use Direct Instruction.

Engelmann, believing that measured outcomes would ultimately speak for themselves, did not concern himself any more with the question of unequal experience than he did with the critiques of radical educators. If students could be taught in all black schools, for instance, the first priority should be teaching. Consequently, while the busing movement gathered momentum in the 1970s, Engelmann opposed it, believing that remediation designed to accelerate the acquisition of school knowledge was far more effective.[52]

The outcomes produced by Direct Instruction programs often *did* speak for themselves. Still, the program was a natural target for those opposed to traditional pedagogy, to so-called deficit models, and to unequal educational experiences. As such, it continued to arouse hostility among educators concerned with social justice, even as Engelmann and his colleagues believed themselves to be promoting equity.

"THE TEACHER BECOMES A TECHNICIAN"

Direct Instruction tended to have a bifurcating effect on teachers, just as it did with parents, policy makers, and administrators. Some loved it. Many hated it. Very few occupied a middle ground. In part, the split was due to Direct Instruction's behaviorist bent and the degree to which the program squared with differing visions of social justice. But more significantly, it was a product of the fact that many saw Direct Instruction—and particularly its scripted curriculum—as a threat to teacher professionalism.

Teacher scripts have a long history in American education. Nineteenth-century texts for teachers occasionally included classroom dialogue, and an 1888 manual by Samuel and Adeline Monroe included complete scripts for teachers to read to their classes.[53] Yet despite the allure that "teacher-proof" curricula held for school reformers, scripting largely remained an exception to the rule in lesson design.

Such resistance among teachers, at least historically, makes sense. Prior to the twentieth century, teachers occupied their positions because of superior knowledge—because they knew what students, and often their parents, did not. Well into the twentieth century, when access to knowledge increased at unprecedented levels, teachers continued to earn dividends from this historical perception. Scripting, however, undermined that.

In addition to its effect on teacher authority, scripting also promised to reduce the responsibilities of those in classrooms. Working with a program like Direct Instruction, teachers would no longer be responsible for lesson design, for expertise about children, or for the task of dealing with the uncertainty of classroom life. As Direct Instruction promoters put it on their Web site: "The popular valuing of teacher creativity and autonomy as high priorities must give way to a willingness to follow certain carefully prescribed instructional practices."[54] And as Engelmann put it: "The teacher is a teacher—not a genius, an instructional designer, or a counselor. The teacher must be viewed as a consumer of instruction material."[55] Engelmann saw this aspect of Direct Instruction as occupationally realistic, and he may have been right. But reducing teacher responsibility also raised serious philosophical compatibility issues insofar as it threatened teacher professionalism.

The program also threatened to reduce the psychic rewards that so many teachers value. As Dan Lortie observed in his study of the teaching profession, "Teachers believe that the teacher is the essential catalyst for student achievement." Teacher leadership, he continued, "stands at the center of this benign and desirable activity; it is portrayed as the sine qua non of student learning. The role of the teacher approaches the heroic."[56] Regarding the problem of authorship, he noted that "the teacher himself wants to establish that he has influenced students [when he knows that] credit might belong to the students themselves or to other teach-ers."[57] Credit in a Direct Instruction classroom, however, would belong to Engelmann and his colleagues—the authors of the script.

Despite all of this, some teachers were willing to make the tradeoff. Instead of feeling less effective as professionals, they felt *more* effective. "If I could follow this program all of the time I would like to teach in kin-dergarten," one teacher commented in 1968.[58] And as another added, "I enjoyed it because of the strict program we had. I wanted to teach them something."[59] In short, whatever the philosophical compatibility problems with Direct Instruction, some teachers found it acceptable because it ad-dressed their fundamental concern with classroom effectiveness and did so in a way that was easy to adopt. For teachers who felt in over their heads, Direct Instruction provided a rule-based method with clear mechanisms for feedback on effectiveness. It reduced uncertainty, it simplified class-room aims to the basics, and, at least in a number of cases, it worked.

Still, there were critics who believed that *no teacher* should use Direct Instruction because of what it would do to the profession. In 1969, for in-stance, school leaders in a midwestern community participating in Proj-ect Follow Through decided to drop Direct Instruction. The argument was that the program had elevated too many teachers' aides to the sta-tus of teachers. Worse, the average aide had been rated by trainers to be as effective as the average teacher in use of the Direct Instruction ma-terials. According to Engelmann, the teacher union "saw the movement of aides teaching as a plot to remove all teachers and replace them with lower-salaried aides."[60] At a time when teachers were trying to profession-alize their occupation, Direct Instruction threatened a setback.[61]

This frustrated Engelmann, whose primary focus remained on mea-surable outcomes, and he frequently excoriated public school leaders for not sharing his concern. The typical school principal, Engelmann argued in 1972, ignored data in favor of ideology and intuition, and instead "sim-ply reassured himself that his school was as good as any in the district, and his teachers were probably better than most." The fact that some children would learn nothing would, as Engelmann saw it, be interpreted by school leaders as "unfortunate but inevitable."[62]

But critics of Direct Instruction were able to make a powerful case that the program would transform teachers into automatons. As Ken Goodman wrote in 1979, "The teacher becomes a technician, part of a 'delivery system' . . . [and] learning is reduced to gain scores on paper-and-pencil tests."[63] A sample from one reading and writing script is illustrative:

1.   "Open your textbook to lesson 2 and find part A.

      "These are regular-order sentences. They have two main parts.

      "Everybody, what's the name of the first part in a regular-order sentence?" (Signal.) Answer: *Subject.*

      "Yes, the first part is called the subject. The name of the second part in a regular-order sentence is the **predicate**."

2.   "You're going to write the subject of each sentence. Remember, the subject **names**.

      "Work sentence 1. Write the number of the sentence and the subject.

      "Don't start with a capital. Raise your hand when you're finished."

      (Observe students and give feedback.)

      "Sentence 1 says: 'The woman wearing a yellow dress was in the elevator.' Everybody, what's the subject?" (Signal.) Answer: *The woman wearing a yellow dress.*

      "What's the predicate?" (Signal.) Answer: *Was in the elevator.*[64]

Negative interpretations of the program—interpretations like Goodman's—argued that such scripts left no room for adjustment, for spontaneity, joy, or adjustment. Teachers would be stripped of many of their responsibilities, and the result would be a net loss in job satisfaction and professional prestige. Engelmann countered that teachers would simply have more time to focus on the actual delivery of instruction. He frequently compared them to actors, and for good reason: the scripts were as thorough as anything on Broadway or in Hollywood.

Yet positive framing alone was not sufficient to solve the problem of teacher professionalism. And although teachers were generally not in a position to adopt or reject Direct Instruction programs—that task was typically the domain of school and district administrators—their cooperation was a key part of any successful implementation. If they wanted to, they could sink any Direct Instruction adoption.

A RETURN TO "BASIC SKILLS"

Whatever the criticism of it, Direct Instruction did have some traction during the 1970s, particularly in the urban context. Its behaviorist slant bothered some. There had been a shift in thinking about what constituted social justice. And it threatened teacher professionalism. But, according to results from Project Follow Through, it raised scores—which to some was a matter of great significance.

Additionally, for district leaders concerned about consistency of implementation, the highly transportable scripts were an alluring answer to the challenge of implementation. And Direct Instruction became even more transportable when its publisher, Science Research Associates (SRA), made the program available for sale in 1972. Marketed as DISTAR, which first stood for "Direct Instruction System for Teaching Arithmetic and Reading," but was soon changed to "Direct Instruction System for Teaching and Remediation," the program reached beyond Follow Through schools to a wider educational audience.[65] Instead of waiting for mimeographed copies, educators could simply purchase materials through SRA.

SRA, then a division of IBM, had modest expectations for DISTAR. The SRA executive who acquired the program, as Engelmann recalled, frankly admitted that DISTAR materials would not be published with mainline materials. It would, he believed, "raise too many hackles."[66] But DISTAR's release coincided with the nascent back-to-basics movement—a backlash against a perceived decline in educational standards—and raised the significance of the program. As one pair of authors wrote in 1976, "One of the most striking phenomena to emerge in North American education in recent years is a strong demand on the part of many parents, school boards, and educators for schools to get back to basics—in reading, writing, arithmetic, and standards of behavior."[67] The belief was not merely that "stricter discipline, minimum competency testing, and a renewed emphasis on traditional subjects and basic skills" would shape up the educational system, Henry Levin wrote in 1982. It was also that such a focus would solve "the economic problems of high youth unemployment and declining productivity growth that many blame on the schools."[68]

Policy talk also led to action. In a poll taken by the *American School Board Journal*, 87 percent of school administrators were in favor of returning to "the basics."[69] Several dozen state legislatures began in the late 1970s and early 1980s to enact legislation on accountability and competency testing.[70] And, given the perception that large portions of the population were failing to acquire basic skills, demands rose "for a return to direct instruction with emphasis on drill and recitation in the basic skills."[71] According to Engelmann, Direct Instruction "tended to be picked up with [federal] Title I funds" in districts with enough low-income students to qualify for such assistance.[72]

For those looking to justify their program selections with data, Direct Instruction products were easy to justify. An analysis of Project Follow Through by Abt Associates found Direct Instruction to be the most effective of the pilot models.[73] Other studies supported the Abt report. In 1980, for instance, David Berliner reviewed the research and found that "although still a nebulous term, 'direct instruction' appears to be one of the most powerful predictors of student achievement."[74] That same year, a review led by George Madaus produced similar results.[75] A 1982 study by Wes Becker and University of Oregon graduate Russell Gersten found that low-income students taught via Direct Instruction outperformed their peers.[76] And another in-house study from 1982, conducted by Gersten and Doug Carnine, found that Direct Instruction "can have a consistent significant positive impact on low-income students in a wide range of settings for a period of seven to ten years."[77]

Not all research on Direct Instruction was positive. A reanalysis of the Abt study, conducted by Ernest House and colleagues and published in the *Harvard Educational Review* in 1978, found that no Follow Through model was better than the others.[78] As Engelmann observed, those looking for grounds to criticize Direct Instruction seized on the House findings. "Man, that was applauded," he recalled. "That was treated as if someone had really come up with some good stuff."[79] Others, too, would challenge the effectiveness of Direct Instruction. Still, positive findings continued to outweigh the negative, and as policy makers looked for research-backed programs, they would frequently turn to Direct Instruction.

In the wake of the 1983 *A Nation at Risk* report, which portrayed American schools being eroded by "a rising tide of mediocrity," policy makers became even more obsessed with and unnerved by low standard-ized test scores.[80] As in previous eras, much of their attention concen-trated on the lack of challenging programs available for talented students. Yet in a new twist, policy leaders were equally focused on performance at the bottom of the educational hierarchy, framing educational failure as a drain on the economy and a challenge to social cohesion. And though the nascent standards movement was largely driven by conservatives, the test scores of low-income and minority students concerned those on the left as well. As Barbara Sizemore wrote in the *Journal of Negro Education* in 1985, "Although many argue against the emphasis on basic skills, one has to remember that in many black poor schools the majority of the children cannot read or compute." Thus, to those dissatisfied with the use of Di-rect Instruction, she suggested that it was a necessary step "for the training function of education even though it may be inappropriate for the enlight-enment function."[81]

This perspective corresponded with the critiques some black educa-tors made of more progressive pedagogies. Liberal educators, Lisa Delpit observed, were opposed to Direct Instruction because of the explicit con-trol exhibited by the teacher.[82] But, as she explained, many nonwhite edu-cators, parents, and students saw things differently. In fact, many believed that so-called progressive instruction was a form of *not teaching* and that black children were, in such classrooms, being cheated out of an education. Black teachers, she wrote, were "anxious to move to the next step, the step vital to success in America—the appropriation of the oral and written forms demanded by the mainstream . . . they are *eager* to teach 'skills.'"[83]

Consequently, some perceived Direct Instruction as increasingly significant during the mid-1980s. In the words of Fran Lehr, the program came to be "in fashion."[84] Of course, not all educators were on board with the Direct Instruction model. Many continued to see it as philosophically incompatible. Others, as Gersten, Carnine, and colleagues found, were concerned that "too much time was devoted to academics" and too little time "set aside for 'fun' or creative activities." Many teachers, however, "altered their reactions to structured educational models after they saw the effects . . . on their students on a day-to-day basis." From teacher interview data collected over two years, the authors concluded that "time and again the teachers marveled at the new academic skills their pupils demonstrated."[85]

AN EFFECTIVE PROGRAM IN SPECIAL CONTEXTS

In the 1980s and 1990s, Direct Instruction remained out of step with a number of trends. In schools of education, for instance—at least those other than the University of Oregon—constructivist approaches based on the work of those like Jean Piaget and Lev Vygotsky had displaced behaviorist approaches. According to Virginia Richardson, constructivism had come to "dominate scholarly and practitioner journals in most subject matter areas."[86] And beyond schools of education, the power of constructivist influence was reflected in documents like the curriculum and evaluation standards released by the National Council of Teachers of Mathematics in 1989 and the National Research Council's *Everybody Counts* report, which stated that "students simply do not retain for long what they learn by imitation from lectures, work sheets, or routine homework."[87] In California, the whole-language movement, led by Direct Instruction critic Ken Goodman, took hold during the late 1980s. The state board of education removed Direct Instruction from its list of approved curricula, and Engelmann, in turn, sued and won. Direct Instruction's legal victory, however, was short-lived. The board, led by William Honig, adjusted its decision-making procedure to comply with legal requirements. But it maintained the effective ban on Direct Instruction and other phonics programs.

Still, Direct Instruction continued to expand in urban settings, and it found another audience in the field of special education. Authors of Direct Instruction texts had long framed their materials as appropriate means of addressing failure. In 1979, for instance, Douglas Carnine and Jerry Silbert wrote in the introduction to their reading textbook that Direct Instruction had "proven particularly effective with handicapped . . . students."[88] And as the population of special education students continued to grow, Direct Instruction was increasingly marketed to that audience. In 1976–1977, 1.8 percent of students were identified as having learning differences. In 1990–1991 that figure had nearly tripled.[89] Consequently, SRA—by then a division of McGraw-Hill—began to pitch Direct Instruction as a research-based method for improving outcomes in special education classrooms. It quickly expanded its Direct Instruction offerings to over two dozen titles.

Thus, while Direct Instruction was hardly mentioned in traditional pedagogy textbooks, it was increasingly identified in special education texts as an effective program for students with intellectual disabilities.[90] Journals in the field portrayed Direct Instruction in a similarly positive light. In 1991, for instance, Barbara Bateman wrote that "the documented success of Siegfried Engelmann and his colleagues' direct instruction reading programs with thousands of hard-to-teach and high-risk children is unsurpassed in the annals of reading history."[91] That same year, the *Journal of Learning Disabilities* devoted two issues to "sameness analysis"—an instructional design principle central to Direct Instruction.[92]

As Direct Instruction was taking root in the world of special education, it was also gaining traction in the urban context. The promise of desegregation had given way to frustration with the failure of busing efforts, the continued phenomenon of white flight, and the further deterioration of urban public schools. In 1983, for instance—the year that *A Nation at*

Risk was released—11 percent of white students dropped out of school. By contrast, 18 percent of black students and nearly 32 percent of Hispanic students dropped out.[93] Students, anecdotal evidence indicated, were graduating from urban public schools unable to perform basic skills. In Chicago, test results portrayed "a school system whose overwhelming numbers of poor students are educationally stunted by the time they reach high school and still handicapped when they graduate or drop out."[94] And, as a 1985 *New York Times* editorial bleakly put it, "It comes as no surprise that an evaluation by the State Education Department lists 417 of New York City's schools as among the worst in the state."[95]

In this context, Direct Instruction was more philosophically compatible than ever, especially as states began to adopt curricular standards and high-stakes end-of-year tests. As Jerry Silbert recalled, Direct Instruction gained prominence in the late 1980s as "accountability systems started to come into place." And teachers and administrators "on the ground level were a little more anxious to go around and find things that worked," he noted.[96] Thousands, for instance, went to the highly publicized Mabel B. Wesley Elementary School, in Houston, which had been using a school-wide Direct Instruction curriculum since 1976. Working with a largely low-income and African American student body, the school was noted for its impressive test scores.[97]

Social justice, as many policy makers framed the issue, demanded that low-income and minority students be taught to read, write, and compute. The back-to-basics movement had led directly into the era of testing and accountability, which served only to heighten rhetoric about the most egregious failings of the public schools. Whether by Direct Instruction or some other program, pressure was increasing in urban districts with low graduation rates and thousands of students performing below grade level to close what was increasingly being referred to as an *achievement gap*. As Marcy Stein, Jerry Silbert, and Douglas Carnine wrote in the preface of their textbook on teaching math: "The need for improvement in mathematics instruction has been well documented by national, even international, evaluations. Moreover, research has also suggested that many teachers are ill-prepared to meet the needs of a diverse student population."[98]

Direct Instruction still imperiled teacher professionalism, and many remained opposed to it for that reason. Yet if its use was to be restricted to failing urban schools and special education classrooms, it constituted a much less significant threat. Direct Instruction might have been further tempered in the eyes of teachers if they had seen an easy way to hybridize the program with more progressive pedagogies—altering scripts, for instance, or including more student-directed activities. But Engelmann has been consistently clear about the rigidity of the Direct Instruction sequence. As he wrote in 1996, "Installation of these 'effective' practices without a systematic instructional sequence will not necessarily lead to highly effective teaching . . . [and] it will not cause superior performance."[99] In fact, Engelmann and his team will, if they feel a site is not adhering faithfully to the Direct Instruction model, pull the program out of schools and districts. Consequently—and unlike other cases considered in this book—adopting Direct Instruction became a viable move only in particular contexts, and only when educators could be convinced of its absolute necessity.

Many districts, though, were able to make persuasive cases for using Direct Instruction. Districts like Baltimore implemented Direct Instruction in the mid-1990s as a remedial and special education program, billing Direct Instruction as particularly necessary for underachieving systems. As the leaders of the Baltimore Curriculum Project noted, "Special education students benefit from Direct Instruction's focus on . . . active student engagement, choral response, continuous assessment, and individual attention."[100] In Fort Worth, Texas, more than 14,000 K–12 students and 430 teachers began using either Reading Mastery—a Direct Instruction product—or a similar program.[101] And as Jersey City mayor and future New Jersey commissioner of education Bret Schundler put it, Direct Instruction–style programs were seen by district leaders as "best for certain children."[102]

In 1996, Chicago Public Schools CEO Paul Vallas "strongly encouraged" low performing elementary schools in the city to adopt Direct Instruction.[103] Although Vallas had decided against his original plan to mandate adoption, the move still rankled opponents. "It's like, they're poor, so they can't learn the same way middle-class kids learn," contended Barbara

Bowman, president of the Erikson Institute for Advanced Study in Child Development. "Winnetka," she added, referring to an upper-middle-class suburb, "ain't using DISTAR."[104] Yet while well-heeled suburban systems were highly unlikely to use Direct Instruction materials, the comparison between Chicago and Winnetka struck some as a false one, particularly when discussing low performing schools or special education classrooms. As one school principal observed: "I don't see Direct Instruction being the answer, the cure-all. But I do see it as a catalyst for getting our kids on the right track."[105]

Many teachers responded positively to the use of Direct Instruction in particular contexts. "An inclusion class lends itself to cooperative learning," one teacher observed, "but if the students show no achievement, I'll switch to more direct instruction with frequent feedback."[106] As another teacher described the choice between constructivist methods and Direct Instruction: "I think a combination of the two is essential to addressing state standards."[107] The American Federation of Teachers even endorsed the use of Direct Instruction in 1998 and 1999 for "remedial reading interventions."[108] It was, in other words, a specialized tool to be used in particular cases.

Not all teachers opened up to Direct Instruction. "A trained monkey could do this program," claimed Janice Auld, president of the North Sacramento Education Association, about adopting a Direct Instruction reading curriculum. As an experienced educator, she found it "humiliating and demeaning."[109] Others made the case that it perpetuated inequality.

Nevertheless, Direct Instruction continued to make inroads in highly challenging settings. In 2001, Bill Honig—the former California school chief who had overseen the adoption of whole language—came out in favor of Direct Instruction, which he called "especially effective for weaker readers and students in special education."[110] Research echoed this position, substantiating the use of Direct Instruction "in remedial programs and those aimed at poor students."[111] As one popular teacher education textbook put it: "What professional demands does research-based direct instruction meet? Most particularly, student success—it helps lower-socioeconomic status children learn . . . Additionally, when teachers use research-based

Direct Instruction, they are seemingly in control, and that is viewed as very important nowadays."[112] In the next decade, such concerns—particularly about bridging the achievement gap—would only intensify.

PRAGMATISM AND DOUBT

The 2001 No Child Left Behind Act (NCLB) dramatically increased pressure on K–12 schools, and particularly urban schools, by ratcheting up testing and accountability measures. This did not transform the way that Direct Instruction was understood; it did, however, amplify the program's perceived significance. Whatever people's feelings about Direct Instruction, it was difficult to argue with the fact that it raised test scores. A 1999 report, for instance, identified fourteen studies on Direct Instruction that met standards for scientific rigor. Of those, seven found that Direct Instruction produced gains in reading, and eleven found that it raised scores in mathematics.[113]

The new century also brought a new focus on "what works." The Individuals with Disabilities Education Improvement Act of 2004 and NCLB both supported "scientifically based research." This, too, magnified Direct Instruction's significance, as it seemed to have a strong empirical research base. In 2003, for instance, a meta-analysis found that Direct Instruction produced robust results across varying contexts and varying study designs.[114] Similarly, a 2005 study by the American Institutes for Research found that of twenty-two elementary school models, only Direct Instruction and Robert Slavin's program "Success for All" could be rated "moderately strong" for their positive overall effects.[115]

These shifts in context drew increased attention from providers of professional development. After all, though such third parties may not have *started* offering Direct Instruction training as a result of increased emphasis on accountability testing and research-supported programs, new federal policies did make Direct Instruction an easier *sell* to schools and districts. As one for-profit promoter of Direct Instruction wrote: "One scientifically based instructional program shown to be effective with special education populations is Direct Instruction. Direct Instruction programs are considered scientifically based but, more importantly, are scientifically validated in that they have been shown to work through rigorous scientific experimentation."[116] Additionally, because Direct Instruction was a scripted program, it was both highly transportable and occupationally realistic—making it attractive to administrators with limited time for conducting faculty professional development.

Shifts in federal policy were also accompanied by increased federal funding, which in turn fostered additional support among intermediaries for moving Direct Instruction into practice. In 2005, for instance, the federal government awarded $3 million to Engelmann's organization—the National Institute for Direct Instruction (NIFDI)—to "build capacity to meet the needs of traditionally underserved students, especially students with disabilities and students with limited English proficiency."[117] NIFDI also offered consultation to schools and districts. For roughly a quarter-million dollars, the organization would help a school implement Direct Instruction; and though costs could be reduced in subsequent years at an existing Direct Instruction site, they would remain substantial.[118] Another organization, the Association for Direct Instruction—founded by Wes Becker in 1981—has fifty consultants working across the nation.

McGraw-Hill, the parent company of SRA, also recognized the opportunities inherent in a new policy climate. "With annual testing in reading and math now mandatory under the No Child Left Behind Act, student performance is getting increased scrutiny," the publisher noted in its 2006 *Investor Fact Book*, "McGraw-Hill Education is strengthening the broadest and most complete lineup in the marketplace."[119] Programs like Direct Instruction, the *Investor Fact Book* indicated, "have proven to be especially effective for students who come from disadvantaged backgrounds, have limited proficiency in English, or have special needs."[120] And the result was financial success for McGraw-Hill. As Engelmann observed, Direct Instruction "proved to be a very profitable program for the publisher."[121] Other publishers got in on the act as well—offering a whole variety of resources for educators. Over one hundred products, for instance, are listed in the back of one Direct Instruction textbook.[122]

In a climate that emphasized quantitative measurement, many saw great strength in a program that on the whole produced clear results. Direct Instruction still raised the hackles of many teachers—a fact that Engelmann almost seemed to enjoy. As he told the *New Yorker*: "We don't give a damn about what the teacher thinks, what the teacher feels."[123] Yet the context of urban education had shifted enough to make Direct Instruction philosophically compatible, at least in some instances. As one teacher and instructional coach noted, "Teachers resent it because it's so scripted. But is it about me being happy or [the students] learning?"[124] And to those who bought into the idea that learning could be measured by tests, Direct Instruction represented a seemingly valuable tool. As a fourth-grade teacher observed: "Students really see their own improvement. It has also made me feel better about my teaching ability and I can actually see it on paper."[125] Even those skeptical of quantitative measures, however, could see a use for Direct Instruction. If test scores were going to be the coin of the realm, then it made sense to figure out how to raise them. Thus, despite the opposition of most professors of education, the fifth edition of *Direct Instruction Reading*—a teacher training textbook—sold one thousand copies a year in the early years of the new millennium.[126]

Still, many educators resisted the allure of Direct Instruction, even if it did promise to improve test scores. As one educator observed: "I don't think there is any question that Direct Instruction is a great way to improve school achievement if that were the only goal in the world."[127] And as a 2004 study found, "Some urban DI teachers expressed great concern over DI's lack of sensitivity to issues of poverty, culture, and race."[128]

At the same time, however, teachers are pragmatic. They know that tests can be taught to, and that much depends on things like accountability scores. School funding depends on such scores. Student confidence is affected. School climate is affected. Teacher salaries can be affected. And there is the lurking fear that such tests actually *do* measure something important. "I do understand why preservice teachers wanted to know why they were not being given the structured and prescriptive method of teaching that purportedly had yielded gains on a mandated assessment," one teacher educator wrote. "I too was once a first-year teacher searching for how to successfully teach a lively group of sixth graders."[129]

As Direct Instruction gained a stronger foothold, political fights over it grew more intense. The executive director of the Reading First program, for instance, lost his job over a perceived attempt "to strong-arm education officials in some states to adopt . . . Direct Instruction, while blocking a nonphonics program, Reading Recovery."[130] A report issued in the wake of the scandal quoted e-mails in which Chris Doherty, the former director, "defended his preferred early-childhood reading programs against their progressive critics in language unsuitable for kids."[131] He resigned soon afterward. Douglas Carnine, who served as U.S. Commissioner of Special Education, and who helped develop Reading First, was also caught up in the imbroglio.

At the district level the story was similar. In Chicago, where test results were mixed—a result that Engelmann attributed to weak cooperation from some principals and poor professional development provided by Malcolm X College—political cover for Direct Instruction quickly dissolved. Consequently, a 2005 school district curriculum committee reviewed six reading programs and selected five for the city, leaving out Direct Instruction. The roughly forty schools using the program were allowed to continue if they had "shown success" with it, but no new schools would be able to adopt the program.[132] Direct Instruction was effectively banned.

Direct Instruction, then, continues to come and go. It is adopted by true believers, by those looking to improve test scores, or by those required to institute a program that "works." And, soon enough, it is opposed by those who see it as an affront to teacher professionalism, by those who see it as culturally insensitive, or by those who see it as out of line with constructivist principles. As Engelmann observed, "Somebody would get in power and know from their own experience, or whatever, that Direct Instruction worked, and they would implement it to varying degrees of fidelity . . . [and] as long as that person stayed in power, the program would stay in place; as soon as that person left, back to the weed patch, immediately."[133] With the exception of some contexts like remedial education, where Direct Instruction has gained real philosophical compatibility, the program moves with the ebb and flow of educator sentiment. Those partial to it see Direct Instruction as significant, occupationally tenable, and highly transportable. Those opposed to it see a challenge to much that they believe in.

CONCLUSION

Half a century after its inception, Direct Instruction continues to incite arguments. It has strong advocates, certainly. But it also has passionate opponents, and the two sides routinely battle each other in school districts, in scholarly literature, and on Internet message boards.[134]

For their part, teachers tend to side with the opposition, usually finding Direct Instruction philosophically incompatible with their beliefs and values. Direct Instruction seems to threaten teacher professionalism. It reeks of an approach to educational psychology long out of favor. And it is used primarily among at-risk populations, creating for them an educational experience quite different than that of their more privileged peers. Consequently, many teachers see Direct Instruction as a program that strips teaching and learning of their deepest rewards—a program that turns teachers into machinists and students into products.

Yet, despite the antagonism that Direct Instruction can inspire, it remains a piece of educational research that teachers are familiar with. It may come and go at particular school sites, but it never fades away. And that is because for teachers and administrators with practical concerns about student achievement, Direct Instruction can be a useful tool—not only because it promises to raise scores, but also because it is seemingly easy to adopt.

At low performing schools attended by the least privileged, many educators have embraced Direct Instruction as a means of teaching basic skills. They do not disagree with those who believe that students should be nurtured intellectually—taught to be analytical thinkers, amateur philosophers, and social critics. Nor do they disagree with the proposition that classrooms should be culturally sensitive and democratic places. But their immediate concerns are with teaching children to read, write, and compute, as well as with maintaining some semblance of order. In short, they do not believe that Direct Instruction is all that teaching should be. But in a particularly challenging context, they are moved first and foremost by the simple justice of literacy and numeracy.

Most educators see only disadvantages in the adoption of Direct Instruction—losses in autonomy, violations of closely held beliefs, and narrowing of aims. But in the most challenging classrooms, teachers see Direct Instruction as more philosophically compatible. In failing schools, and in special education classes, teachers are faced with significant challenges—challenges that can seem overwhelming in the face of high-stakes accountability measures. As a result, many teachers are receptive to Direct Instruction. As one educator wrote in *Early Childhood Education*, even though she would "like to see a stake driven in the heart of DISTAR," it "does have a place."[135] And as one teacher "in the trenches" concluded: "In inner city schools, direct instruction is the best method."[136]

The program has also maintained a high level of perceived significance across its half-century of existence. From its earliest days, Direct Instruction produced strong empirical results, and that trend has continued into the present. Three decades after the end of Project Follow Through, for instance, a team of researchers concluded that "when the instructional task calls for the teaching of discrete skills and knowledge in an interactive and guided format, DI remains a proven approach."[137] And though some studies have undermined that conclusion, Siegfried Engelmann has been an aggressive and tireless champion for Direct Instruction throughout his long career. Working to promote positive findings about Direct Instruction, Engelmann and his team have succeeded in making the program visible to K–12 educators and policy makers.

Finally, Direct Instruction's road-ready packaging has made it both occupationally realistic and easily transportable. Because it comes in the form of a year-long, course-specific, scripted curriculum, Direct Instruction does not require integration with existing lesson plans or new content knowledge; hence, many teachers see it as easy to implement. And, because it is seemingly "teacher-proof," Direct Instruction has had a powerful appeal among policy makers and administrators inclined toward central-ization and concerned with matters like efficiency and uniformity.

Direct Instruction has its enemies. But it also has its champions. And perhaps more importantly, it has the characteristics crucial for winning a foothold in educational practice—at least in particular settings.

It is not known by all teachers, nor is it loved by all who use it. Yet it has bridged the divide between research and practice. And, as a method of last resort, it endures.

CHAPTER FIVE

"Less of an Impact on the Educational World"

Ideas Without a Foothold

Most ideas from education research have failed to win a place in teacher practice; therefore, choosing to examine particular cases from among that vast well might seem inherently arbitrary.

Yet evaluated alongside the four ideas considered earlier in this work, some failures are particularly surprising. Some cases, in other words, bear such a striking similarity to their better-known counterparts that they seem to disprove any claims about the importance of specific characteristics. Consider the case of the Taxonomy of Educational Objectives for the Affective Domain. Developed virtually in parallel with the Taxonomy of Educational Objectives for the Cognitive Domain (Bloom's taxonomy), and by most of the same scholars, it seems unlikely that something about the idea *itself* played a crucial role in whether or not it gained a foothold in K–12 classrooms. Instead, it seems to suggest that historical contingency—chance—is the truly decisive factor.

The importance of chance cannot be dismissed. Fortunate timing can often bring about otherwise unforeseeable, unpredictable, or unlikely outcomes. But timing is not everything.

The four ideas considered in this chapter diverged in slight yet significant ways from the four examined earlier in the book. As a result, their impact on education practice was substantially different. This is not to suggest that the ideas unrecognized by most teachers are intrinsically less valuable. The objectives for the affective domain are no less sound than those for the cognitive domain. Robert Sternberg's triarchic theory is no less valid a theory of intelligence than Howard Gardner's. Merlin Wittrock's notion of generative intelligence is no less rigorous or "constructivist" than the project method. And the behavior analysis model is no less complete a basic skills program than its Project Follow Through counterpart, Direct Instruction. Instead, the implication is that neither pure luck nor the quality of research alone dictates the impact of an idea on teacher practice.

Simply put: perceived significance, philosophical compatibility, occupational realism, and transportability—factors mediating between the world of research and the world of practice—matter. And though the presence of those factors is no guarantee that scholarship will move from the ivory tower into the classroom, their absence virtually precludes such an outcome.

THE TAXONOMY FOR THE AFFECTIVE DOMAIN

The *Taxonomy of Educational Objectives, Handbook I: The Cognitive Domain* was a resounding success, and made its editor a famous name in education. Yet Bloom's taxonomy was not his alone—nor, for that matter, was it his only taxonomy. In fact, *Handbook I*, as its title indicated, was designed as the first of a three-part series that would also include the so-called "affective" and "psychomotor" domains.[1]

Unlike Bloom's taxonomy, *Handbook II* had three authors (rather than five), and no lead editor. And, with David Krathwohl assuming lead authorship—Bloom and Benjamin Masia were listed as second and third authors of the work, respectively—*Handbook II* could not accurately be called Bloom's. It was, instead, Krathwohl's: a branding problem that would only reveal itself over time.

Otherwise, however, much in the second volume—released in 1964—echoed the first. The opening pages repeated the aims of the overall project; part one of the work explained the decision-making process of its authors; and part two provided a detailed outline of the taxonomy. The central organizing concept for the second taxonomy was "internalization" rather than "complexity," as it had been for the first, and five divisions instead of six were identified: receiving, responding, valuing, organization, and characterization by a value or value complex.

Despite the similarities between the two taxonomies, however, Krathwohl's made only a fraction of the penetration into practice that Bloom's made. As one teacher wrote in 1974, "Behavioral objectives were for filing, not using." And, as he concluded, "If someone asks what your objectives are, you mutter something about 'forgetting the affective domain and just teaching some U.S. history,' and leave it at that."[2] But even such talk of ignoring Krathwohl's taxonomy indicated a deeper engagement than was typical in the world of practice. As a Google Ngram graph indicates (see figure 5.1), references to Krathwohl's taxonomy blipped briefly in the mid-1970s and then seemed to disappear.[3] In fact, the 1994 text *Fostering the Love of Reading: The Affective Domain in Reading Education* did not reference the Krathwohl taxonomy anywhere in the main text.[4]

The quality of the research could not account for the difference. The participants, after all, were mostly the same as those who had authored the volume on the cognitive domain. Furthermore, the rigor of the scholarship undergirding Bloom's taxonomy was hardly the key draw. As one scholar noted, research had "cast doubt on the validity of some of the basic assumptions that were made by Bloom in compiling the taxonomy."[5]

Timing—another possible explanation—also holds little explanatory power. While Krathwohl's taxonomy came second, it was a companion volume rather than a competitor: something that should have given it a practical *advantage* in entering the teacher knowledge base. Further, although it was not published until eight years after Bloom's taxonomy, the earlier work had taken several years to penetrate practice, thereby significantly reducing the interval between volumes.

Nevertheless, Bloom's became the taxonomy of note. As Henry Ellington observed in 1984, the taxonomy for the cognitive domain was "by far the more influential," making "a considerable effect on both curriculum planning and assessment."[6] Krathwohl's, by turn, would in many ways be forgotten.

FIGURE 5.1

Textual references to "Bloom's Taxonomy" and "Krathwohl's Taxonomy," 1950–2005

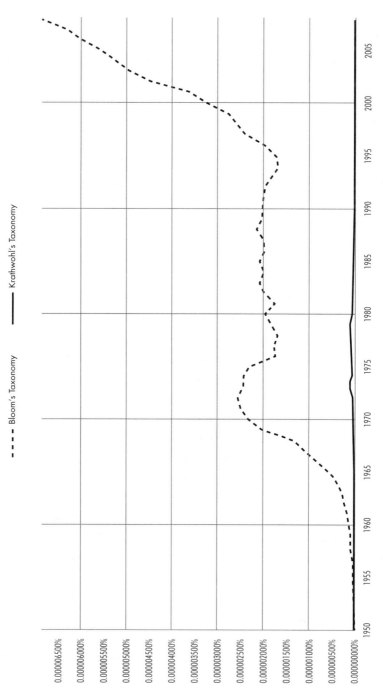

The y-axis in this graph indicates the relative frequency with which a word or phrase appears in the several million books scanned in Google's digitization project.

On What Is Learned in School

In many parts of the world, and in the United States for much of its history, affective aims superseded cognitive aims in importance. As David Tyack has suggested, during the nineteenth century "civic education was the public school's most crucial purpose."[7] In a popular teachers' manual from the 1830s, Orville Taylor wrote that the chief duty of educators was "to make men moral."[8] The broader society, he argued, "expects that teachers will make children and youth social, honorable, and benevolent members."[9]

The nineteenth-century fixation on character education did eventually fade. And in the twentieth century, as schools were increasingly presented as drivers of social mobility and the national economy, the importance of the cognitive domain steadily grew. Still, even in the wake of World War II, the notion that schools should produce socialized and moral citizens continued to persist. To the authors of the Taxonomy of Educational Objectives, then, it made sense that the affective domain would be addressed alongside the cognitive and psychomotor domains.[10]

As the twentieth century wore on, however, Americans became increasingly focused on what schools could do to build student knowledge. The rhetoric of economic survivalism grew more hysterical as the Cold War–inspired notion of international competitiveness took root in the national psyche, drawing attention to the ostensibly fundamental concern of academic achievement. Additionally, near-universal enrollment in secondary education and rapidly expanding opportunities in higher education further amplified the growing expectation that schools would function as meritocratic ladders to socioeconomic opportunity, provided that students could reveal their brainpower.

Not surprisingly, the pursuit of affective aims began to seem less relevant to the work of education. Put another way, the focus on the development of intelligence was pushing the development of character out of schools. As one teacher wrote in 1968, "The nature of the affective goals renders them far more personal, and hence more individual, than those in the cognitive domain."[11] Krathwohl and colleagues could feel this shift, noting, "Teachers and examiners do not regard it as appropriate to grade students with respect to their interests, attitude, or character development."[12] But they did not anticipate how dramatic the swing away from affective aims would ultimately be.

Two major factors in that shift were the basic skills movement in the 1970s and the standards movement of the 1980s and 1990s. Each entirely ignored the affective domain, concentrating attention on cognitive growth and the acquisition of traditional content.[13] Only the lowest level of Krathwohl's taxonomy—receiving—entered into the thinking of reformers, who focused the attention of educators through bold rhetoric and increasingly assertive policy.

The language of the affective domain certainly continued to exist. A science Web site hosted by Carleton College, for instance, noted that professors would like for students "to respond to what they learn, to value it, to organize it, and maybe even to characterize themselves as science students, science majors, or scientists."[14] But such a perspective was increasingly rare in the latter decades of the twentieth century, remaining largely the province of boutique programs, exclusive private schools, and higher education—or, in Carleton's case, all three.

Eventually, the past—and all of the concern with the affective domain that characterized it—would be forgotten. As one author wrote in 2010, "Knowledge and skills are traditionally perceived as a more important outcome than attitudes and values; it is believed that the latter ones should be developed at home but not at school."[15] Her judgment about the status of "attitudes and values" was correct, even if the history lesson was flawed. After all, attitudes and values were the chief concern of eighteenth- and nineteenth-century educators. Still, whatever the case may have been in the past, K–12 teachers no longer perceived scholarship on the affective domain as being significant.

The rising importance of the cognitive domain, associated with individual and national achievement, was not the only contextual shift influencing perception of Krathwohl's taxonomy. In the second half of the twentieth century, Americans became increasingly uncomfortable with the teaching of values in public schools. Between the end of the Second World War and 1964, when *Handbook II* was published, international and domestic transformations—the escalation of the Cold War, expansion of

U.S. involvement in Vietnam, the Civil Rights movement, the counterculture movement of the 1960s, and the rise of Goldwater Republicanism, to name just a few factors—accelerated a new vision of schooling in America.

Consequently, educators saw the problem with the new taxonomy not as one of significance, but of philosophical compatibility. On the left, notions of social pluralism undermined the notion of a shared understanding of the purpose of schooling. On the right, antigovernment sentiment and the obsession with freedom from coercion made nineteenth-century conceptions of character education seem, in the words of David Tyack, "distant and strange."[16]

Thus, when Krathwohl's taxonomy was released in 1964, it seemed to some wholly inappropriate. One early reviewer, for instance, wondered "whether objectives and tests of this kind have a legitimate place in public education." Sounding more like an author in a right-wing magazine than in the *Journal of Educational Measurement*, he wrote that there were "strong reasons" for regarding the affective domain "as private property; as the essence of personal freedom." As he concluded: "There is nothing so close to the fulcrum of one's controlling motives as his personal values."[17] And two decades later, a conservative commentator asked, "Do educators in public schools have the right to programmatically enter the 'affective domain' of the child without the prior informed consent of parents?"[18]

Difficult to Implement, Difficult to Use

By and large, teachers knew what was meant when Bloom and colleagues referenced knowledge, comprehension, application, analysis, synthesis, and evaluation on their taxonomic pyramid. Analysis and synthesis could be confused for each other, and certainly the entire scheme could be radically oversimplified and reinterpreted. But at the most basic level, Bloom's taxonomy was simple and straightforward.

Krathwohl's taxonomy, on the other hand, was far more difficult to approach. Receiving and responding were uncomplicated enough, but what did "valuing" mean? And how was valuing, at the third rung on the ladder, different from "characterization by a value or value complex"? Finally, why was "organization" included on a taxonomy of objectives for the affective domain? As the authors of a Web site would later observe, "The differences between the levels, especially between 3, 4, and 5, are subtle, and not so clear as the separations elsewhere in the Taxonomy."[19]

The descriptions of the various hierarchical levels, at least as provided by the *Handbook*, did not clarify things. At "the peak of the internalization process," Krathwohl and colleagues wrote, are "those objectives which concern one's view of the universe, one's philosophy of life, one's *Weltanschauung*."[20] The use of German vocabulary aside, Krathwohl's taxonomy simply seemed to rely on a more specialized set of definitions than Bloom's had. As one observer wrote in 1968, *Handbook I* had deployed "a technical vocabulary common to logic and philosophy." *Handbook II*, by contrast, employed "a set of terms and constructs rather different from those familiar to educational theory and practice." As a consequence, readers might wonder "whether processes described by these new terms are really relevant to educational practice."[21]

Again, Krathwohl and colleagues were aware of the general problem. As they wrote, the affective domain had been "much more difficult to structure," and the result was a product they were "much less satisfied with."[22] It is not clear, however, that they understood the degree to which the new taxonomy was difficult to transport across informal networks of educators, curriculum designers, test developers, and scholars. As a teacher educator observed in 1970, "Part of the time available for practice in constructing questions was interfered with because of the terminology, which was difficult for preservice teachers to comprehend."[23] And, as educational psychologist Robert Travers wrote in 1980, "When one turns to the taxonomy of the affective domain, one is confronted with the fact that what is being classified is not clear at all."[24] Even the transportable pyramid image (see figure 5.2) would be of little use.

It was also not clear how any of this could be applied in the classroom. Education professor Morton Alpren made the case in 1974 that if the affective movement "was to succeed, its proponents should think about and express the differences in the components so that they could then begin to address themselves better to the curriculum."[25] Yet while Bloom's taxonomy had easily been translated into lesson plans and evaluation rubrics, it

FIGURE 5.2

Taxonomy of Educational Objectives for the Affective Domain

was less clear how Krathwohl's would be storable and sharable among educators. As one scholar observed, "few public schools" were able to "operationalize the evaluation of affective goals."[26]

The problems with the affective domain, however, went beyond the philosophical questions it raised about the purpose of school or the transportability issues brought about by its technical terminology. In fact, perhaps the biggest obstacle in moving Krathwohl's taxonomy into practice was that it was occupationally unrealistic. That is not to imply that Bloom's was crafted with great concern for the daily work of K–12 teachers; it was not. Yet Bloom's, by fortunate accident, was seen by educators as something that could be easily added on to existing practice without overhauling the nature of the occupation.

Krathwohl's taxonomy, by contrast, would have required significantly reimagining the nature of teaching. Once more, its authors were not completely naïve about potential complications. "A teacher will rarely have the same students over a sufficient period of time to make measurable changes in certain affective behaviors," they wrote. Consequently, they noted, "measures of a semester's or year's growth would reveal little change." That fact alone would not absolutely preclude Krathwohl's taxonomy from being implemented. They might have suggested, for instance, that goals be further broken down to allow teachers to observe progress within the school year. But instead, they recommended the creation of "an evaluation plan covering at least several grades and involving the coordinated efforts of several teachers."[27] Such efforts would require the creation of systems and structures in the age-graded school that K–12 reformers had long sought but failed to produce—a tall order indeed.

There was also the question of how the affective objectives would be evaluated. As one scholar noted in 1970, "A search of the literature revealed that there is almost a complete absence of instruments to measure affective outcomes of instruction."[28] And as a teacher educator put it that same year: "The affective products cannot be measured as yet, nor for that matter have they been exactly defined."[29] Thus, even if teachers saw the affective domain as an appropriate target for instruction, even if schools were able to successfully create long-term scope and sequence plans for the affective domain, and even if scheduling could be redesigned to promote teacher coordination, they would still be left with the difficult task of designing assessments.

Without clear and discrete outcomes to look for, teachers could hardly be expected to see the affective domain as something usable in the classroom. Many teachers no doubt considered aspects of the affective domain to be, as one teacher put it, "essential for learning."[30] Yet the objectives would not be useful, he wrote, unless "their successful fulfillment may be measured."[31] And as another author argued, "It can be assumed that among the areas which most teachers consider difficult or impossible to measure are the behaviors which belong to the affective domain."[32]

By the 1970s, then, when Bloom's taxonomy was continuing to make inroads into the formal curriculum and into informal networks of educators, Krathwohl's was already being forgotten—exiled to the territory of "not my job" by teachers. As one teacher concluded, "We cannot continue to provide most of the motivation past level 2.10."[33] Producing student compliance ("acquiescence in responding"), it seems, was the most that could be asked of teachers. Anything beyond that—student willingness to respond, student satisfaction in response, acceptance of a value—was seen as either inappropriate, impractical, or impossible.

Ultimately, Krathwohl's taxonomy entered into a negative feedback loop—a world-upside-down version of the phenomenon that made Bloom's taxonomy a known entity among successive generations of teachers. Because it had achieved recognition, Bloom's taxonomy was widely included in teacher training textbooks, curriculum guides, professional development seminars, and the like. Such inclusion, in turn, endowed it with even greater legitimacy, which led to further adoption.

Krathwohl's taxonomy, on the other hand, was not translated into institutional structures and did not travel well by word of mouth. It remained in the research literature and, because of its connection with the broader taxonomic project, was linked to the powerful Bloom brand. But layers of time would seal it away from practice, with each passing decade further trapping it in the world of research. It became, for teachers, a museum piece—a curio worth only a glance before moving on.

STERNBERG'S TRIARCHIC THEORY

In education research circles, Robert J. Sternberg's name is often listed near that of fellow psychologist Howard Gardner. Similarly, Sternberg's triarchic theory, which posits three facets of human intelligence, is often grouped with Gardner's theory of multiple intelligences.

Yet despite this connectedness with Gardner and multiple intelligences, mention of Sternberg or the triarchic theory in K–12 classrooms is unlikely to produce much recognition. On the U.S. Department of Education's Education Resources Information Center database, the triarchic theory produces forty-two hits—nearly fourteen hundred fewer than a search for multiple intelligences returns. And a Google Ngram (see figure 5.3) reveals an equally stark difference between references to Sternberg's idea—which made modest inroads among practitioners—and references to Gardner's.

Given the surface-level similarities between Gardner and Sternberg, this difference in uptake is surprising. For instance, Gardner taught at

FIGURE 5.3

Textual references to "Multiple Intelligences" and "Triarchic Theory," 1980–2008

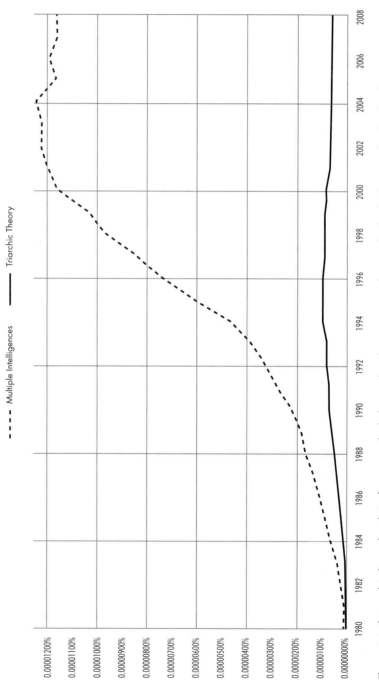

- - - - Multiple Intelligences — Triarchic Theory

The y-axis in this graph indicates the relative frequency with which a word or phrase appears in the several million books scanned in Google's digitization project.

Harvard, while Sternberg taught at Yale; and both men held prestigious endowed chairs. Like Gardner, Sternberg has won tens of millions of dollars in grants. And both men are stars in the field. In fact, among psychologists, Sternberg has arguably had a far greater impact than Gardner. On a 2002 list of the one hundred "most eminent" psychologists of the twentieth century, Sternberg was ranked sixtieth.[34] And in a separate list from the same issue of the *Review of General Psychology*, Sternberg tied for twenty-fourth in the "25 Psychologists Most Frequently Cited in Introductory Psychology Textbooks."[35] Gardner did not rank. Additionally, the Institute for Scientific Information has rated Sternberg as one of the most highly cited authors in psychology and psychiatry, locating him in the top .05 percent of all authors. Thus, as Gardner observed, "If you asked one hundred psychologists which theory was a better psychological theory, I have a feeling he would win easily."[36]

The two men also worked at almost exactly the same time, embraced comparable ideas, and published at similarly prolific rates. Gardner's book *Frames of Mind: The Theory of Multiple Intelligences* was released in 1983—just two years before Sternberg's *Beyond IQ: A Triarchic Theory of Intelligence* and hardly an advantage, as it would take several years to catch on among practitioners.[37] Both books rejected the behaviorist tradition, instead embracing cognitivism. Both works posited a multifaceted view of intelligence. And both were written for general audiences. Not surprisingly, then, several early reviews mentioned both books together.[38] And today, *Frames of Mind* and *Beyond IQ* are paired under the "Frequently Bought Together" heading on Amazon.com.

So what explains the fact that K–12 educators are far more likely to know Howard Gardner and multiple intelligences than they are to know Robert Sternberg and his triarchic theory?

What's in a Name?

In *Beyond IQ*, Sternberg laid out a theory outlining a broader conception of intelligence. Like multiple intelligences, Sternberg's triarchic model identified multiple facets of human intelligence—facets as engaged by social environments as by mathematical equations. Unlike multiple intelligences, however, the triarchic theory emphasized process over domain. Rather than identify the manifestations of intelligence, as Gardner did—logical-mathematical, say, or bodily-kinesthetic—Sternberg identified mental procedures that often worked in tandem during the performance of intelligent acts.

The first piece of the intelligence pie, as Sternberg identified it, was the componential—the facet of intelligence that constituted the "internal world of the individual."[39] In other words, this third of the triarchic theory described what had traditionally been taken for the whole of intelligence. Sternberg labeled it *componential* for the three separate components that collectively constituted it. Knowledge acquisition components were the processes used in gaining and storing new knowledge—the components necessary for learning how to do things. Metacomponents were executive functions associated with decision making—the components necessary for planning what things to do and how to do them. And performance components were the basic operations involved in any cognitive act—the components required for carrying out the work of metacomponents. Collectively, the three components specified what Sternberg called "the mental mechanisms that lead to more and less intelligent behavior."[40] In short, someone with high marks in the componential category would make for an excellent test taker.

The second facet of intelligence in the triarchic model was the experiential, which described how people approach new and unfamiliar tasks. But because not all experiences involve new situations, Sternberg also included in this facet of intelligence the ability to manage similar scenarios in an economical manner—automatizing responses to familiar situations. Those particularly gifted in the experiential aspect would not only adapt nimbly to new tasks, but would also respond efficiently to old ones. Sternberg described such intelligence as "creative," though it may be more helpful to imagine someone with high marks in the experiential category as an expert solver of the *New York Times* crossword puzzle—nimbly riddling out any new form of deception and efficiently deploying standard word-deciphering tactics.

The third aspect of the triarchic model was the contextual dimension. Being able to connect one's internal world to external reality, Sternberg

contended, was a distinct aspect of intelligence, separate from the componential or the experiential, and was associated with practical giftedness. As
he saw it, the contextual facet of the model was made up of three kinds of
interactions with one's environment: adapting to it, shaping it, and select-
ing more suitable surroundings. Constituting what some would call street
smarts, Sternberg described these interactions as those "that characterize
intelligent behavior in the everyday world."[41] For an even more specific (if
fictional) example, we might imagine the case of J. Pierrepont Finch, who,
in the musical *How to Succeed in Business Without Really Trying*, rises from
window washer to chairman of the board of the World Wide Wicket Company, relying solely on his ability to think in context.

The triarchic theory, thus, was quite complex. Understanding the nu-
ances of the theory, the distinctions between the subtheories and their
various components, and the way that the facets worked together in the
performance of intelligent acts required no small degree of concentration
while reading—an important difference between it and Gardner's theory.
Not surprisingly, then, when distinguished educational psychologist Lee J.
Cronbach reviewed *Beyond IQ*, he concluded that "the central overview of
Sternberg's results is best suited to psychologists and advanced students."[42]

Sternberg made things no easier in his approach to naming or organization. *Triarchic* is an obscure word—the adjectival form of *triarchy*, which
itself is a less common synonym for *triumvirate*. And outside of those familiar with Roman history, readers would be pressed to know that it referred to a government with three individuals at the helm. As Howard
Gardner observed: "The name isn't very good."[43] Compare this with the
naming of Gardner's theory, which immediately signaled the central concept of multiple intelligences.

The naming of the three subtheories, too, was problematic. Rather
than using vernacular language to describe the kind of intelligence being deployed, Sternberg described them more literally—a facet of intelligence comprising three components, a facet that dealt with novel and
repeated experiences, and a facet that related individuals to their environ-
mental context. Tellingly, many people simply used Gardner's phrasing
when discussing Sternberg's work. As Albert Shanker—the former head of

the American Federation of Teachers, and no intellectual slouch—wrote in 1990: "Howard Gardner and Robert Sternberg tell us that people have multiple intelligences and that different ones predominate in different people."[44] But perhaps most indicative of the linguistic complexity of the theory, as well as the limits that such complexity placed on uptake, is the fact that Sternberg and others eventually dropped the language of componential, experiential, and contextual. Gradually, the triarchy at the heart of the theory stopped referring to the three subtheories and started referencing the three different types of giftedness *associated* with each subtheory: analytical, creative, and practical.[45]

Finally, there was the issue that some found *Beyond IQ* a slog. According to a reviewer in the *British Journal of Educational Studies*, readers were "likely to find the literary style somewhat labored."[46] Lee Dembart, a *Los Angeles Times* reviewer, was more critical: "There is a good book in here struggling to be free," he wrote. "A better editor would have helped Sternberg, the book, and the readers."[47] *Frames of Mind*, by contrast, was a page turner. Even Sternberg, in a highly critical review of Gardner's book, conceded that *Frames* was "a beautifully written, well-organized, engaging review of the literature on human talents." Gardner, he added, is "quite simply, one of the best writers in the field of psychology. He has a knack for writing in a way that is engaging and challenging, but never condescending."[48] And as Gardner himself matter-of-factly observed, "I'm a more engaging writer than [Sternberg] is, and I am better able to draw people in."[49]

Sternberg took issue with the research undergirding multiple intelligences. Gardner, he wrote, "never applies [his] criteria in a careful or convincing way" and "provides no evidence that his particular list is better than any plausible alternative." Ultimately, he concluded, "Gardner's 'theory' is not truly a psychological theory, since it does not contain a set of interlocking constructs that together can explain, at some level, some domain of human performance."[50] Other notable scholars agreed. As Stanford University's Richard Snow wrote, *Frames of Mind*, though written "with flowing, glowing prose," was "more journalism than science."[51]

Yet none of that would present a significant enough obstacle to keep multiple intelligences out of schools. The transportability problems inherent in the triarchic theory, however—its naming, its organizational scheme, and the writing style of the key text—would pose significant challenges for educators attempting to share Sternberg's research through informal networks.

Not "Intuitively Satisfying"

Sternberg was not merely seeking to converse with the scholarly community. Had he been, his work would have been an unqualified success. Instead, he was seeking to engage a broader audience, and he worked to reach out to educators and general readers.

In 1986, for instance, only one year after the publication of *Beyond IQ*, and seven years before the appearance of Gardner's *Multiple Intelligences: The Theory into Practice*, Sternberg wrote *Intelligence Applied*. The book, as he put it, was "a distillation and simplification of material in . . . *Beyond IQ*" and included exercises, examples, and tips for developing the various facets of intelligence.[52] As one reviewer enthusiastically observed, Sternberg was departing "from the usual practice of those who specialize in cognitive research and [taking] on the practical task of providing a service to people."[53]

Two years later, Sternberg wrote *The Triarchic Mind: A New Theory of Human Intelligence*. While *Beyond IQ* had been written for a general audience, it was published by Cambridge University Press—a prestigious house that carried more weight in scholarly communities than in corner bookshops. *The Triarchic Mind*, on the other hand, was published by Viking—a popular press that would aggressively market the book to a wide audience. And revealing some of his motives for the book in his acknowledgments, Sternberg thanked Mindy Werner, his editor at Viking, whom he praised for "making the book more readable and lively."[54]

These works, as well as several articles Sternberg wrote during the 1980s, had some of the innate appeal that multiple intelligences did. Sternberg, for instance, addressed the fact that "many of us know people who, although often slow in performing tasks, perform them at a superior level," implying that people could be smart in different ways.[55] He talked about "real-world kinds of intelligence" mattering as much as "the academic kinds of intelligence measured by traditional tests."[56] And he implied that tests were problematic, working only for "some of the people some of the time."[57]

Yet much of what Sternberg was saying was old news, at least to teachers. Others had made the argument that IQ was not a complete measure of intelligence, and much of their work had become standard reading in teacher preparation programs.[58] Perhaps most commonly used by the mid-1980s was Stephen J. Gould's book, *The Mismeasure of Man*—a history of the mental testing movement published in 1981 and written for a general audience.[59] Gardner and several additional scholars had presented alternate models for describing intelligence. And others, like Benjamin Bloom and colleagues, had categorized various kinds of cognitive acts. In fact, in a 1998 chapter on "Applying the Triarchic Theory of Human Intelligence in the Classroom," Sternberg listed four levels of thinking distinctly reminiscent of Bloom's: memory (*knowledge* in Bloom's taxonomy; *remembering* in Krathwohl and Anderson's 2001 revision), analytical (*analysis* in Bloom), creative (*synthesis* in Bloom; *creating* in Krathwohl and Anderson), and practical (seemingly connected to *application*).[60]

Beyond this, some of the triarchic theory may not have felt inherently *true* to educators. Sternberg gradually made the language of the theory more accessible, labeling the facets of intelligence as analytical, creative, and practical, and making the case that teachers could nurture each facet in students of all ages and abilities. Yet while it may have seemed evident to American teachers that all students could learn to think analytically, the proposition that they might also learn to think creatively and practically was less obvious. As Alfonso Montuori and Ronald E. Purser have argued, the modern view of creativity is built around the idea that the artist must struggle against and rise above "the limiting, stultifying forces of the conforming masses." Consequently, creativity is often understood to be nurtured not through education, but through disengagement from the social environment."[61] Similarly, the traits involved in what Sternberg described as practical intelligence—traits like motivation, perseverance, independence, and self-confidence—are commonly perceived in the United States to be inborn. As a result, Sternberg's work may not have felt immediately "right," even if it was methodologically rigorous. As Marie Winn wrote in the *New York Times*, the triarchic theory was simply less "intuitively satisfying" than multiple intelligences.[62]

Sternberg might have persuaded more teachers to take a longer look at the triarchic theory if he had pitched it as a bulwark against the encroachments of standardized tests, or if a corps of intermediaries had taken to the idea as they did to the theory of multiple intelligences. There was clear interest among teachers in resisting the tyranny of measurement, and some, like longtime classroom teacher Dan Kirby, saw *Beyond IQ* as an argument "like Gardner's" for moving "beyond mere academic aptitude and into the real world."[63] But Sternberg did not make those appeals. In fact, he supported the practice of testing on the grounds that "we simply do not have strong alternatives yet."[64]

Howard Gardner, meanwhile, was charismatically tapping directly into teacher concerns. At every opportunity, he signaled to teachers that he was on their side, that he should be trusted, and that his research was relevant to their interests. "Much of what I write about can be identified with the educational tradition of John Dewey," he wrote in *The Disciplined Mind*, signaling as clearly as possible his allegiance with teachers. Whether framing multiple intelligences within the construct of "progressive or neo-progressive education" or criticizing E. D. Hirsch—an advocate of a more traditional core curriculum—Gardner consistently worked to reveal the extent to which his idea squared with the professional concerns and philosophical dispositions of K–12 teachers.[65]

Of course, Gardner's work was also transportable enough that professional development providers took to the idea. Sternberg, by contrast, was often the sole promoter of his idea, and not always a particularly effective one. In 1987, for instance, he wrote an article in the practitioner-friendly journal *Phi Delta Kappan* about critical thinking—a favorite teacher topic. Yet rather than highlighting the triarchic theory throughout the piece, Sternberg mentioned his major research project only in passing.[66] Why? It seems that Sternberg may have believed that scholarly ideas catch on as a product of their merits. Gardner, on the other hand, seemed quite aware of the importance of visibility in gaining perceived significance for his idea.

Sternberg certainly was concerned with affecting practice. As he would later recall: "In my days at Yale, I spoke once or twice a week, so was traveling almost all the time, it seemed." Yet while he gave scores of workshops to K–12 educators across the country, the triarchic theory never sparked the same interest as multiple intelligences. As he put it, "I guess I was not as good a salesman as I might have wished."[67]

Eventually, Sternberg moved on from the triarchic theory, busying himself with other projects. Gardner, meanwhile, continued making multiple intelligences even more visible, accessible, and transportable.

A Footnote for Multiple Intelligences

The most significant hurdle keeping the triarchic theory out of K–12 classrooms was figuring out how it would actually be implemented. In part, that was a product of the nature of the theory, which, according to a *New York Times* review, was "a formula for what has to be computed, rather than for how the computation might be carried out by mind or machine."[68] Equally, however, it was a consequence of the nature of academic research, which is generally more oriented toward explaining than instructing. As Sternberg put it, "Teachers often don't know how to implement the theories in the classroom, and they recognize (correctly) that incorrect implementations of a theory can do more harm than good."[69]

Sternberg did address issues like lesson design, but in doing so, he displayed a relatively naïve understanding of teacher autonomy. As he wrote of *Intelligence Applied*, the book was intended as "a yearlong course that trains intellectual skills in general and critical-thinking skills in particular."[70] Teachers at the K–12 level, however, have little space in the curriculum to add entire units, much less yearlong courses.

Sternberg revealed a similar disregard for occupational realism when he and his Yale colleagues partnered with Gardner and his Project Zero team in the late 1980s to create what they called the Practical Intelligence for School program. The Harvard part of the curriculum emphasized "individual subject-matter infusion of skills within the content class." In so doing, its aim was to enrich the traditional curriculum without overhauling its basic structure. By contrast, the Yale portion of the curriculum—Sternberg's part—was designed to be "taught by content teachers separately for two to three periods per week, ideally for a period of a year."[71] In short, huge chunks of time would need to be allocated for the program, staffing assignments would need to be reconsidered, testing would be thrown into flux, and curricula would need to be entirely redesigned.

Other occupational constraints would also make Sternberg's practitioner-oriented work seem unrealistic. As Gardner put it, "I don't think there was a particular way in which [the triarchic theory] was useful for classrooms and especially people [who] work with younger kids."[72] Teachers with only one free prep period per day, staff meetings to attend, and piles of grading awaiting them were unlikely to voluntarily engage in sustained group inquiry into the triarchic theory. At the same time, even Sternberg's simplified materials were more complex than what might be covered in a one-shot professional development workshop. In the 1996 book *Teaching for Thinking*, for instance, Sternberg described three different "teaching strategies": didactic, fact-based questioning, and dialogical. The work also identified seven levels of responses to questions, four "prongs" for "intellectual-skills development," three separate processes involved in insight, and twenty stumbling blocks that get in the way of thinking.[73]

It is worth acknowledging that, at least early on, Gardner was no better at creating practitioner-friendly materials. Certainly, multiple intelligences was a more straightforward concept with a more transportable set of terms, and it was intuitively satisfying. But *Frames of Mind*, like *Beyond IQ*, made no mention of practical applications, focusing instead on debates within the field of psychology. Gardner also took significantly longer than Sternberg to write about how his theory might be applied in classroom settings.

What Gardner had that Sternberg did not, however, was an army of intermediaries willing to loosely interpret his theory for classroom use. "As I saw it," Gardner later recalled, "I had issued an 'ensemble of ideas' (or 'memes') to the outer world, and I was inclined to let those 'memes' fend for themselves." It was not his concern, he added, "to isolate MI theory from MI practice."[74] Gardner was not interested in defending the purity of his idea; he was content to let various intermediaries make what they wanted of the theory, even if that meant substantially altering it in the process.

Gardner, then, largely abstained from translating multiple intelligences for the classroom, allowing interpreters to mold the idea as they wished. Yet he frequently lent his name to such projects, writing glowing forewords and prefaces for several of the more radical readings of his work. Gardner's rationale in doing so was simple: "No one," he wrote in 1995, "not even its creator, has a monopoly on MI wisdom or foolishness." Just as practice is enriched by theory, he asserted, theory should be allowed to transform "in the light of the fruits and frustrations of practice." And ultimately, he concluded, a community with a sense of ownership over multiple intelligences was "the best guarantor that the theory will continue to live in the years ahead."[75]

Sternberg did work to interpret the triarchic theory for educators. Yet because his research was not obviously transportable, he wrote most of those pieces himself, or with a coauthor. And in so doing, Sternberg adhered closely to the complexity of his research. This eventually changed. In works like the second edition of *Teaching for Successful Intelligence*, the triarchic theory is significantly easier to use. In fact, Sternberg even began tying the triarchic theory to Gardner's work, despite his earlier criticism of multiple intelligences. In a 2007 issue of *Educational Leadership*, for instance, Sternberg wrote that "successful intelligence is not the only theory on the basis of which we might create new, broader assessments. Howard Gardner's theory of multiple intelligences provides another basis for such assessments, and other theories could be used as well.[76] And in 2008, he argued that "each of the [triarchic] processes can be applied in each of Gardner's domains."[77]

By that time, however, multiple intelligences had been in schools for two decades and was seemingly all the scholarship on intelligence that educators needed or wanted. Without the time or the support to track the various and often competing research on intelligence, teachers turned to the known quantity of Gardner and the name brand of multiple intelligences—scholarship that seemed not only reliable, but accessible. Thus, even by tying his work explicitly to Gardner's, Sternberg would not be able to gain traction for the triarchic theory in practice. Instead, he would secure for it a place as a footnote to multiple intelligences—the kind of scholarship that seemed to support Gardner's, rather than the other way around.

WITTROCK'S GENERATIVE LEARNING MODEL

Merlin Wittrock's idea of generative learning, like William Kilpatrick's project method, offered K–12 educators a research-based model for learning-by-doing in the classroom. Suggesting that traditional didactic instruction was inherently flawed, it characterized learning as an interactive process that teachers could structure in their classrooms. As scholar Barbara Grabowski defined it, generative learning activities required that students have the "opportunity to mentally 'play with' information to create a personal understanding of the subject to be learned."[78]

Like the "wholehearted purposeful activity" outlined by Kilpatrick, generative learning techniques called for student self-direction and exploration within particular curricular blocks. But whereas the project method had presented cognition as a black box, generative learning detailed a specific mechanism by which students learned through activity. Knowledge, Wittrock argued, was constructed as a learner made cognitive connections—between different ideas, and between new ideas and prior knowledge. Thus, generative learning broadly endorsed constructivist and pedagogically progressive approaches to student activity, while seemingly offering clearer instruction about classroom application. Additionally, the theory was rooted in a distinctly modern methodology—cognitive science—that carried as much weight in the late twentieth century as the more philosophical anchoring of the project method did in the early part of the century. Consequently, generative learning may have seemed likely to win a foothold in practice equal to, if not greater than, that of the project method.

In some circles, particularly in the world of educational psychology in the late 1970s and early 1980s, generative learning became well known and commonly referenced. As Richard Mayer wrote in a 2010 issue of *Educational Psychologist*, "The impact of Wittrock's generative theory as it developed over the past thirty-five years can be clearly seen in today's science of learning." By the early twenty-first century, he argued, educational psychologists widely agreed that "meaningful learning is best understood as an active process in which the learner engages in generative cognitive processing during learning along the lines proposed by Wittrock."[79]

Yet generative learning never took root beyond the confines of its academic subfield, and certainly not in K–12 classrooms. It was a success, without question. A search of the journal database JSTOR, for instance, returns nearly two hundred hits for generative learning—a clear signal of the idea's penetration into the scholarly literature. Wittrock himself was highly respected within his field, serving as president of the division of educational psychology of the American Psychological Association, and in 1986 he earned the association's Thorndike Award for distinguished research contributions. In the wider world of education, however, generative learning garnered little attention—far less than the project method.

As a Google Ngram reveals, mentions of the project method outnumber mentions of generative learning by several orders of magnitude. Certainly, mentions of the project method declined over time, and particularly so after the ostensible death of pedagogical progressivism in 1957—when the movement's leading journal followed the Progressive Education Association into oblivion.[80] Even still, mentions of the project method, to say nothing of one-off monikers like project-based learning, have consistently outnumbered mentions of generative learning by at least a factor of two (see figure 5.4).

So how do we account for the failure of generative learning to gain traction in K–12 classrooms? The simplest explanation, were it accurate, would be that Wittrock never worked to engage the world of practice. After all, that is true of many productive scholars. Yet that was not the case with Wittrock and generative learning. In addition to writing dozens of practice-oriented manuscripts, Wittrock engaged in decades of outreach to working educators, including service as chair of the Los Angeles Unified School District's Committee on Research and Evaluation. In other words,

FIGURE 5.4

Textual references to "Project Method" and "Generative Learning" 1950–2005

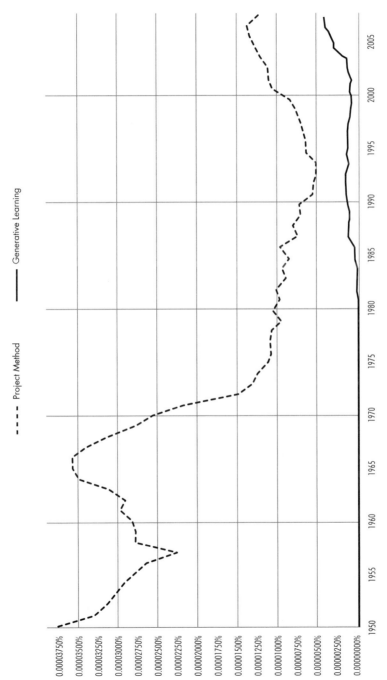

The y-axis in this graph indicates the relative frequency with which a word or phrase appears in the several million books scanned in Google's digitization project.

he was a highly engaged scholar, and he worked diligently to reveal the usefulness of his idea. Why is it, then, that generative learning never made a dent in the knowledge base of working teachers?

Theory into Method?

Wittrock, who taught at UCLA from 1960 until his death in 2007, was concerned primarily with outlining the process of knowledge acquisition, and generative learning was his crowning achievement. At the core of generative learning was a simple theory: that bits of knowledge acquired power and meaning only through a web of connections that stitched them together. Learners, consequently, needed to establish relationships among various parts of information, as well as between that information and their own existing knowledge. Wittrock spent much of his career detailing and substantiating this theory, and his work significantly shaped the field of cognitive science.

Yet Wittrock was also concerned with educational practice, and he frequently described what effective instruction would look like in a classroom where generative learning was taken seriously. He did so, however, by using much of the same conceptual language that characterized his research. As he wrote in a 1978 article in *Educational Psychologist*, "Effective instruction does not teach, in the usual sense of the word." Instead, he asserted, "it facilitates the learners' ability to construct meaning from experience."[81] Such statements may have inspired researchers to dream up cognitive experiments. But insofar as such statements were comprehensible among teachers, they likely seemed totally unrelated to the K–12 classroom.

Generative learning did possess a certain philosophical compatibility. Its core message was that understanding could not be given directly to students, and that it must be the product of engagement in activities that fostered appropriate mental processes.[82] Such a theory squared well with pedagogical progressivism—highly influential in teacher talk, if not always equally in teacher practice. It also aligned with much of what teachers observed in their classrooms, and specifically with the fact that what is *taught* is not always what is *learned.*

In terms of what those appropriate mental processes were, however, Kilpatrick's answer was much simpler than Wittrock's. The idea of projects was easy to understand, easy to apply, and easy to share, at least in some recognizable form. Not surprisingly, the project method gained significant traction with educators.

But in Wittrock's model, cultivating cognition was a much more complicated undertaking. "Generative teaching," he and coauthor Marilyn Kourilsky wrote in 1992, "involves knowing the learners' preconceptions of the subject matter and leading the learners to revise these preconceptions by teaching them to generate meaning from instruction." Additionally, it would seek "to foster a distinctive type and quality of student motivation (and attention) that emphasizes taking control and responsibility for being active and attentive in learning."[83] It was hardly an easy concept to understand.

Thus, while Wittrock's discussions of generative teaching may have been faithful to his model of learning, applications of the model were hardly self-evident. Perhaps even more problematically, the idea was difficult to spread by word of mouth—the means by which most teachers share knowledge. Consequently, as one set of researchers wrote in 2008: "Designing instruction based on this basic assumption . . . is not as simple or straightforward as it may first appear."[84]

Abstract and Fine-Grained

In an effort to move generative learning into classrooms, Wittrock wrote a number of pieces oriented toward practice. Yet he did so largely within scholarly journals and focusing on particular subjects, rather than through a discipline-general book for a lay audience or through publications like *Phi Delta Kappan*, *Instructor*, or *Education Week*.

Despite his interest in affecting practice, Wittrock was a scholar. As two educational psychologists wrote of him after his death, "Throughout his career, he conducted carefully designed research at the edge of the dominant paradigm and published his work in high-impact journals."[85] He did not, however, conduct professional development or moderate his research in an effort to make it more accessible. Nor did he cultivate partnerships

with intermediaries who might have made generative learning more occupationally realistic for K–12 classroom use. The effect of this was that
generative learning penetrated a narrow band of the practice-oriented literature, but not the broader teacher knowledge base.

The strongest connection with practice was within the scholarly literature on teaching reading. Such work includes Wittrock's "The Teaching
of Reading Comprehension According to the Model of Generative Learning," as well as applications of the model by others who saw it as relevant
to reading instruction. Perhaps this was because Wittrock's instructions to
reading teachers were more specific than those to teachers of other subjects. As he wrote in 1981, "Teachers can facilitate reading comprehension
by inducing the readers to attend to the text, to relate their knowledge
and experience to it, and to build associations, abstractions, and inferences
from it."[86] Whatever the reason, the vast majority of references to generative learning are within the field of reading education.

Generative learning did not need to be confined to the teaching
of reading comprehension; its potential connection with other subject
areas was just as strong. In fact, as Thomas Romberg wrote in 2010,
Wittrock's article "A Generative Model of Mathematics Learning" was
"influential to the mathematics education community at large."[87] Other
works, addressing other subjects—articles like "Generative Teaching: An
Enhancement Strategy for the Learning of Economics in Cooperative
Groups"—further displayed the potential applications of the idea. Yet at
no point did Wittrock bring his separate discipline-specific research together to create a one-stop shop for teachers broadly looking to better
understand curriculum design across subject areas. And given the nature
of teacher training and professional development—generally done with
the entire faculty, rather than with small groups sorted by discipline—
generative learning was at a significant disadvantage against ideas with
broader scope.

Further hindering the adoption of generative learning ideas in practice
was the fact that though much of Wittrock's research was fine-grained, it
was simultaneously abstract and difficult to pin down. "In the generative
model," he wrote ambiguously in 1979, "comprehension depends upon

cognitive transformations or elaborations learners perform upon stim-uli."[88] Instruction, consequently, would involve "stimulating the learners' information processing strategies, aptitudes, and stores of relevant specific memories in relation to the information to be learned."[89]

Even Wittrock's more prescriptive interpretations of generative learn-ing were relatively abstract. In a 1992 article, for example, he outlined four key generative teaching principles that required attention, including "one another's preconceptions," "knowledge and perception," "motivation," and "attention and generation."[90] As a result, third-party interpreters of gen-erative learning—who might otherwise have helped move the idea into practice—were left with vague language to use and little guidance about the kinds of classroom activities they might encourage. As one set of schol-ars wrote in a conference abstract: "Learners build deeper knowledge by physically and mentally manipulating models and information while ac-tively seeking to organize and integrate informational relationships be-tween what is seen, heard, felt, read, and mentally processed."[91] These were hardly the kinds of ideas that teachers were likely to discuss at the lunch table, much less apply immediately in their classrooms.

Thus, the theory was both abstract and fine-grained. Movement from the ivory tower into the schoolhouse, however, requires precisely the op-posite. It demands that an idea take a big-picture perspective—raising its perceived significance—while also being application-oriented enough to maintain a sense of occupational realism. Whereas Kilpatrick's mag-num opus (his concise article "The Project Method") would be circu-lated among hundreds of thousands, Wittrock's articles—with titles like "Generated Meanings in the Comprehension of Word Problems in Math-ematics" and "Verbal and Graphical Strategies in the Teaching of Econom-ics"—would live on only in scholarly citations.

Not Even a Footnote

Even if Merlin Wittrock made a determined effort to disseminate genera-tive learning and its potential classroom applications, teachers' use of the idea would require major expenditures of effort and instructional time. Ac-cording to Barbara Grabowski, it would be necessary to spend "more time and effort" on "identifying important factors about the learner than is traditionally spent in the instructional design process."[92]

Given such uncertainty about occupational fit, Wittrock would have needed to aggressively market generative learning and promise significant results. Yet, perhaps guided by scholarly sensibility, he made only modest claims about the idea. In a 1985 article in *Studies in Science Education*, for instance, Wittrock contended that "any model to do with human learning is an oversimplification of reality." The generative learning model, he added, "is no exception."[93] Hardly a ringing endorsement.

Had Wittrock been stationed at Harvard—or better, at Teachers College in the 1920s—his name might have endowed generative learning with greater authority, or attracted third-party professional development providers willing to make exaggerated claims about the idea. Such authority and assistance would have been essential given Wittrock's hesitance to self-promote and his commitment to faithfully complex representations of his scholarship. Yet Wittrock was at UCLA—an excellent public university, but one more often known by the general public for its winning basketball tradition than for its stellar roster of research faculty.

One consequence of this was that although Wittrock's doctoral students often went on to have successful careers in higher education, they often did not wield the influence of students from even more prestigious schools. Benjamin Bloom's students, by contrast, scattered across American universities, running teacher education programs and advancing Bloom's research agenda.

But perhaps a more significant consequence of Wittrock's middling prestige was that many of those referencing generative learning would not even bother to cite him in their work. Grant Wiggins and Jay McTighe, for instance, mentioned "generative learning" in several publications (though not in their runaway bestseller, *Understanding by Design*). Yet not only did Wiggins and McTighe fail to mention Wittrock by name, they failed to even *cite him* in their bibliography.

This, sadly, is understandable. For those looking to associate themselves with big names and known entities, there was lower-hanging fruit than Wittrock available. For those looking to support their constructivist programs, for instance, John Dewey and Jean Piaget had already become the go-to figures. In *Understanding by Design*, Wiggins and McTighe observed that Piaget so "wisely said that 'to understand is to invent.'"[94] And they cite Dewey numerous times. Similarly, for those looking to connect their work to cognitivist scholarship, the classic citation had already become Jerome Bruner by the 1970s. As one group of authors wrote in *The High School Journal* in 2000, "The term constructivism most probably is derived from Piaget's reference to his views as 'constructivist,' as well as from Bruner's description of discovery learning as 'constuctionist.'" Other terms, they noted, were "also used to refer to constructivist views of learning, including: generative learning."[95] Yet Wittrock was not mentioned, and generative learning was given no real review. Not even worth a footnote, the idea had become an afterthought.

THE BEHAVIOR ANALYSIS MODEL

The behavior analysis model, developed out of the University of Kansas by Don Bushell and colleagues, was in many ways like its Project Follow Through counterpart Direct Instruction. Like Direct Instruction, the behavior analysis model was classified by the study's evaluation team as a "basic skills" model. Also like Direct Instruction, it was conspicuously behaviorist in orientation. And perhaps most strikingly, the behavior analysis curriculum was composed of several scripted programs, including some of the very same instructional materials used in Direct Instruction.

There was also the matter of results. According to the original Abt analysis of Project Follow Through, behavior analysis finished second to Direct Instruction in reading, math, and spelling, as measured by the Metropolitan Achievement Test. And it finished third behind Direct Instruction and the Bank Street model in language.[96] Other subsequent interpretations of the data from Project Follow Through produced similar conclusions.[97]

Yet despite these similarities, Direct Instruction persisted in a way that behavior analysis did not. Long after the end of Project Follow Through,

Direct Instruction lived on as a widespread (if not always popular) curricular program—adopted by educators looking for quantifiable results in challenging contexts. The behavior analysis model lived on, too. Only, it did so largely outside of K–12 classrooms, with the exception of some penetration into the highly specific subfield of autism education.

A New Skinner Box

Behavior analysis was born in the world of psychology. With its roots in the work of those like Edward Thorndike, it grew under B. F. Skinner at Indiana University in the late 1940s. In 1964, the American Psychological Association created a new division for the Experimental Analysis of Behavior (today, the Division for Behavior Analysis).

That work was largely theoretical in nature. In the late 1960s, however, a group of scholars led by Sidney W. Bijou and Donald Baer led the development of a new field: Applied Behavior Analysis.[98] Bijou taught at the University of Washington, working in Seattle with Baer from 1957 to 1965 before moving on to the University of Illinois. Baer, too, left Washington, settling at the University of Kansas, where he partnered with scholars like Montrose M. Wolf and Todd R. Risley.

The behavior analysis model used in Project Follow Through was developed out of Kansas, but not by Baer, Wolf, or Risley. Instead, the model was spearheaded by Donald Bushell, who codirected a behavior analysis pilot program at the Juniper Garden Parent Cooperative Preschool. Juniper Garden was a Head Start Research and Demonstration Project in Kansas City, Kansas, and the model used positive reinforcement in order to teach reading, arithmetic, handwriting, and spelling. Social praise and tokens were given to children for correct responses, and teachers used programmed reading systems like DISTAR or Sullivan Programmed Phonics in which tasks were broken down into their constituent parts. When students made mistakes, "corrective procedures" were implemented to ensure progress.

The distinctive feature of the model, as one report put it, was the use of tokens to reinforce desired behaviors. Children would earn tokens for good work and behavior and then, later in the day, exchange them for individually chosen reward activities.[99] As a 1971 report on behavior analysis model implementation in Philadelphia described it: "This model employs a direct application of the behavior analysis and behavior shaping techniques of B. F. Skinner through the instrumentation of a 'token' economy and a reward system of activities offered as contingency of appropriate responses."[100] What did that look like in the classroom? A report on a behavior analysis model project in Arizona sketched a scene of students cashing in their tokens at the end of the day: "The children in the math group gather around the teacher, counting out tokens . . . 'Bonita, what are you going to do? The dolls? Let's see if you have ten tokens. Good.' 'I'm sorry, Alice, you only have seven and dolls cost ten tokens. Let's see if you can earn ten tokens next time. Puzzles? That's fine—puzzles take five tokens, so you have how many left over? Two; that's right.'"[101]

In a sense, the classroom would be something like one of B. F. Skinner's operant conditioning chambers—or, as they were informally known, Skinner boxes. Operant chambers, by design, contained features that would detect particular behaviors and deliver what Skinner called *primary reinforcers*—rewards that would create strong behavioral associations between particular kinds of behaviors and particular kinds of outcomes.

The classroom did differ in important ways from a Skinner box. Children, unlike animals, were present by choice and free to leave, at least by proxy of their parents. Unlike conditioning with animal subjects, in which behaviors were chosen for their experimental value, classroom activities would be designed to align with socially valued knowledge and behavior. And, while Skinner boxes characteristically isolated animals, classrooms were intended to remain vibrant social spaces.

Still, with behaviorism on the decline throughout the 1960s and 1970s, the association of a classroom with a Skinner box became philosophically incompatible. Direct Instruction, too, suffered from antibehaviorist sentiment, suffering criticisms that it treated children like animals. But behavior analysis established an even closer relationship with behaviorism, even in its very name. Further, there was the centrality of tokens in the classroom—visible symbols at the core of the model that were easily equated with bird feed doled out to obedient pigeons. By contrast, pedagogical progressivism was built around the idea that children's ideas, attitudes, and skills are transformed by education—that students are empowered by "learning to learn" rather than conditioned to operate in particular ways.

Much of progressive sentiment is the product of experiences in classrooms, whether because of interactions with students, or professional socialization. But progressive sentiment is also unquestionably a product of teacher training. Behavior analysis conflicted strongly not just with sentiments about students, but also with professional training. In the Follow Through site in Philadelphia, for instance, all teachers preferred the progressive Bank Street model to the behavior analysis model. Among teachers with advanced degrees, however, the tilt toward Bank Street was even stronger. And this preference for the Bank Street model was particularly pronounced when teachers were asked how closely each model related to their beliefs about how children learn.[102]

In addition to challenging common teacher philosophies, the behavior analysis model also threatened to erode teacher professionalism and strip teaching of one of its core psychic rewards. Direct Instruction threatened teacher professionalism by taking lesson design and, to some extent, lesson delivery, out of teachers' hands. But behavior analysis went one step further by reducing the relationship between teacher and student to a transactional one.[103] As sociologist Dan Lortie noted in his study of the teaching profession, "It is of great importance to teachers to feel they have 'reached' their students—their core rewards are tied to that perception." Other sources of teacher satisfaction, he observed, "pale in comparison."[104] Reaching students, however, meant leveraging relationships in order to, as one teacher put it, "instill a love of learning from within."[105] As Lortie argued, "They believe it takes a teacher to stimulate intellectual curiosity and interest in school."[106]

Tokens, however, would displace the teacher as the central arbiter in the relationship between students and learning. And though Skinner himself believed that teachers engage in their work "primarily because of economic reinforcement," the reality was that many did not wish to see the relational centerpiece of their practice disappear.[107]

What's a Token Worth?

Behavior analysis had a distinct appeal. When effectively applied, the token system promised to motivate students and condition classroom-appropriate behaviors. And, as the 1975 study of Philadelphia participants revealed, nearly half of teachers trained in behavior analysis felt positively about the model. Yet there were other obstacles standing between the behavior analysis model and widespread classroom use.

One such obstacle was the transportability of the model. Some of this was rooted in the language of behavior analysis. As Carl Binder put it in 1991, "The terminology of functional behavior analysis is a powerful and precise tool for analyzing and understanding behavior, and for developing effective teaching methods and materials. As technologists, we should maintain the precision of that language because of its technical advantages. But it is not the language we should use to describe our products to the general public, or even to other educators."[108] In short, the terminology central to the model's success among experts was impenetrable among laypeople.

The model also required expanded adult presence in the classroom—something unlikely to occur outside of Project Follow Through. As Don Bushell wrote in 1968, "Behavior modification with social reinforcement requires constant monitoring of the subject's responding." Such monitoring, he added, could be done only "on a very limited scale in a classroom by a single teacher," and Follow Through sites utilized both paraprofessionals and parent volunteers.[109] Once Follow Through was over, however, the requirement for additional personnel made the behavior analysis model occupationally unrealistic in K–12 classrooms.

Behavior analysis was also not particularly easy to implement. Merely introducing tokens was not enough. According to a description of the model in an Arizona Follow Through site, the role of the teacher was to "observe the children carefully enough to know what backup activities are most attractive to them and to set prices accordingly" for reward activities. Prices and activities would need to vary in order "to sustain interest" among students.[110] And, unlike Direct Instruction, there was no script to fall back on. As Binder noted, "Direct Instruction programs and materials are actual products." By contrast, "lists of behavioral principles and terminology do not seem tangible."[111] Behavior analysis model users, then, would have to develop their own practices and materials—something they were unlikely to do uniformly if at all.

Perhaps most importantly, the research on effectiveness was hardly as robust as that supporting Direct Instruction. According to the Abt analysis, the behavior analysis model produced measurable gains in student achievement and in the acquisition of so-called affective skills. Yet outcomes for the development of cognitive skills, when measured against a control group, were negative. Subsequent interpretations of the data found the behavior analysis model even less effective, calling into question not only that particular model, but all "basic skills" designs.

Particularly damaging was the reanalysis conducted by Ernest House and colleagues in 1978. Published in the *Harvard Educational Review*, it asserted that neither Direct Instruction nor the behavior analysis model produced significant results, and the report was widely discussed.[112] The difference between the two models, however, was that the backers of Direct Instruction launched a decades-long campaign to vindicate their program.

Immediately after the publication of the House report, Wes Becker wrote a response published in the *Harvard Educational Review*. And that was only the start. Becker, Engelmann, and their former students, including Doug Carnine and Russell Gersten, set up a research shop at the University of Oregon that produced a slew of scholarship backing Direct Instruction. In 1980, Becker and Carnine published their own reanalysis of Project Follow Through, showing that students in Direct Instruction schools outperformed their peers on both the Metropolitan Achievement Tests and the Wide Range Achievement Test.[113] In 1982, Becker and Gersten published a study in the well-regarded *American Educational Research*

Journal revealing that fifth and sixth graders who had participated in Direct Instruction classrooms were still reaping the benefits.[114] And Gersten, working sometimes alone and sometimes with colleagues, published positive findings on Direct Instruction nearly every year through the 1980s.[115]

The research on Direct Instruction continued through the end of the twentieth century and into the twenty-first. Consequently, summaries of research on it often conclude that while some studies find negative or inconclusive results, "the preponderance of evidence shows otherwise."[116] And as a Web site for the University of North Carolina at Wilmington's Hillcrest Reading Program explains: "The research base for Direct Instruction and *Teach Your Child to Read in 100 Easy Lessons* is extensive, stretching back nearly forty years."[117]

By contrast, while research into applied behavior analysis has continued, little empirical work was done on the effectiveness of the behavior analysis model after the end of the Follow Through program. As a result, the program began to fade from the scene. And, without a group of savvy advocates working constantly to defend the behavior analysis model, educators codified their displeasure with the philosophically incompatible program. In the mid-1980s, for instance, the National Association for the Education of Young Children created a set of "developmentally appropriate practices" and located behavior analysis among the "inappropriate" programs available for use.[118]

Equally damaging to behavior analysis was the fact that it simply receded from the mainstream literature, in periodicals oriented toward both scholars and the public. According to Edward K. Morris of the University of Kansas—a behavior analysis stronghold—the model is, by all dominant accounts in the field, "dead." And while Morris's course on behavioral science "offers an alternate history by recounting a different tradition in psychology," such efforts are hardly enough to impact classrooms in any large-scale manner.[119] Other schools that do work in behavior analysis—schools like Florida State University, Southern Illinois University, and Western Michigan University—may have excellent programs, but they lack the prestige required to reach a national audience.

The one place that the behavior analysis model has truly won a foothold is in the world of autism education. And, given the nature of the behavior analysis model, that should not be surprising. The autism subfield, even more than the larger field of special education, has a close connection to the field of applied psychology. Hence, those delivering education and treatment are often the graduates of specialized training programs in which behaviorism is alive and well and in which behavior analysis has high levels of perceived significance. Additionally, the features of autism are such that behavioral conditioning is frequently perceived as appropriate. According to the National Institutes of Health, autism is characterized by social impairments, communication difficulties, and restricted, repetitive, stereotyped patterns of behavior.[120] The goals of applied behavior analysis—shaping and reinforcing new behaviors, such as learning to speak and play, or learning to control antisocial behavior—align neatly with the disorder.[121] And finally, autism classrooms operate separately from traditional classrooms, making a significant programmatic shift to the behavior analysis model not only philosophically tenable, but occupationally possible.

Outside of autism education, however, behavior analysis never gained a significant foothold in K–12 classrooms or in the common knowledge base of teachers. It is not mentioned in mainstream teacher education textbooks, even in a critical manner, as is often the case with Direct Instruction. It has not won a segment of the market, as Direct Instruction did in low performing urban schools. It has no clear champions churning out research and publicizing results. And, without having entered into structures that might extend the life of the idea, it has faded from view. Despite its similarities to Direct Instruction, behavior analysis has gone the way of Tucson Early Education Model, or the cognitive curriculum model, or any of the other Project Follow Through models that have not persisted in the four decades since the origin of the undertaking.

CONCLUSION

The four ideas discussed in this chapter shared a great deal with those ideas considered earlier in the book. Krathwohl's taxonomy, the triarchic theory, generative learning, and behavior analysis were, in obvious ways, quite similar to their better-known counterparts—Bloom's taxonomy, Gardner's multiple intelligences, the project method, and Direct Instruction. Yet, unlike the latter series of ideas, the former are largely unknown to K–12 teachers.

Each of the four ideas examined in this chapter possessed qualities seemingly advantageous for locating them in classrooms. Most noticeably, each had solid grounding in scholarship and was intentionally targeted at the world of practice. And each experienced its own limited success in gaining traction among K–12 teachers. In fact, in a system with a greater overlap between those with the capacity for consuming research and those with control over its implementation, all four ideas considered in this chapter might have managed to take hold in educational practice. Yet educational research and practice, at least in the United States, is not characterized by such overlap. Consequently, for scholarship to enter the knowledge base of teachers it must possess traits that compensate for a dysfunctional system.

The presence or absence of those traits is not an assurance that an idea from scholarship will be adopted or rejected by practitioners. Instead, those traits might be thought of as bridges. With all four in operation, there is still no guarantee that an idea will not encounter other roadblocks, veer off course, or be waylaid by the unforeseen. Still, the conditions are such that real movement is possible. By contrast, with those bridges out of commission, the challenge of moving an idea from the research university into the schoolhouse is virtually insurmountable.

Stepping back to look at the cases considered in this chapter, it is clear that whatever the strengths of these ideas *as works of scholarship*, they lacked the characteristics crucial for crossing the divide into practice. Even at the most basic level of being perceived as significant, these ideas fell short—not because they represented flawed or inconsequential scholarship, but because they failed to send appropriate signals of quality and relevance to practitioners. Generative learning and behavior analysis, for instance, possessed weak proxies for quality. Krathwohl's taxonomy lacked an obvious significance for the daily work of classroom teachers. And the triarchic theory was eventually viewed as superfluous because of its resemblance to a piece of research—in its particular case, multiple intelligences—that had already taken root.

These cases also reveal the critical importance of philosophical compatibility. After all, even if an idea gains visibility, teachers must still accept it. Yet it is clear that ideas like behavior analysis—an idea that challenged dominant notions about the way children learn—contrasted too strongly with prevailing sensibilities to ever gain widespread traction in K–12 classrooms. Krathwohl's taxonomy, too, had philosophical compatibility problems, at least insofar as it seemed to suggest that all children should learn to behave in similar ways—a challenge to notions of social pluralism, as well as to conservative ideas about freedom. Generative learning and the triarchic theory, by contrast, actually had some philosophical allure. Still, because Wittrock and Sternberg failed to make the compatibility of their ideas explicit, they forfeited much of their potential appeal.

Even if teachers find an idea philosophically compatible, more challenges await, as they must also be able to put it into practice without significant levels of support. Consequently, if educational scholarship is to affect practice it must square with the various constraints on teachers, and particularly those on their time. Often, then, what succeeds is what can be added on to existing practice. But few pieces of scholarship reflect this consideration. The triarchic theory, for instance, at least as presented in Sternberg's early efforts to promote it, would have required new subjects in the school day and extensive training for teachers. Behavior analysis, too, demanded new teacher knowledge, as well as a large expenditure of time on the model's token system. Generative learning, for its part, would have required class sizes small enough that teachers could customize instruction for each learner. And at least one implementation proposal for Krathwohl's taxonomy involved coordination across multiple grades and teachers—another occupationally unrealistic proposition.

Finally, without systematic conduits between research and practice, ideas have to travel easily. As this chapter demonstrates, each of the four ideas did gain traction on a small scale, yet ultimately failed to spread. In part, this was because they all generally lacked a simple and transportable core. Generative learning, for instance, is difficult to describe in a paragraph, much less a sentence. They also lacked simple language, relying on technical or nontransparent terms like *componential*, as the triarchic theory did. And, instead of being storable and sharable, they were often ethereal and complex. Behavior analysis and Krathwohl's taxonomy, for instance, had very few "products" and were less easy to structure than Direct Instruction—a scripted curriculum package—or Bloom's taxonomy, which was frequently used as a straightforward rubric for assessment design.

Given all of this, it should come as no surprise that the four ideas discussed in this chapter failed to substantially take root in practice. Whatever the quality of the scholarship, they lacked the bridges required for traversing the often swampy terrain of the American educational system. Thus, they remained inaccessible to K–12 teachers. They lived on, certainly— but they did so only within the confines of the ivory tower.

What Do We Know
and What Might We Do?

To the inexperienced, first encounters with the field of educational research can be quite surprising. Where they expect to find practical and applied scholarship, they often discover a field devoted to the theoretical. And where they expect to find best practices readily adaptable for classroom use, they frequently encounter scholarship that feels irrelevant to their needs. What, they may ask, does any of this have to do with teaching? The answer, quite commonly, is "very little."

Historians have offered explanations for the prevalence of such research. The low status of educational scholarship, derived from its practical orientation and its proximity to a feminized occupation, drove professors of education in the early twentieth century to seek legitimacy through an emphasis on the ersatz scientific aspects of their work. Such educationists mimicked purer and more theoretical fields, rooted much of their work in other disciplines, and became particularly obsessed with testing and measurement. All the while, they labored to distance themselves from low-status K–12 teachers and their chalk-covered hands. And given the nature of education as a field of inquiry drawing on many disciplines, they produced an avalanche of often disparate research—little of which was intended for use by classroom educators.[1]

This does much to explain the troubled relationship between research and practice in education. Still, it does not account for the large body of educational research that *does* seek to affect practice. Most scholarship in the field may not be intended for classroom use, but much of it is. Library shelves and electronic databases teem with research on how to teach elementary history or high school physics or middle school English, how to develop critical thinking skills or language proficiency, and how to reach gifted or high-needs populations. And while many scholars resign themselves to working on the margins, many labor tirelessly in the hopes of shaping classroom practice. Their chief aim is to influence the instructional core by affecting the teacher knowledge base.

Other commentators have offered an alternative explanation for why educational scholarship so often fails to gain traction among practitioners. Even if the majority of research were reoriented in the direction of practice, they argue, a slew of roadblocks would still preclude it from entering the knowledge base of teachers. The teaching profession, it has been repeatedly demonstrated, is simply not culturally or structurally positioned to absorb research.[2] Further, the occupation is configured in a manner that gives teachers significant control over implementation of curricular and pedagogical policy, regardless of their low capacity for consuming research. Thus, while scholarship may occasionally penetrate policy documents or teacher talk, it rarely gains a foothold in the place that matters most—the classroom.

Such accounts have helped establish a picture of why the vast majority of educational scholarship fails to take hold among teachers, and in turn why it has such a weak effect on educational outcomes. Yet they do not explain why scholarship sometimes *does* enter practice, nor do they offer explanations for what it means that educational research sometimes bridges the gap.

As the cases considered in this book reveal, educational scholarship has continued to enter classrooms across the twentieth century—shaping how teachers perceive their students, design lessons, deliver instruction, and conduct evaluations. It has done so even when the original research has been largely theoretical in nature. It has done so even without support from policy makers. And it has done so without altering the nature of the teaching occupation.

How can that be?

KEY CHARACTERISTICS

Scholarship can move from the ivory tower into the schoolhouse—and particularly, into the working knowledge base of teachers—without overhauling either sphere. But in order to do so, it must possess a particular set of attributes that function to adapt it for a challenging environment. Such characteristics would, of course, be unnecessary if those with the capacity for consuming research were also those with control over its implementation. If policy elites truly controlled what goes on inside K–12 classrooms, they would simply issue mandates about instructional practice. And if teachers possessed the time, skills, authority, and inclination to engage with educational research, they would adopt ideas on their own terms, without the need for intermediaries. In lieu of these alternate realities, however, these characteristics—perceived significance, philosophical compatibility, occupational realism, and transportability—serve as detours for moving research into practice.

The first of those characteristics, *perceived significance*, gives teachers greater access to educational scholarship by bringing it to their attention. Teachers are, generally speaking, interested in research. Many are eager to apply concepts learned in graduate school or in professional development workshops to their classrooms, and many are receptive to the idea of research-informed practice. Yet the structure of the occupation provides little support for teachers to sift through or engage with research in a deep or sustained way, and they operate in a sphere almost entirely separate from that inhabited by scholars. Further, nothing like a central ministry of education exists to channel research into practice via guidelines and directives.

Consequently, when teachers come into contact with educational scholarship—whether through preservice preparation, continuing education, professional development, or informal inquiry—it can be a tremendous challenge to decipher what ideas are of consequence. When is it worth adopting a new idea and when is it not? Many teachers, unable to answer that question to their own satisfaction, abandon the search.

A shorthand measure of value, however, can change that. If some signal of significance can be perceived by teachers, they can—and, as this book demonstrates, *do*—become active agents in the process of their own professional development. Rather than resisting or undermining change, they embrace it. They allow it to affect the instructional core.

The problem with this, of course, is that no codified signal exists. As a result, teachers rely on proxies for quality—like the enthusiastic endorsement of enterprising professional development providers—that can be highly imperfect. A back-alley detour, in short, can sometimes lead teachers astray.

Each of the four cases at the heart of this book met some standard of rigor by proxy and, as a result, connected classroom teachers with educational research in a powerful, if imprecise, way. Multiple intelligences and Bloom's taxonomy came out of elite research universities and won powerful advocates among professional development providers and curriculum designers, respectively. The project method was created at Columbia University's Teachers College—a citadel of progressive education at the peak of its influence—and was taught to thousands of aspiring academics and administrators. And Direct Instruction, from its origins, established a seemingly unassailable empirical record, which in turn was heavily promoted by its author and his research team. Additionally, each idea eventually achieved a kind of name-brand status—inspiring confidence among teachers who equated recognition with quality and who, consequently, worked to modify their classroom practice.

But research quality is not the sole determinant of significance. In fact, teachers are equally attentive to whether scholarship addresses a question central to the profession. Research must not only indicate something about its quality, but also speak to the fundamental concerns of the educators adopting it. The four key cases in this book met that test as well. Whether by addressing concerns about student thinking, the nature of knowledge, the challenge of curriculum design, or the science of pedagogy, each idea won perceived significance because it sent a clear signal of its relevance.

Of course, even if they see research as significant, teachers may still disagree with it based on their professional opinions. Thus, while significance might theoretically be achieved through brute force—driven by an assertive principal, a district mandate, or a state directive—it can still fall short when it comes to affecting teacher practice. When they close their classroom doors, teachers can conveniently forget a piece of scholarship, reject a policy, or alter a curriculum. This, certainly, can be a good thing; teachers often possess situated knowledge that administrators and policy makers do not. But teacher response to ideas generated outside the classroom can also be shaped by a general set of beliefs and concerns that has little to do with the quality of those ideas. Such reactions can keep even good ideas at bay.

Insofar as teaching attracts certain kinds of people—particularly those who care about children and who, although not always well paid, want to be seen as professionals—there exists a common core of interests and anxieties that shape the way teachers see the world. Consequently, if research is going to take hold among teachers, it must possess a sense of philosophical compatibility. If it does not, even if the idea is ostensibly "proven," it stands little chance of survival in classrooms.

This is not to say that teachers simply reject out of hand any idea that promotes a degree of philosophical discomfort. Teachers can be every bit as willing to be challenged as professionals working in other occupations, though it is worth noting that teachers can face more public scrutiny than those working in other industries. Still, an intellectual willingness to be challenged is hardly a sufficient counterweight to one's deeply held beliefs and personal biography.

Each of the four key ideas considered in this book, beyond being perceived as significant, was also seen as philosophically compatible with common teacher beliefs. Multiple intelligences endorsed the notion that all students can learn, while also buffering teachers from the standards and accountability movement. Bloom's taxonomy managed to appeal to both progressives and traditionalists through its philosophical openness. The project method squared with romantic visions of children, as well as with progressive ideas about learning by doing. And Direct Instruction, though initially resisted because it seemingly deprofessionalizes teaching and rests on a cultural deficit model, was eventually seen as promoting the equity mission of serving low-income, minority, and handicapped students. To teachers, these ideas were both true and useful.

But just because an idea is theoretically plausible, or even appealing, does not mean that teachers will see its benefits outweighing its costs and integrate it into classroom practice. The profession is characterized by a host of persistent practical demands and structural limitations, all of which complicate the adoption of new ideas. Teachers face severe time constraints given their various obligations to teach, lesson plan, grade student work, and perform administrative duties. And American teachers spend more hours in the classroom than most of their counterparts in the industrialized world—roughly 80 percent of each day. Unlike their peers in nations heralded for their success in international tests—places like Japan, Finland, and Singapore—American teachers have little time to engage with educational scholarship, share knowledge with one another, overhaul lessons, or observe colleagues.

Thus, if research is going to be put to classroom use, it must be easy to add it on to existing practice, it must allow teachers to maintain most of their previous work, and it must be adaptable to the particular contexts of different classrooms. In other words, it must be occupationally realistic with regard to the constraints within which teachers operate. Multiple intelligences and Bloom's taxonomy could each be worked into existing approaches with the simple addition of a new set of options for student performance or questions to provoke discussion. And implementing the project method or Direct Instruction actually seemed to make the job easier for teachers, with the former calling for student-directed, hands-on work and the latter providing the teacher with a set of ready-made lessons designed for hard-to-teach students. In short, teachers saw each of these ideas as having the potential for a life not just in teacher talk, but in teacher work.

Finally, if an idea is going to enter the professional knowledge base of teachers, it must have an easy way of traveling. There are very few teachers engaged with the world of educational research, and very few educational researchers connected to networks of K–12 teachers. Popular scholarly journals possess circulations in the thousands, while the majority of high-traffic educational blogs and Web sites—reaching hundreds of thousands—are maintained by amateurs, many of them teachers, without research expertise. Professional development, ostensibly designed to move research into practice, is usually delivered over the course of a handful of noncontiguous days and tends to be led by third-party providers unaligned with either the district or a research institution. To make matters worse, professional development is conducted in highly disparate fashion across schools and districts, hindering ideas from taking root in a broad way.

Scholarship, then, must have transportability among a multitude of actors—professional development providers, teacher educators, administrators, and teachers themselves. It must, to put it another way, possess an internal characteristic that compensates for a lack of structural support. One key element in transportability is a simple core that can be easily understood by practitioners and that will persist as a lowest common denominator across different contexts and interpretations. The use of straightforward language, for instance, matters. But even more important is the extent to which an idea is "storable and sharable," to use a borrowed phrase.[3] Translated into a structure, an idea can travel through documents like textbooks and curriculum frameworks. It can move into the teacher knowledge base, and endure.

All four of the major cases considered in this work were highly transportable. Howard Gardner originally posited seven "intelligences," for instance, and Benjamin Bloom and his colleagues identified six levels of thought. The project method and Direct Instruction, though they did not rely on such simple subdivisions, were equally storable and sharable. The former suggested, through its name alone, that students learned best through hands-on activity, and the idea could be clearly lodged in easily recognizable lessons. Direct Instruction, for its part, was delivered in the form of a scripted curriculum, and though it sometimes raised the ire of teachers, it was always recognizable. And all four ideas were easily translated into rubrics, diagrams, charts, and forms, which not only increased the potential for transfer, but also promoted persistence.

Bloom's taxonomy, multiple intelligences, the project method, and Direct Instruction are in many ways quite distinct from each other. The ideas were shaped by different methodologies and in different eras. And they developed in unique historical contexts, taking root in unique ways.

Yet despite these differences, the ideas shared a core set of crucial characteristics. In possession of those attributes, they stood a chance at moving from the world of research into the world of practice—a chance that other, similar ideas never had.

Possession of those four characteristics, of course, is no guarantee that a piece of scholarship will make the long leap into practice. There must also be an element of luck in the mix. But in the hostile territory between the ivory tower and the K–12 classroom, these characteristics are essential. In a terrain marked by dead ends and wide chasms, they serve as alternate routes.

RADICAL PROPOSALS AND REAL CONSTRAINTS

As the case studies at the heart of this book reveal, scholarly research can possess specific kinds of characteristics that make it uniquely suited for particular environments. Therefore, even in the field of education, which is characterized by a series of seemingly fundamental obstacles precluding the movement of research into practice, ideas can bridge the gap in some meaningful way. But they can do so only with the right mix of *internal* traits, which compensate for gaps in the research-to-practice pathway.

Still, it is important to remember that these characteristics are not by any means ideal, and should not be counted on to automatically channel the best research into practice. Merely creating research that mimics these pieces of boundary-crossing scholarship, then, is not a solution. We must, instead, develop systems and structures that make it easier for high-quality scholarship to possess those characteristics, at least if the aim is to affect the knowledge base of working teachers.

There are those who will resist this kind of approach, seeing it as both too messy and too complicated. Why settle, they might argue, for a mechanism resembling a Rube Goldberg machine when we can design something sleeker and more efficient? The question is worth considering.

Those who envision a more forceful, systematic, and uniformly constructive connection between research and practice have proposed a number of approaches that would more tightly link the ivory tower and the

K–12 classroom. One proposition with significant support in the scholarly community, for instance, is for "hands-on research." Respected figures like Marilyn Cochran-Smith and Susan Lytle have argued persuasively in favor of a "knowledge for teaching" that is developed both inside and outside the classroom. Scholars like Eleanor Duckworth have made the case that teaching should be reconsidered as a form of research.[4] And myriad thinkers have argued that teachers should engage in highly specific site-based research particular to their problems and interests. Though the momentum behind this movement has flagged somewhat, it continues to intrigue.

Such approaches, which attempt to blur the lines between research and teaching and between the ivory tower and the classroom, have a number of strengths. Perhaps first among them is the philosophical compatibility of such a proposition; practice-based research, after all, would be created by, or at the very least alongside, those charged with implementing it. Still, the potential philosophical appeal of such research is hardly a counterweight to the occupationally unrealistic proposition of radically overhauling the teacher workday or transforming cultural understandings of teaching and research—necessities for pursuing this kind of effort in any vigorous way. Additionally, while hands-on research may get around the perceived significance issue at a single school, it presents a major transportability issue because of how site-specific each act of research would be. The wheel would have to be consistently reinvented, and the products of such efforts might be of highly mixed quality from site to site. Finally, there is the question of whether such research, conducted on a site-by-site basis, would be any good. As Fred Kerlinger put it, the risk of such movements is that they might "distract us from adequate research" or "substitute superficial and mediocre activities" for more robust forms of inquiry.[5]

Others seeking to create a research-to-practice superhighway (rather than relying on a series of detours and back alleys) have proposed moving in the opposite direction—running even further from a "wisdom of practice" and toward a "science" of education. Efforts like the federally sponsored What Works Clearinghouse, for instance, have sought to use "gold-standard" research methodologies to establish the credibility of particular ideas and then compile them in a centralized location.

By carefully defining what counts as rigorous research and centrally warehousing it, backers of such plans have certainly addressed issues of perceived significance and transportability. Yet such an approach hardly clears all of the hurdles standing between a research idea and its use in K–12 classrooms. Modeled after the randomized control trials used in medicine, gold-standard research is highly technocratic and bears the distinct patois of outsiders to the teaching profession, potentially exacerbating the problem of philosophical tenability. Similarly, given the challenge of conducting experiments in education, the approach is limited in what it can measure—creating a potential misalignment between the questions research can answer and the questions teachers are interested in. Finally, gold-standard research does nothing to address occupational realism, focusing on the evaluation of educational "interventions" with little concern for practicality or feasibility in average classrooms.

Altering the nature of research, one might conclude, does not represent a viable solution for reforming the research-to-practice pathway in education. In fact, it seems likely to aggravate the tension between policy makers and K–12 teachers by endowing research with greater prestige without winning for it a greater foothold in classroom practice. So what else might be done? Two other solutions, focused on teaching, are also worth considering, though they are no more promising.

The first of those propositions is true centralization. In such a scenario, the state would assume responsibility for identifying high-quality research and moving it into practice. In service of that aim, the state might provide training for teachers and structure connections between K–12 schools and research universities. It might create new offices, with the specific charge of preparing scholarly research for application in classrooms. It might even take on the responsibility for conducting research itself, bringing scholars interested in application under the newly broadened wing of the state. Yet reality constrains these many possibilities. Given the constitutionally limited authority of the federal government, the challenge of building capacity in fifty different state offices of education, the legacy of local control, the independent nature of most colleges and universities, and the diverse nature of American schools—no two of which ever seem to be quite alike—it would be surprising to see the federal government, or even state governments, attempt any of this. In other words, it is a highly unlikely scheme.

The second proposition is an overhaul of the teaching profession. Starting from a blank slate, we might imagine teachers who receive extensive training in the evaluation of research, who teach only half the day and spend the other half in professional development, who return to graduate school periodically, and who interact regularly with scholars. We might similarly imagine teachers citing research in lesson plans, tracking particular efforts with colleagues, or developing affinity-based research networks. But tradition, financial constraints, and the problem of scale—to name only the most obvious challenges—constitute nearly insurmountable obstacles. Such a scenario would require a mutually supportive cultural conversion and structural transformation that, while not unimaginable, would have to take place across several generations.

So it seems that while working within the constraints of the existing system is not ideal, it presents a more realistic prospect for improving the research-to-practice pathway than do the most prominent alternatives. Thus, it is worth taking seriously the question of how we might productively manipulate certain characteristics in order to improve them. Currently, they function as informal and unmarked detours—linking research ideas with K–12 classrooms, but doing so inelegantly and unevenly. How, we should ask, might these detours be paved, widened, and made more direct? How might they be integrated into our official maps?

WORKING WITH WHAT WE HAVE: A PROPOSAL

Working within existing systems is always a complex venture—less straightforward, if often more realistic, than wiping the slate clean. But despite such inherent complexity, those interested in connecting educational research with practice might make great strides toward their aim. Specifically, they might build on what we know about the way research enters practice by developing systems and structures that more easily allow scholarship to possess the characteristics crucial for reaching teachers. And whatever the complexity of such work, the upside of affecting the instructional core merits the expenditure of effort.

It is important to remember that the characteristics crucial for moving research into practice—perceived significance, philosophical compatibility, occupational realism, and transportability—are not designed for that purpose, and thus they are imperfect at channeling high-quality and high-impact scholarship into K–12 classrooms. Still, they are not unimprovable. Instead, it seems that the problems associated with those characteristics arise because weak research can possess those traits and, as is more often the case, strong research can lack them. Consequently, any efforts to more tightly link scholarship with practice must also improve the availability and reliability of those crucial characteristics. The question, then, is what that might look like.

Improving Perceived Significance

As the cases in this book reveal, perceived significance is a crucial condition for moving educational research into practice. After all, whatever the inherent merits of particular scholarship, practitioners must—in the words of Cynthia Coburn and colleagues—"still look for it, notice it, and attend to it."[6] Generally, teachers gauge significance through a series of proxies, relying on indicators like institutional affiliation as signals of research merit. Yet such proxies are inconsistent markers of quality and relevance. As such, they can lead teachers to perceive significance where there may be none. But perhaps more problematically, reliance on such proxies can lead teachers to overlook scholarship with potential for improving classroom practice. Similarly, teachers are more likely to favor ideas that are general, expansive, and seemingly common to all teachers regardless of grade level and subject matter—even if such scholarship is so broad as to be impracticable. This, obviously, is problematic. Yet it is not unrealistic to imagine the characteristic of perceived significance being strengthened, and particularly so that it more consistently directs teachers toward scholarship of quality and relevance.

One way to enhance both the frequency and the efficacy of perceived significance is to increase teacher capacity for vetting research. After all, even if districts were to mandate the use of a particular piece of scholarship, teachers would still need to see it as significant enough to actually engage with. To be clear: this does not mean that teachers must become dedicated consumers of scholarly journals or experts in evaluating research methodologies. Such an outcome is highly unlikely. But teachers might be trained to engage with educational scholarship in a regular and critical way. And even if such preparation produced only increased regard for research among teachers and the use of better proxies for quality—proxies like journal selectiveness or citation frequency instead of those like institutional prestige—it would increase the degree to which practitioners perceived meaningful scholarship as significant.

Responsibility for such a shift might also be delegated to departments and colleges of education. In the past two decades, academics have seen their grip on teacher preparation slipping and their very existence called into question. A focus on orienting teachers toward research, though, might help them make a stronger case for their work. This, certainly, would require adjustments to the current curriculum, which is already crowded with requirements. Yet such moves are long overdue, particularly given the increasing difficulty of answering the question "what does traditional teacher education do that alternative preparation cannot?"[7]

If more high-quality scholarship is going to be perceived as significant for classroom practice, teachers will also need the support of a range of other actors. Districts, for instance, might target key teachers who are respected by their peers and who see research as helpful rather than a hindrance—something that other nations like England, where it is called the "cascade" model, have done.[8] Some of these teachers maintain blogs and use social media and therefore might be positioned as brokers to raise the significance of research. In turn, districts might support these teachers by giving them reduced teaching loads, connecting them with local scholars, or sponsoring their enrollment in graduate programs. Districts might further match such teacher leaders with affinity groups organized around the subjects and grade levels they teach. In so doing, they might assist educators in building smaller and more specific bodies of knowledge, as well as in seeing new kinds of scholarship as significant to their work.

Much might also be done by intermediaries in terms of directing teachers toward relevant and high-quality scholarship. District-level research librarians or research coordinators, for instance, might help raise the profile of particular—and often more domain-specific—pieces of scholarship that suit their particular needs. Working with groups of educators organized by grade level or subject area, they could serve as liaisons between the ivory tower and the classroom, sifting through scholarship and presenting curated collections to classroom teachers. Federally or state-funded research offices, supported either directly or through bodies like the Regional Educational Laboratories, could play a similar role by aggregating, sorting, summarizing, and making available scholarship of potential use to teachers. Such bodies might even take this one step further by emulating the work of Her Majesty's Chief Inspector of Schools in England—an office that evaluates schools and provides direct feedback to administrators, as well as to individual teachers, about improving educational practice.[9]

Hiring new staff and creating new positions at the federal, state, or district level would obviously create new expenditures. Yet those costs would likely amount to no more than what is currently spent on professional development provided by unregulated and largely self-interested third parties. According to one estimate, public schools spend roughly $20 billion a year on in-service days and on training, with little evidence of lasting positive impact.[10] Furthermore, many moves might be made at minimal cost. Some scholars, for instance, have called for the development of standards around continuing education and accreditation of providers.[11] Improving the federal Education Resources Information Center—an unwieldy online database that presents all research on equal footing, with no guidance about what is more or less useful, and no way for teachers to comment on it—is another example of low-hanging fruit waiting to be picked.

Ultimately, much responsibility for addressing the issue of perceived significance will fall to researchers. Beyond developing seemingly relevant research agendas, scholars will need to begin to think carefully about where they publish and how they take other steps to promote their research in the world. Those working in colleges and universities will not need a reminder that the kinds of publications credited in the tenure review process are almost always distinct from those with the potential to affect practice. Times have changed since William Kilpatrick built his reputation among scholars and practitioners with a single, highly readable article. Yet the choice between winning respect in the research community and affecting practice is, in many ways, a false one. Howard Gardner frequently wrote in periodicals oriented toward teachers and, at least early in his career, was an active contributor to scholarly journals. In the past several decades, Siegfried Engelmann has written almost exclusively in venues for practitioners, and has taken full advantage of the Internet in writing directly to practicing teachers. Other tenured scholars, like Carol Tomlinson of the University of Virginia—William Clay Parrish Jr. Professor and Chair of Educational Leadership, Foundations, and Policy—maintain Web sites with their own writing, that of other educators, and resources for professional development.

Enterprising scholars might also pursue a number of other routes in raising the perceived significance of their work. They might found new journals, or at least sections of journals focused on classroom applications of scholarly ideas. They might engage the public by learning to blog and tweet. They might establish research centers focused on particular fields—teaching elementary math, for instance, or serving English language learners. Or they might push their colleges and universities to forge partnerships with districts, creating projects like the University of Chicago's Consortium for Chicago Schools Research—a scholarly collaborative that focuses exclusively on the city's public schools. Perhaps most ambitiously, they might challenge their institutions to begin awarding credit for the kind of work that matters to them—something currently being done at schools like Michigan State and Syracuse, where tenure and promotion policies have recently shifted to recognize public scholarship as much as publishing in scholarly journals. In short, such work requires creative thinking and a degree of activism. But it is possible.

Improving Philosophical Compatibility

Beyond addressing how significance is perceived, teachers, scholars, and policy makers might also begin an open conversation about the matter of philosophical compatibility. Like those working in many other fields, teachers are attracted to their profession for particular reasons, they are acculturated in specific ways, and their views are shaped by a common set of on-the-job experiences. This, certainly, is not a new revelation, and it has been well documented by sociologists from Dan Lortie onward. Yet the impact of this phenomenon on efforts to move research into practice is rarely discussed. Specifically, what it means is that teachers see research from a distinct viewpoint—one particular to their craft and which differs from that of scholars, policy makers, or laypeople. As a result, most research ends up being less viable than it might be, and some scholarship is more alluring than perhaps it should be. Further, those ideas adopted among teachers are often disconnected from any collective goal or systemic purpose.

Teachers are aware that they bring a certain worldview with them. In fact, many no doubt see their insider perspective as an advantage in thinking about improving classroom instruction—a perspective they view as troublingly underrepresented in education policy. Nevertheless, they might have productive discussions—in their preservice programs, as well as once on the job—about why they are inclined in particular directions with regard to research, and about how they might act with self-knowledge to advance their profession.

Teacher preparation programs seem a natural place for these kinds of discussions to take place. And though departments and colleges of education would have to navigate some complex terrain in ensuring faculty were prepared for such a task, they might look to exemplary programs at home and abroad for instruction. Teachers in Finland, for instance, are trained to use research and research-derived competencies—a practice that begins, according to one study, with "a positive attitude" toward research.[12] In a similar vein, schools of education might seriously reconsider the place of the doctorate of education. Shifting away from a model that some have termed the "PhD-lite," leaders at such institutions might build on the work of scholars like Lee Shulman, who has sought to reorient EdD programs around the use of research in the classroom.[13]

Other actors might also play a role in making more high-quality scholarship philosophically compatible among classroom teachers. At the district level, research coordinators—perhaps graduates of revamped EdD programs—might assist groups of teachers organized by grade level or by department in examining the use of research. Additionally, they might spearhead projects carried out in partnership with teachers and professional researchers. Some scholars, like Ann Brown and Joe Campione of the University of California Berkeley, have engaged productively in such partnerships, which not only made scholarship more philosophically compatible, but also helped teachers see research in action. More recently, Anthony Bryk and Louis Gomez have proposed to create "networked improvement communities" in which researchers, practitioners, and designers work together to solve problems.[14] In Japan, the widespread practice of "lesson study"—in which small groups of teachers meet regularly over the course of several weeks to investigate a topic, often with the assistance of an expert—has been both successful and sustainable. In Singapore, such teams are referred to as "learning circles," and generally meet for longer periods of time.[15] Whatever the particular approach taken by the district, the simple move of making the research office less marginalized would represent a significant step forward.

Unions, too, might help develop the structures necessary for teachers to thoughtfully hybridize research, explaining for their members the potential appeal of scholarship that might otherwise be perceived as the work of outsiders. In other fields like nursing and social work, professional organizations have won significant buy-in for research through effective framing, and particularly through the assertion that research must always be combined with practitioner expertise. This could happen through union Web sites like the National Education Association's "Tools and Ideas" page, and through publications like the American Federation of Teachers' *American Educator*. Or more ambitiously, unions might work together with policy makers to foster enthusiasm about research by cultivating a designation that could be adopted by schools or districts—a label like "Research School" that might promote teacher cooperation and institutional pride.[16] Whatever form such work might take, though, unions have a great deal to gain from a project that would publicly renew their purpose in a period of intense scrutiny. Such work would not be new to them; the

American Federation of Teachers, from the time of Albert Shanker's leadership onward, has displayed an organizational understanding of the upside of such a move. But where previous efforts stalled, a renewed focus on research-based practice might help teacher unions stave off the fierce criticism they have faced from both conservatives and neoliberal reformers in the twenty-first century.

Improving Occupational Realism

Compared to the challenge of addressing issues of perceived significance and philosophical compatibility, attending to occupational realism is a relatively straightforward proposition. Whatever the merits of the scholarship, ideas from research that do not square with occupational constraints are unlikely to enter the teacher knowledge base; insofar as they stand any chance at all, they are liable to be significantly transformed. The reverse is also true: even if an idea lacks a substantial evidentiary base, it may gain a foothold in practice if it fits with the organization and scope of the teacher workday.

Not surprisingly, some have called for remaking the teaching profession in a manner that would allow for more consistent engagement with scholarship. But while such a shift might make more research occupationally realistic, or at least *allow* more high-quality research to be occupationally realistic, it is for the most part implausible. In lieu of overhauling the profession, however, interested parties might use their knowledge about occupational constraints by jointly cultivating a new perspective on the relationship between research and practice. Specifically, they might establish consensus around the idea that connecting teachers with scholarship is a time-consuming and ongoing work in progress. Structurally, this might be brought to life through the creation of professional learning communities, or other groups of educators—organized by school, district, or affinity—working together over the course of several years, meeting regularly, and moving slowly toward a significant end goal.[17] Districts could play a key role in this process by providing release time and salary incentives for participating teachers.

Scholarship itself might be made more occupationally realistic through research projects specifically designed for use in practice. We might imagine, for instance, research teams at colleges and universities consulting for schools or districts and collaborating in both the creation and study of new models—work not unlike that done by James Comer of Yale University through his School Development Program. This could also take the form of educational researchers serving sabbatical terms as scholars-in-residence at districts, leading teams of teachers interested in addressing particular district- or school-based issues—and even learning something themselves about how real K–12 classrooms operate.[18] Conversely, research groups might form strategic partnerships with K–12 teachers, seeking their input and feedback on particular projects.

Traditional forms of research could also be made more occupationally realistic if they were intentionally transformed for classroom use. As in countries like New Zealand—where the Best Evidence Synthesis program has created high-quality, practice-oriented overviews of research—this might be done at the state level, or, where capacity exists, at the district level. But such work also might be done by scholars and their research teams. Funded by the state, or by private foundations concerned with impact, scholarly collaboratives might take a more active role in making their research occupationally realistic for teachers by translating some of their own work into classroom-ready products. Recently, for instance, the Stanford History Education Group created a curriculum based on research by its members—a small team of professors and graduate students. The curriculum is made up of lessons "designed to stand alone and supplement what teachers are already doing in their classrooms."[19] Primary documents are included and have already been excerpted for readability. And lessons are grouped by traditional categories found in textbooks. To date, the curriculum has been downloaded over a million times.

Providers of professional development might also continue to play a role in fostering occupational realism. Yet rather than operating as entrepreneurial and largely unaccountable free agents, they might better serve schools and teachers if they were directed by district, state, or federal guidelines. Such guidelines might require that third parties partner with colleges or universities, that they align their work with state and district resources, or that they collect and report data on outcomes. Alternatively, we might imagine third parties working under the umbrella of coordinating organizations with ties to states or districts. The work done on the Common Core State Standards initiative under the oversight of the National Governors Association and the Council of Chief State School Officers, for instance, is an example of the kind of measured work that might be done by conscientious third parties.

Improving Transportability

The last of the four crucial characteristics—transportability—may appear to be the most difficult to intentionally cultivate. Ideas that are complex, that cannot be diagrammed, and that have a large number of moving parts are at an inherent disadvantage when stacked against those like the project method, which can seemingly travel through name alone. And, whatever the interest of scholars in cultivating transportability, it is unlikely to ever be clear at the outset of a project just how transportable its outcomes will be. Nevertheless, the manner in which scholars communicate their findings is well within their control, and as the cases in this book reveal, issues like language matter a great deal. What an idea is called, how it is explained, and the naming of its component parts are all worth considering carefully. Collectively, scholars might determine standards of organizational clarity and simplicity that might serve as a framework for all who are interested in greater transportability.

Equally important in this regard is the form that scholarship takes. All too often, the product of research is, in the words of Howard Gardner, the "obscure monograph."[20] There are reasons for that, ranging from the complexity of new knowledge to the dictates of the tenure process. Yet if scholarship is to move among practitioners, it must take other forms. Easily transportable versions of research, whether derived by its original author or by another party, would hardly capture the fullness and detail of serious scholarship. A one-page "Commentary" piece in *Education Week*, for instance, is no substitute for a book-length manuscript, or even for a research article. It might, however, get more high-quality research a foot in the schoolhouse door. And though teachers might initially understand such scholarship only shallowly, they might develop deeper and more complex understandings as they engage with it on a sustained basis through lesson study, in conjunction with research coordinators, or by working with teacher mentors. Such work is easily done by scholars, but other actors might play key roles as well. Research coordinators at the district and state level could certainly make research more transportable by adapting it for easier dissemination. And teachers, perhaps working together with journalists—as in one U.K. program—might increase transportability by rewriting and summarizing relevant journal articles.[21]

Scholarship might also be made more transportable by making *individuals* more transportable. Principals, for instance, might build scholarly expertise in particular areas and rotate across schools in a district the way that members of the foreign service move across posts. Such a proposal would be even more effective if the position of "assistant principal in charge of research" were created, allowing lead principals to stay in place and cultivate a sense of continuity at the school site. Teacher knowledge of research might also be made more transportable, particularly if engaged teachers were granted research leaves, with the understanding that their classrooms would—upon their return—become sites for peer observation. Districts might also incentivize such teachers to maintain blogs on district Web sites, detailing the use of educational research in their posts. And district research coordinators or research librarians, if those positions were created, could also maintain such blogs on school or district Web pages.

Even if none of these actions were to be taken, however, it would be a victory merely to recognize the tradeoffs inherent in transportability. As the cases considered in this work demonstrate, an idea that travels in its most basic form has a greater chance of proliferating, yet in doing so it loses much of its value. Being conscious of such complexities will not, on its own, transform teachers into critical consumers of research, nor will it radically transform the way that scholars approach their work. But it might do a great deal. And, as is the case with each of these characteristics, understanding the way the world *currently works* is the absolute prerequisite for beginning to move forward.

PROGRESS, SLOW AND STEADY

It should be abundantly clear that these proposed reforms do not represent a perfect fix. And none, on its own, will do much to tighten the connection between educational research and the knowledge base of K–12 teachers. Collectively, however, such practical and realistic adjustments might lay the groundwork for progress of a slow and steady sort.

Energetic principals and innovative district leaders might piece together plans that include new partnerships with local colleges and universities, research librarians coordinating staff development, key teachers exploring issues of interest and working with affinity groups, learning circles organized by grade level or subject area, and research-oriented leaders rotating across schools.

Engaged scholars might gain new relevance and impact by learning to blog and tweet, founding new open-access journals oriented toward affecting practice, reorienting teacher education toward research, consulting for districts, and even writing curricula for K–12 schools.

Finally, policy leaders at the state and federal level might support this work by adapting and synthesizing research for practitioners, funding collaborations between scholars and K–12 teachers, establishing guidelines around professional development, and encouraging colleges and universities to orient their programs—from teacher licensure to doctoral training—toward the aim of moving educational scholarship into the classroom.

Each party, in sum, has a role to play, as do actors like foundation heads and professional development providers. And were they to work together, the results might be quite powerful.

A NOTE TO SKEPTICS

The preceding slate of proposals is merely a rough outline of what teachers, administrators, scholars, and policy makers might do to more closely connect research with practice—food for thought more than prescriptions for filling. Still, that is unlikely to satisfy skeptics, who will have initial misgivings about any vision so ambitious. Thus, it is worth addressing several of the questions that might be asked of even a sketch so rough.

Perhaps the most obvious question is whether such a project will bring better ideas into practice. After all, educational scholarship is notoriously vast in its quantity and varied in its quality. So it is important to note that although the potential benefits of linking the ivory tower and the schoolhouse are multiple—from the ways it might encourage teacher professional growth to the ways it might foster cooperation across various spheres of influence in American education—such linkages alone are not enough. A positive impact on K–12 schooling can be realized only if the scholarship in question is both relevant and high quality.

Yet as this concluding chapter should indicate, it is possible to improve upon existing systems and structures such that high-quality research might more easily possess the four characteristics crucial for making the jump into K–12 classrooms, and such that low-quality research might not. To put it another way: the aim is not to spray schools with a fire hose; rather, it is to introduce both conduits and filters such that what arrives at the schoolhouse door can effect change in a positive direction.

It is also worth noting that, whatever the concerns of skeptics, even an idea like multiple intelligences—an idea with many thoughtful critics—has done much good in K–12 schools. It has given teachers some professional common ground. It has facilitated discussions by providing a framework and a common language. And it has raised questions and prompted discussions that moved beyond the research. All of these things are important contributions, even if the research base for multiple intelligences is less than fully convincing. Thus, while it is important to build stronger systems and structures, it is also important to appreciate the full range of ways that scholarship can have a positive influence on practice.

Skeptics, of course, might ask another tough question, about the depth of implementation. As scholars like Larry Cuban have convincingly shown, reform often penetrates the way teachers *talk* more than it does the way teachers *teach*. And that was often—though not always—true for the scholarly ideas considered in this book. What, then, will move scholarship past rhetoric and into practice with any kind of consistency?

Language, without a doubt, will always be easier to change than action. Still, there are particular elements in this slate of proposals designed to promote deeper knowledge of new ideas by strengthening occupational realism and transportability. Just as the characteristics of perceived significance and philosophical compatibility signal an idea's *importance* to teachers, occupational realism and transportability help compensate for the structural limitations that so often keep teachers from *understanding* research. They do so imperfectly, as the case studies in this book reveal. But as the preceding proposal outlines, all of these characteristics can be further improved. Thus, reforms like lesson study, teacher release time, salary incentives, scholars-in-residence, research coordinators, research librarians, teacher mentors, research-expert principals, and research sabbaticals might *intensify the impact* of occupational realism and transportability. Consequently, they might not only get more high-quality research past the schoolhouse door, but also give good ideas a chance to take hold and bloom.

Finally, skeptics might wonder about the central role teachers play in this proposal—not only because there are over three million of them to manage, but also because teachers have many times in the past resisted reform. Dealing solely with policy makers, by contrast, would make for a much simpler process. There are fewer of them to persuade, and they are often eager to initiate change. They tend to be more connected to the world of scholarship than teachers are. And they have stronger professional networks with one another—networks across which coordination might be achieved. Additionally, one could argue that a whole slew of research findings might be applied without the need for teacher cooperation. Improved governance, for instance, more effective data collection and analysis, or more robust student services might each be designed centrally at the state or district level and pursued via top-down mandate.

Yet however simple it would be to bypass teachers, the fact remains that the instructional core of education is resistant to such an approach. And while improvements to elements like governance structures, data systems, or support services are worth pursuing, such work is only complementary—if not peripheral—to the work that teachers do inside their classrooms.

Policy elites, of course, have tried it all. A reform like the small schools movement, for instance, was popular—if not entirely successful—because it sought to transform instruction while ignoring teachers completely.

Conversely, the standards and accountability push of the past two decades has sought, through aggressive policy changes, to pry open the classroom door in order to address teacher practice. In many ways it succeeded in doing so. But policy structures in education are highly ineffective when it comes to influencing the instructional core. Teachers work in isolation and maintain high levels of autonomy, making their cooperation an inescapable precondition of any effort to affect practice. And even if teachers cooperate with reform efforts, the process of instructional improvement is still contingent upon teacher capacity to execute. After all, the decisive factor in improving educational outcomes is not policy per se, but policy in *practice*. Reforms that fail to recognize this—the standards movement included—are destined to bring change without improvement.

There is no escaping the centrality of teachers—at least with regard to what happens once the bell rings, students take their seats, and classroom doors swing shut. Accordingly, reformers seeking to improve the instructional core in education must cultivate educators as willing and able partners, working collectively to expand what teachers know. Linking the world of scholarship with that of practice offers a way forward on this front—engaging educators in the process of professional growth through an ongoing exchange of ideas.

There are alternatives, certainly. Policy elites continue to float proposals that would overhaul teacher recruitment and training—altering what teachers know through a process of selection and preservice preparation. Others, more pessimistic about the prospect, have begun to press for eliminating teachers entirely and moving toward computer-based instruction.

Yet whatever the merits of other proposals, the vision of linking the ivory tower and the schoolhouse has perhaps the greatest potential upside. Not only does it promise to develop teacher competency in long-term fashion, but it also offers an existing resource—the educational research community—for doing so. And unlike most reform efforts, which pull stakeholders in different directions and tug at the seams of fragile partnerships, the vision of connecting research and practice is one that might foster cooperation and collaboration among all parties. It is a reform that *might actually work*.

EPILOGUE

A Consensus Agenda

As the conclusion of this book suggests, we might take what we know about the movement of research into practice and begin to act on it. Still, it is important to recognize that there are no obvious or certain steps to take in this process—no silver bullets or quick fixes. The intended contribution of this book, then, is not to serve as an instruction manual. Instead, it is to structure an informed dialogue about the relationship between research and practice in the American educational system.

Obviously, the upshot of such dialogue is better educational outcomes. But there is a less obvious payoff that would have more far-reaching consequences, and that is a common sense of purpose among key stakeholders. Policy makers blame teachers for their failure to adequately implement seemingly rational plans. Teachers, in turn, reproach policy makers for failing to recognize the realities of classroom teaching. And both groups criticize scholars for their failure to produce relevant and usable research. Viewing one another as misguided and out of touch, each set of actors tends to work at cross-purposes, wasting both time and resources in casting about blame.

But what if they could begin working toward a shared aim?

And what if, by recognizing the complexity of reality, they could begin making progress toward that aim?

It is not impossible to imagine a world in which teacher unions, state and federal offices, schools of education, districts, school administrators, and classroom teachers engage in genuine partnership for the sake of advancing a common goal. Such common ground has certainly been elusive in modern American schooling. But the work of connecting research with practice is a uniquely alluring opportunity. After all, despite the well-documented and problematic history of bridging educational scholarship with practice, the dream of perpetual progress still carries significant weight across a society enriched by the fruits of research—from the way we communicate, to the way we care for the sick, to the way we evaluate professional athletes. Further, the work of connecting research with practice requires not just action, but *coordinated* action. Unlike most policy proposals, it is an enterprise predicated on the building of understanding more than it is on the expansion of power; it is an enterprise that requires professional sympathy.

Without such a common aim, policy makers and teachers will continue to face off against each other, education researchers will continue to wallow in irrelevance, and the national mood around our public schools will continue to sour. As the rhetoric of decline dominates, efforts to shift blame will only further fracture relationships between various stakeholders—and the ultimate blow will be felt by a system long under fire. It is a system that, for all its faults, has served hundreds of millions of Americans to great effect. But it is a system that rests upon a foundation of faith as much as it does on bricks and mortar.

In 1940, 85 percent of adults polled by George Gallup agreed "that young people today are getting a better education in school than their parents got."[1] Three-quarters of a century later, however, the tides had shifted dramatically. Today, only 41 percent of Americans believe schools are improving; half believe them to be worse.[2] In short, the bedrock of the American school system—public faith in a public good—is no longer what it once was, even as the vast majority of Americans continue to look to that system for the education of their children.

Ultimately, we do not need schools to improve overnight, nor are most schools in need of especially dramatic improvement. And the same might be said of the teachers who constitute the heart of any school. Instead, what we need is an agenda for moving forward. Slowly, perhaps. But together.

Introduction

1. Richard Elmore and colleagues have defined the *instructional core* as "the relation-ship between the teacher and the student in the presence of content." See Elizabeth A. City et al., *Instructional Rounds in Education: A Network Approach to Improving Teaching and Learning* (Cambridge, MA: Harvard Education Press, 2009), 22. For more on the re-sistance of the instructional core to change, see Richard F. Elmore, *Building a New Struc-ture for School Leadership* (Washington, DC: The Albert Shanker Institute, 2000).

2. The use of educational research *outside* of teacher practice is, without question, more prevalent. But it is important to note that such work is still characterized by chal-lenges. One common complaint, for instance, is that policy makers "work backward"— choosing a course of action and then assembling a research base to justify the decision.

3. Evidence from research also indicates that teachers do not prefer scholarship of any particular methodology or genre. See, for instance, Mary M. Kennedy, "A Test of Some Common Contentions About Educational Research," *American Educational Re-search Journal* 36, no. 3 (1999): 511–541.

4. Anthony S. Bryk and Louis M. Gomez, "Reinventing a Research and Develop-ment Capacity," in *The Future of Educational Entrepreneurship: Possibilities for School Re-form*, ed. Frederick M. Hess (Cambridge, MA: Harvard Education Press, 2008); David F. Labaree, "The Dysfunctional Pursuit of Relevance in Education Research," *Educational Researcher* 37, no. 7 (2008).

5. See, for instance, Terry Moe, *Special Interest: Teachers Unions and America's Public Schools* (Washington, DC: Brookings Institution Press, 2011).

6. David K. Cohen, "Teaching Practice: Plus Que Ça Change . . ." in *Contributing to Educational Change: Perspectives on Research and Practice*, ed. Philip W. Jackson (Berkeley, CA: McCutchan); John W. Meyer and Brian Rowan, "Institutionalized Organizations: Formal Structure as Myth and Ceremony," *American Journal of Sociology* 83, no. 2 (1977): 340–363.

7. Thomas R. Guskey, *Evaluating Professional Development* (Thousand Oaks, CA: Corwin, 1999).

8. Linda Darling-Hammond, Ruth Chung-Wai, and Alethea Andree, *How High-Achieving Countries Develop Great Teachers* (research brief, Stanford Center for Op-portunity Policy in Education, August 2010).

9. M. Fernanda Astiz, Alexander W. Wiseman, and David P. Baker, "Slouching Towards Decentralization: Consequences of Globalization for Curricular Control in National Education Systems," *Comparative Education Review* 46, no. 1 (2002); William H. Clune, "The Best Path to Systemic Educational Policy: Standard/Centralized or Differentiated/Decentralized," *Educational Evaluation and Policy Analysis* 15, no. 3 (1993); Mona Mourshed, Chinezi Chijioke, and Michael Barber, *How the World's Most Improved School Systems Keep Getting Better* (New York: McKinsey and Company, 2010), 20; Hans N. Weiler, "Comparative Perspectives on Educational Decentralization: An Exercise in Contradiction?" *Educational Evaluation and Policy Analysis* 12, no. 4 (1990).

10. Milton Rokeach, *Beliefs, Attitudes, and Values: A Theory of Organization and Change* (San Francisco: Jossey-Bass, 1968).

11. National Education Association, *Status of the American Public School Teacher 2005–2006* (2010), tables 26, 28, 29, and 31.

12. OECD, *Education at a Glance 2011: OECD Indicators*, table D4.2, http://dx.doi.org/10.1787/888932465417.

13. Cynthia E. Coburn, Meredith I. Honig, and Mary Kay Stein, "What's the Evidence on Districts' Use of Evidence?" in *The Role of Research in Educational Improvement*, ed. John D. Bransford et al. (Cambridge, MA: Harvard Education Press, 2009), 69.

14. For more on the "black box" of the classroom, see Larry Cuban, *Inside the Black Box of Classroom Practice: Change Without Reform in American Education* (Cambridge, MA: Harvard Education Press, 2013).

Chapter 1

1. Gary L. Peltier and David W. Noonan, "Influential Publications in Education 1950–2002," *The Clearing House* 76, no. 4 (2003): 215.

2. Reprinted in "The Way We Were?" *University of Chicago Magazine* 91, no. 4 (1999).

3. John W. Boyer, *The Organization of the College and the Divisions in the 1920s and 1930s* (University of Chicago, 2002).

4. Benjamin S. Bloom, *All Our Children Learning* (New York: McGraw-Hill, 1981), 245.

5. Benjamin S. Bloom, The Relationship Between Educational Objectives and Examinations Designed to Measure Achievement in General Education Courses at the College Level (doctoral dissertation, University of Chicago, 1943).

6. Lorin Anderson, "Benjamin S. Bloom: His Life, His Works, and His Legacy," in *Educational Psychology: A Century of Contributions*, ed. Barry J. Zimmerman and Dale H. Schunk (Mahwah, NJ: Lawrence Erlbaum Associates, 2003), 369.

7. Chauncey S. Boucher and A. J. Brumbaugh, *The Chicago College Plan* (Chicago: University of Chicago Press, 1940), 91–92.

8. Ralph Tyler, *Basic Principles of Curriculum and Instruction* (Chicago: University of Chicago Press, 1949), 43.

9. Edwin Kiester Jr., "Ralph Tyler: The Educator's Educator," *Change* 10, no. 2 (1978): 28–35; Eliot Eisner, "Benjamin Bloom," *Prospects: the Quarterly Review of Comparative Education* 30, no. 3 (2000).

10. Mary Ann Dzuback, *Robert M. Hutchins: Portrait of an Educator* (Chicago: University of Chicago Press, 1991); Clark Kerr, *The Uses of the University* (Cambridge, MA: Harvard University Press, 1963).

11. Alvin C. Eurich, "A Renewed Emphasis upon General Education," in *The Thirty-Eighth Yearbook of the National Society for the Study of Education, Part II: General Education in the American College*, ed. Guy Montrose Whipple (Bloomington, IL: Public School Publishing Co., 1939), 3.

12. W. S. Gray, ed., *General Education: Its Nature, Scope, and Essential Elements* (Chicago: University of Chicago Press, 1934).

13. Dzuback, Robert M. Hutchins, 154.

14. Eliot Eisner, "Benjamin Bloom," *Prospects: the Quarterly Review of Comparative Education* 30, no. 3 (2000).

15. Benjamin S. Bloom, ed., *Taxonomy of Educational Objectives, The Classification of Educational Goals, Handbook I: Cognitive Domain* (New York: David McKay, 1956), 4.

16. For more, see David R. Krathwohl, "A Revision of Bloom's Taxonomy: An Overview," *Theory into Practice* 41, no. 4 (2002): 212.

17. Benjamin S. Bloom, "A Taxonomy of Educational Objectives" (opening remarks for the meeting of examiners at Monticello, Illinois). In David R. Krathwohl, ed., *Summary Report, College and University Examiner's Taxonomy Conference* (Champaign, IL: Bureau of Research and Service, College of Education, University of Illinois, 1949).

18. Krathwohl, Summary Report.

19. Benjamin S. Bloom, "Reflections on the Development and Use of the Taxonomy," in *Bloom's Taxonomy: A Forty-Year Retrospective*, ed. Lorin W. Anderson and Lauren A. Sosniak (Chicago: University of Chicago Press, 1994), 4.

20. David R. Krathwohl, "Reflections on the Taxonomy: Its Past, Present, and Future," in *Bloom's Taxonomy: A Forty-Year Retrospective*, ed. Lorin W. Anderson and Lauren A. Sosniak (Chicago: University of Chicago Press, 1994), 186.

21. Bloom, ed., Taxonomy of Educational Objectives, 62.

22. Ibid., 89.

23. Ibid.

24. Ibid., 116.

25. Ibid., 120.

26. Ibid.

27. Ibid., 136.

28. Ibid., 144.

29. Ibid.

30. Ibid., 161.

31. Ibid., 162.

32. Ibid.

33. Ibid., 177.

34. Ibid., 185.

35. Ibid., 197.

36. Ibid., 198.

214 NOTES

37. Ibid., 185.

38. "Classifying Teaching Aims: The Cognitive Domain," *Improving College and University Teaching* 4, no. 4 (1956): 95.

39. E. I. Sawin, [untitled review], *The Elementary School Journal* 57, no. 6 (1957): 343–344.

40. Bloom, ed., Taxonomy of Educational Objectives, 21.

41. Julian C. Stanley and Dale Bolton, "A Review of 'Bloom's Taxonomy of Educational Objectives' and J. R. Gerberich's 'Specimen Objectives Tests Items: A Guide to Achievement Test Construction'," *Educational and Psychological Measurement* 17, no. 4 (1957): 631–634.

42. Leon Lessinger, "Test Building and Test Banks Through the Use of the 'Taxonomy of Educational Objectives'," *California Journal of Educational Research* 14 (1963): 195–201; Robert W. McFall, "The Development and Validation of an Achievement Test for Measuring Higher Level Cognitive Processes in General Science," *Journal of Experimental Education* 33 (1964): 103–106; Russell P. Kropp and Howard W. Stoker, *The Construction and Validation of Tests of the Cognitive Processes as Described in the Taxonomy of Educational Objectives* (Tallahassee: Florida State University, Institute of Human Learning and Department of Educational Research and Testing, 1966); Russell P. Kropp, Howard W. Stoker, and W. L. Bashaw, "The Validation of the Taxonomy of Educational Objectives," *Journal of Experimental Education* 34 (1966): 69–76.

43. John W. Lombard, "Preparing Better Classroom Tests," *The Science Teacher* (1965): 33–38; Francis P. Hunkins, "Bloom's Taxonomy as a Test Construction Guide," *Ideas Educational* 4, no. 2 (1966): 13–16; Clifford B. Elliott, Philip R. Merrifield, and O. L. Davis Jr., "Cognitive Dimensions of Lesson Objectives Set by Secondary Student Teachers" (paper presented at the Annual Meeting of the American Educational Research Association, Chicago, 1966); Isobel L. Pfeiffer and O. L. Davis Jr., "Teacher-Made Examinations: What Kinds of Thinking Do They Demand?" *NASSP Bulletin* 49 (1966): 1–10; Thomas A. Romberg, *Derivation of Subtests Measuring Distinct Mental Processes Within the NLSMA Algebra Achievement Test* (unpublished doctoral dissertation, Stanford University, 1968); Joe Milan Steele, "Assessing Intent and Practice in Instruction" (paper presented at the Annual Conference of the American Educational Research Association, Minneapolis, MN, March 2–6, 1970); M. Frances Klein, "Use of Taxonomy of Educational Objectives (Cognitive Domain) in Constructing Tests for Primary School Pupils," *Journal of Experimental Education* 40, no. 3 (1972): 38–50.

44. Mary Lee Marksberry, Mayme McCarter, and Ruth Noyce, "Relation Between Cognitive Objectives from Selected Texts and from Recommendations of National Committees," *Journal of Educational Research* 62 (1969): 422–429.

45. Norris M. Sanders, *Classroom Questions: What Kinds?* (New York: Harper and Row, 1966).

46. Sidney J. Drumheller, "A Model for Applying the Bloom Taxonomy of Educational Objectives in Curriculum Design," *National Society for Programmed Instruction Journal* 6, no. 5 (1957): 10–13.

47. Richard C. Cox and Carol P. Widemann, *Taxonomy of Educational Objectives: Cognitive Domain. An Annotated Bibliography* (Washington, DC: U.S. Office of Education, 1970).

48. David R. Krathwohl, Benjamin S. Bloom, and Bertram B. Masia, *Taxonomy of Educational Objectives, The Classification of Educational Goals, Handbook II: Affective Domain* (New York: David McKay, 1964), 12.

49. Kropp, Stoker, and Bashaw, "Validation of the Taxonomy of Educational Objectives," 69.

50. Hulda Grobman, "The State of the Art: Curriculum Development and Evaluation," *Journal of Educational Research* 64, no. 10 (1971).

51. Ibid., 438.

52. Evelyn Klinckmann, "The BSCS Grid for Text Analysis," *BSCS Newsletter*, no. 19 (1963).

53. L. M. Lessinger, "Test Building and Test Banks Through the Use of the *Taxonomy of Educational Objectives*," *California Journal of Educational Research* 14 (1963): 195–201.

54. Los Angeles City Schools, *The Art of Questioning in Reading*, Division of Instructional Services Report no. 117 (1966).

55. Victor W. Doherty, "Procedure for Growth," *Educational Leadership* 23 (1965): 247–249.

56. Ambrose A. Clegg Jr., "Classroom Questions and Higher Cognitive Abilities" (paper presented at the Annual Meeting of the American Educational Research Association, Chicago, IL, February 1968); Ambrose A. Clegg Jr., George T. Farley, and Robert J. Curran, *Training Teachers to Analyze the Cognitive Level of Classroom Questioning*, Research Report No. 1, Applied Research Training Program, University of Massachusetts, June 1967.

57. C. B. Elliott, *Cognitive Dimensions of Lesson Objectives Set by Secondary Student Teachers* (unpublished master's thesis, Kent State University, 1965); Morton D. Waimon and Henry J. Hermanowicz, "Helping Prospective Teachers Classify and Study Teaching Behavior," *Teachers College Journal* 38 (1966): 97–102; C. B. Elliott, Philip R. Merrifield, and O. L. Davis Jr., "Cognitive Dimensions of Lesson Objectives Set by Secondary Student Teachers" (paper presented at the annual meeting of the American Educational Research Association, Chicago, February 1966); Duane C. Scribner, "Learning Hierarchies and Literary Sequence," *English Journal* 56 (1967): 385–393.

58. Jean Marie Wood, *A Survey of Objectives for Teacher Education*. Report prepared for the Commission on Teacher Education, Association for Supervision and Curriculum Development (San Bernardino, CA: San Bernardino City School System, 1960).

59. Barbara Davis, "Memo to Ben Bloom—Items That May Be of Interest; Applications of the Taxonomy," April 25, 1988, box 23, Benjamin Bloom Papers, University of Chicago (Chicago Illinois), 1.

60. Richard W. Paul, "Bloom's Taxonomy and Critical Thinking Instruction," *Educational Leadership* 42, no. 8 (1985): 36.

61. Bloom, ed., Taxonomy of Educational Objectives, 40.

62. Lawrence Cremin, *The Transformation of the School: Progressivism in American Education, 1876–1957* (New York: Vintage, 1964); Diane Ravitch, *Left Back: A Century of Battles over School Reform* (New York: Touchstone, 2000), 16.

63. Piaget's *Origins of Intelligence in the Child* was translated into English in 1953, and Vygotsky's *Thought and Language* was translated and published in 1962; Educational Policies Commission, *The Central Purpose of American Education* (Washington, DC: Educational Policies Commission of the National Education Association, 1961).

64. See, for instance, Larry Cuban, *How Teachers Taught: Constancy and Change in American Classrooms 1890–1990*, 2nd ed. (New York: Teachers College Press, 1993).

65. Nancy Roberts, "Further Verification of Bloom's Taxonomy," *Journal of Experimental Education* 45, no. 1 (1976): 16.

66. Romiett Stevens, "The Question as a Measure of Efficiency in Instruction: A Critical Study of Classroom Practice," *Teachers College Contributions to Education*, no. 48 (1912); Hubert C. Haynes, *The Relation of Teacher Intelligence, Teacher Experience, and Type of School to Types of Questions* (unpublished doctoral dissertation, George Peabody College for Teachers, 1935); Frank J. Guszak, "Teacher Questioning and Reading," *The Reading Teacher*, no. 21 (1967): 227–234; Joan E. Schreiber, *Teachers' Question-Asking Techniques in Social Studies* (unpublished doctoral dissertation, University of Iowa, 1967); James J. Gallagher, "Expressive Thought by Gifted Children in the Classroom," *Elementary English*, no. 42 (1965): 559–568.

67. Elliot W. Eisner, "Do Behavioral Objectives and Accountability Have a Place in Art Education?" *Art Education* 26, no. 5 (1973): 3.

68. Arthur Bestor, *Educational Wastelands* (Urbana: University of Illinois Press, 1953), 151.

69. Bestor, *Educational Wastelands*, 54; John Dewey, "The Child and the Curriculum," in *The School and Society and the Child and the Curriculum*, ed. Philip W. Jackson (Chicago: University of Chicago Press, 1902/1990), 181–209.

70. Eisner, "Behavioral Objectives and Accountability," 3.

71. Bestor, Educational Wastelands, 166.

72. Ibid., 53, 54. Antecedent steps, according to Bestor, included "knowledge," "synthesis," and "analysis."

73. David Tyack, *The One Best System: A History of American Urban Education* (Cambridge, MA: Harvard University Press, 1974).

74. Guy Montrose Whipple, ed., *The Thirty-Eighth Yearbook of the National Society for the Study of Education, Part II: General Education in the American College* (Bloomington, IL: Public School Publishing Co., 1939), 4.

75. Ernest Havemann and Patricia S. West, *They Went to College* (New York: Harcourt, Brace and Co., 1952).

76. Paul L. Dressel, "General and Liberal Education," *Review of Educational Research* 24, no. 4 (1954).

77. Wilford M. Aikin, *Adventure in American Education, Volume I: The Story of the Eight-Year Study* (New York: Harper & Bros., 1942).

78. Aikin, Adventure in American Education.

79. Aura E. Severinghaus, Harry J. Carman, and William E. Cadbury Jr., *Preparation for Medical Education in the Liberal Arts College* (New York: McGraw-Hill Book Co., 1953); Robert H. Knapp and H. G. Goodrich, *Origins of American Scientists* (Chicago: University of Chicago Press, 1952).

80. Paul Dressel et al., *General Education: Explorations in Evaluation* (Westport, CT: Greenwood Press, 1954), 17.

81. Robert Maynard Hutchins, "The Outlook for Public Education," in *No Friendly Voice* (Chicago: University of Chicago Press, 1936): 107–108.

82. Bloom, ed., Taxonomy of Educational Objectives, 6–7.

83. Ibid., 17–18.

84. See, for instance, David Labaree, *The Making of an American High School: The Credentials Market and the Central High School of Philadelphia, 1838–1939* (New Haven: Yale University Press, 1988).

85. National Center for Education Statistics, "High School Graduates, by Sex and Control of School: Selected Years, 1869–70 through 2018–2019," *Digest of Education Statistics*, http://nces.ed.gov/programs/digest/d09/tables/dt09_103.asp.

86. Department of the Interior, Bureau of Education, *Cardinal Principles of Secondary Education: A Report of the Commission on the Reorganization of Secondary Education*, appointed by the National Education Association, Bulletin, 1918, no. 35 (Washington, DC: United States Government Printing Office, 1918), 7–16.

87. W. W. Charters, *Curriculum Construction* (New York: Macmillan, 1923), 44–46.

88. Special Committee on the Secondary School Curriculum for the American Youth Commission, *What the High Schools Ought to Teach* (Washington, DC: American Council on Education, 1940), 10–16, 19–29; David L. Angus and Jeffrey E. Mirel, *The Failed Promise of the American High School: 1890–1995* (New York: Teachers College Press, 1999), 76.

89. Lloyd W. Warner, Robert Havighurst, and Martin Loeb, *Who Shall Be Educated?* (New York: Harper and Brothers, 1944); A. B. Hollingshead, *Elmstown's Youth: The Impact of Social Classes on Adolescents* (New York: John Wiley and Sons, 1949).

90. Russell W. Rumberger, "Dropping Out of High School: The Influence of Race, Sex, and Family Background," *American Educational Research Journal* 20, no. 2 (1983): 199–220; Christopher Jencks et al., *Inequality: A Reassessment of the Effect of Family and Schooling in America* (New York: Basic, 1972).

91. Sophie Bloom, "Foreword," in *Benjamin S. Bloom: Portraits of an Educator*, ed. Thomas R. Guskey (Lanham, MD: Rowman & Littlefield Education, 2006), xii.

92. Thomas R. Guskey, "Closing Achievement Gaps: Revisiting Benjamin S. Bloom's 'Learning for Mastery,'" *Journal of Advanced Academics* 19, no. 1 (2007): 8–31.

93. Los Angeles City Schools, *The Art of Questioning in Reading*, Division of Instructional Services Report no. 117 (1966), 1.

94. M. Frances Klein, "Use of Taxonomy of Educational Objectives (Cognitive Domain) in Constructing Tests for Primary School Pupils," *Journal of Experimental Education* 40, no. 3 (1972): 38–50.

95. Clifford B. Elliott, *Cognitive Dimensions of Lesson Objectives Set by Secondary Student Teachers* (unpublished master's thesis, Kent State University, 1965).

96. Stuart R. Johnson, *Relationships Among Cognitive and Affective Outcomes of Instruction* (unpublished doctoral dissertation, University of California, Los Angeles, 1966).

97. See, for instance, Marcelle H. Nerbovig and Herbert J. Klausmeir, *Teaching in the Elementary School*, 3rd ed. (New York: Harcourt, Brace and Co., 1969); Alex B. Crowder and Olive Boone Wheeler, *Elementary School Mathematics: Methods and Materials* (Dubuque, IA: W. C. Brown Co., 1972); Michael J. Dunkin and Bruce Jesse Biddle, *The Study of Teaching* (New York: Holt, Rinehart and Winston, 1974); Walter Pierce and Michael Lorber, *Objectives and Methods for Secondary Teaching* (Englewood Cliffs, NJ: Prentice-Hall, 1977); Dan W. Anderson et al., *Competency-Based Teacher Education* (Berkeley, CA: McCutchan Publishing, 1973); James M. Cooper et al., *Classroom Teaching Skills: A Handbook* (Lexington, MA: D. C. Heath and Co., 1977); Iris McClellan Tiedt et al., *Teaching Thinking in K–12 Classrooms: Ideas, Activities, and Resources* (Boston: Allyn and Bacon, 1988), 61.

98. Cooper et al., Classroom Teaching Skills, 15.

99. *Praxis Study Guide for Principles of Learning and Teaching*, 2nd ed. (Princeton, NJ: Educational Testing Service, 2004).

100. Ralph E. Kellogg, *An American History Test Bank* (San Diego: San Diego County Secondary Curriculum Council, 1964).

101. Gerald D. Baughman and Albert Mayrhofer, "Leadership Training Project: A Final Report," *Journal of Secondary Education* 40, no. 8 (1965): 369–372.

102. See, for example, Department of Education, *Taxonomy of Mathematics IX Objectives with Illustrative Test Items: A Summary Description* (Edmonton, Alberta: City of Edmonton, 1968); Donald H. Bernard, *Exam Questions Using Bloom's Taxonomy* (Tallahassee: Florida Department of Education, 1974).

103. Benjamin Bloom, "Applications of the Taxonomy," 1988, box 23, Benjamin Bloom Papers, University of Chicago (Chicago Illinois), np.

104. George A. Miller, "The Magical Number Seven, Plus or Minus Two: Some Limits on Our Capacity for Processing Information," *Psychological Review* 63 (1956): 81–97.

105. Lauren A. Sosniak, "The Taxonomy, Curriculum, and Their Relations," in *Bloom's Taxonomy: A Forty-Year Retrospective*, ed. Lorin W. Anderson and Lauren A. Sosniak (Chicago: University of Chicago Press, 1994), 117.

106. Bloom, "Applications of the Taxonomy."

107. Krathwohl, "Reflections on the Taxonomy: Its Past, Present, and Future," 189.

108. Tiedt et al., Teaching Thinking in K–12 Classrooms, 63.

109. Robert R. Newton, "The High School Curriculum: Search for Unity and Coherence," *The High School Journal* 62, no. 7 (1979): 289.

110. See, for instance, B. F. Skinner, "The Science of Learning and the Art of Teaching," *Harvard Educational Review* 24 (1954): 86–97.

111. Robert M. Gagné, "The Learning Basis of Teaching Method," in *The Psychology of Teaching Methods: Seventy-Fifth Yearbook of the National Society for the Study of Education*, ed. N. L. Gage (Chicago: University of Chicago Press, 1976): 30.

112. Newton, "The High School Curriculum," 290.

113. See Ellen Condliffe Lagemann, *An Elusive Science: The Troubling History of Education Research* (Chicago: University of Chicago Press, 2002).

114. Bloom, "Reflections on the Development and Use of the Taxonomy," 1.

115. Ibid., 7.

116. Sandra Clark, "The Curriculum Builder's Game Adapted for the Secondary English Program," in *The Growing Edges of Secondary English*, ed. Charles Suhor, John Sawyer Mayher, and Frank J. D'Angelo (Urbana, IL: National Council of Teachers of English), 30.

117. The concept of an "add-on" is taken from David Tyack and Larry Cuban, *Tinkering Toward Utopia: A Century of Public School Reform* (Cambridge, MA: Harvard University Press, 1995); Robert R. Newton, "The High School Curriculum: Search for Unity and Coherence," *The High School Journal* 62, no. 7 (1979): 290.

118. http://theapple.monster.com/topics/2303-do-real-teachers-care-about-blooms-taxonomy/posts.

119. Richard W. Paul, "Bloom's Taxonomy and Critical Thinking Instruction," *Educational Leadership* 42, no. 8 (1985): 36–37.

120. Robert J. Kloss, "Toward Asking the Right Questions: The Beautiful, the Pretty, and the Big Messy Ones," *The Clearing House* 61, no. 6 (1988): 248.

121. Bloom, ed., Taxonomy of Educational Objectives, 19.

122. Gabriela Flores, "How Bloom's Taxonomy Will Help Me to Improve My Teaching," *TeacherGaby* blog, July 24, 2012, http://teachergaby.wordpress.com/2012/07/24/how-blooms-taxonomy-will-help-me-to-improve-my-teaching/.

123. 6-Gun Annie, comment on "How Is Bloom's Taxonomy Useful in Teaching?" October 18, 2008, http://au.answers.yahoo.com/question/index?qid=20081018131050AA9JoBP.

124. See, for instance, William G. Miller, Jack Snowman, and Takeshi O'Hara, "Application of Alternative Statistical Techniques to Examine the Hierarchical Ordering in Bloom's Taxonomy," *American Educational Research Journal* 16, no. 3 (1979): 241–248; I. Leon Smith, "IQ, Creativity, and the Taxonomy of Educational Objectives: Cognitive Domain," *Journal of Experimental Education* 38, no. 4 (1970).

125. Krathwohl, "Reflections on the Taxonomy," 188.

126. Amelia E. Kreitzer and George F. Madaus, "Empirical Investigations of the Hierarchical Structure of the Taxonomy," in *Bloom's Taxonomy: A Forty-Year Retrospective*, ed. Lorin W. Anderson and Lauren A. Sosniak (Chicago: University of Chicago Press, 1994), 78.

127. Grant Wiggins and Jay McTighe, *Understanding by Design* (Alexandria, VA: Association for Supervision and Curriculum Development, 1998).

128. http://theapple.monster.com/topics/2303-do-real-teachers-care-about-blooms-taxonomy/posts.

129. Barbara Davis, "Memo to Ben Bloom," 2.

130. Lorin W. Anderson and David R. Krathwohl, eds., *A Taxonomy for Learning, Teaching, and Assessing: A Revision of Bloom's Taxonomy of Educational Objectives* (Boston: Allyn & Bacon, 2001).

131. Delaware Department of Education, "Framework for Curriculum Design," https://www.doe.k12.de.us/infosuites/staff/ci/content_areas/files/VPA%20Framework%20for%20Curriculum%20Design.doc.

132. New Jersey State Department of Education, "New Jersey World Languages Curriculum Framework," 1999, http://www.state.nj.us/education/frameworks/worldlanguages/.

133. See, for instance, South Dakota Department of Education, "Science Content Standards," 2005, http://doe.sd.gov/contentstandards/documents/South%20Dakota%20Science%202005.pdf, and South Dakota Department of Education, "Social Studies Content Standards," 2006, http://doe.sd.gov/contentstandards/documents/Full_Social%20Studies.pdf.

134. Beverly Joyce Love, *The Inclusion of Bloom's Taxonomy in State Learning Standards: A Content Analysis* (unpublished doctoral dissertation, Southern Illinois University, 2009).

135. Bloom, "Applications of the Taxonomy."

136. Peter Kneedler, *Critical Thinking in History and Social Science* (Sacramento: California State Department of Education, 1985).

137. Lorin W. Anderson, "Research on Teaching and Teacher Training," in *Bloom's Taxonomy: A Forty-Year Retrospective*, ed. Lorin W. Anderson and Lauren A. Sosniak (Chicago: University of Chicago Press, 1994), 133; Susan S. Stodolsky, *The Subject Matters* (Chicago: University of Chicago Press, 1988).

138. Julie Pyburn, "Pondering on the New Bloom's Taxonomy and Digital Learning Theory," *Pyburn's Ponderings* blog, February 17, 2012, http://www.coetail.com/jkpyburn/tag/new-blooms-taxonomy/.

Chapter 2

1. Susan Baum, Julie Viens, and Barbara Slatin, *Multiple Intelligences in the Elementary Classroom: A Teacher's Toolkit* (New York: Teachers College Press, 2005), 7.

2. Howard Gardner in Mary Eberstadt, "The Schools They Deserve: Howard Gardner and the Remaking of Elite Education," *Policy Review*, 1999, no. 7: 7.

3. Howard Gardner, *Multiple Intelligences: The Theory into Practice* (New York: Basic Books, 1994), xi.

4. Howard Gardner, *Frames of Mind: The Theory of Multiple Intelligences* (New York: Basic Books, 1983), 9.

5. Gardner, *Frames of Mind*, xiii.

6. Ibid., 10.

7. Ibid., 11.

8. Howard Gardner, "Intelligence in Seven Steps," in *Creating the Future*, ed. Dee Dickinson (Aston Clinton, England: Accelerated Learning Systems, Inc., 1991), 68–75.

9. Howard Gardner, "Reminiscences" (recording, Spencer Foundation Oral History Project, Oral History Research Office, Columbia University, 1990).

10. Gardner, *Frames of Mind*, 390.

11. Ibid., 391.

12. Ibid., 392.

13. Gardner, Multiple Intelligences, xii, xiii.

14. Ibid., 69.

15. Charlie Euchner, "Private-School Officials Fear Reforms May Infringe Upon Their Autonomy," *Education Week*, December 21, 1983.

16. Blake Rodman, "Independent Schools Fear Reforms Threaten Their Autonomy," *Education Week*, March 13, 1985.

17. See Lawrence Cremin, *The Transformation of the School: Progressivism in American Education, 1876–1957* (New York: Alfred Knopf, 1961).

18. Launa Ellison, "Using Multiple Intelligences to Set Goals," *Educational Leadership*, October 1992: 72.

19. Lynn Olson, "Children 'Flourish' Here," *Education Week*, January 27, 1987.

20. Gardner was awarded a MacArthur Fellowship in 1981.

21. Larry Cuban, "Assessing the 20-Year Impact of Multiple Intelligences on Schooling," *Teachers College Record* 106, no. 1 (January 2004): 142.

22. Although international comparative tests like PISA would not emerge for at least another decade, *A Nation at Risk* is a clear example of how policy elites drew together perceived declining American achievement and the threat of rising international competition in making the case for education reform. Such rhetoric of crisis was not new, being prevalent during the Cold War.

23. Glen Macnow, "Poll Shows Public Support for Reforms," *Education Week*, August 17, 1983.

24. Tricia Furniss, "Educators Urge That Arts Be Added to 'Basics,'" *Education Week*, October 12, 1983.

25. For an example of concern about educating the whole child, see the U.S. Department of Education's first annual "Exemplary Private School Recognition Project," administered in 1984, according to Terrel H. Bell, as a means of identifying "distinguished schools that are doing an exceptionally fine job, so we can focus on what they are doing that is right."

26. Tina Blythe and Howard Gardner, "A School for All Intelligences," *Educational Leadership*, April, 1990: 36.

27. James Bellanca and Robin Fogarty, *Blueprints for Thinking in the Cooperative Classroom*, 2nd ed. (Thousand Oaks, CA: Corwin Press, 1991), restated in Robin Fogarty

and Judy Stoehr, *Integrating Curricula with Multiple Intelligences: Teams, Themes, and Threads* (Thousand Oaks, CA: Corwin Press, 2008), xii.

28. Thomas R. Hoerr, *Becoming a Multiple Intelligences School* (Alexandria, VA: Association for Supervision & Curriculum Development, 2000), x.

29. In 1905, for instance, psychologist G. Stanley Hall wrote in his book *Adolescence* of the "great army of incapables" who he believed "should be in schools for dullards or subnormal children." Such sentiments were seemingly supported by the work of educational psychologists like Lewis Terman and Edward Thorndike, suggesting that inherited IQ scores marked people and groups for their stations in life and that differences between groups were products of heredity. While this thinking was common through the 1940s—exemplified in the Education Policies Commission's publication *Education for All American Youth*—it was challenged by scholars and activists with increasing vigor in the 1950s and 1960s. Research about student disaffection, inequitable distribution of resources, and social disadvantage, for instance, made the case that low-income and minority students had been dramatically underserved educationally. *Racial Isolation in Public Schools, I and II*, produced by the U.S. Commission on Civil Rights in 1967, is exemplary of such work. Politically, the push for social justice and equal opportunity further undermined the position that intelligence and success in school were causally related. And ultimately, policy makers' increasing acceptance of the language of the civil rights agenda—if not necessarily all of its goals—was perhaps the most significant driving force behind this shift.

30. Howard Gardner and Thomas Hatch, "Multiple Intelligences Go to School: Educational Implications of the Theory of Multiple Intelligences," *Educational Researcher* 18, no. 8 (November 1989): 6.

31. Blythe and Gardner, "A School for All Intelligences," 34.

32. Gardner, Multiple Intelligences, 69.

33. Timothy C. Urdan and Scott G. Paris, "Teachers' Perceptions of Standardized Achievement Tests," *Educational Policy* 8, no. 2 (June 1994): 137–156.

34. See, for instance, *An Open Letter to America on Schools, Students, and Tomorrow* (Washington, DC: National Education Association, 1984); *Tomorrow's Teachers: A Report of the Holmes Group* (East Lansing, MI: The Holmes Group, Inc., 1986); *A Nation Prepared: Teachers for the 21st Century: The Report of the Task Force on Teaching as a Profession* (Hyattsville, MD: Carnegie Forum on Education and the Economy, 1986).

35. This was through precursors to Bush's proposed America 2000 legislation and Clinton's Goals 2000 legislation.

36. Thomas Hoerr, "Applying MI in Schools," *New Horizons for Learning*, http://www.newhorizons.org/strategies/mi/hoerr2.htm.

37. Ibid.

38. Howard Gardner, foreword to *Multiple Intelligences: Best Ideas from Research and Practice*, by Mindy Kornhaber, Edward Fierros, and Shirley Veenema (Boston: Pearson, 2004), xiii.

39. Ibid., xii.

40. Gardner, *Frames of Mind*, 392.

41. David Lazear, *Eight Ways of Teaching: The Artistry of Teaching with Multiple Intelligences* (Palatine, IL: Skylight Publishing, Inc., 1991); David Lazear, *Multiple Intelligence Approaches to Assessment* (Tucson, AZ: Zephyr Press, 1994).

42. Carolyn Chapman, *If the Shoe Fits: Developing Multiple Intelligences in the Classroom* (Arlington Heights, IL: SkyLight Publications, 1993); Carolyn Chapman, *Multiple Assessments for Multiple Intelligences* (Arlington Heights, IL: SkyLight Publications, 1994); Carolyn Chapman and Lynn Freeman, *Multiple Intelligences Centers and Projects* (Arlington Heights, IL: SkyLight Publications, 1996).

43. Sally Berman, *A Multiple Intelligences Road to a Quality Classroom* (Palatine, IL: Skylight Publications, 1996); Anna T. O'Connor and Sheila Callahan-Young, *Seven Windows to a Child's World* (Arlington Heights, IL: Skylight Publications, 1994); James Bellanca, *Active Learning Handbook for the Multiple Intelligences Classroom* (Palatine, IL: Skylight Publications, 1997); Robin Fogarty, *Problem-Based Learning and Other Curriculum Models for the Multiple Intelligences Classroom* (Arlington, Heights, IL: Skylight Training and Publishing, Inc., 1999); Robin Fogarty and James Bellanca, *Multiple Intelligences: A Collection* (Arlington Heights, IL: SkyLight Publications, 1995).

44. John Davies, "A Reluctant Guru on Matters Between the Ears: Howard Gardner Talks to John Davies About His Theory of Human Intelligence," *The Thesis*, January 19, 1996.

45. Robin Fogarty and Judy Stoehr, *Integrating Curricula with Multiple Intelligences: Teams, Themes, and Threads* (Thousand Oaks, CA: Corwin Press, 2008), xvii.

46. Bruce Campbell, Linda Campbell, and Dee Dickinson, *Teaching and Learning Through Multiple Intelligences* (Seattle: New Horizons For Learning, 1992).

47. University of Idaho College of Agricultural and Life Sciences, "Multiple Intelligences Indicator," http://www.agls.uidaho.edu/fcsed/FCS461/Multiple_Intelligences_1a.pdf; Brett Bixler, "A Multiple Intelligences Primer," http://www.personal.psu.edu/staff/b/x/bxb11/MI/MIQuiz.htm; Walter McKenzie, "Multiple Intelligences Inventory," http://surfaquarium.com/MI/inventory.htm; C. Branton Shearer, "Multiple Intelligences Research and Consulting Inc.," http://www.miresearch.org/.

48. Thomas Armstrong, *Multiple Intelligences in the Classroom* (Alexandria, VA: Association for Supervision and Curriculum Development, 1994); Thomas Armstrong, *Seven Kinds of Smart: Identifying and Developing Your Multiple Intelligences* (New York: Plume, 1999); Thomas Armstrong, *In Their Own Way: Discovering and Encouraging Your Child's Multiple Intelligences* (New York: Tarcher/Penguin, 2000); Thomas Armstrong, *You're Smarter Than You Think: A Kid's Guide to Multiple Intelligences* (Minneapolis, MN: Free Spirit Publishing, 2002); Thomas Armstrong, *The Multiple Intelligences of Reading and Writing: Making the Words Come Alive* (Alexandria, VA: Association for Supervision and Curriculum Development, 2003).

49. Thomas Armstrong, "Client List," http://www.thomasarmstrong.com/clients.htm.

50. Thomas Armstrong, "Multiple Intelligences: Seven Ways to Approach Curriculum," *Educational Leadership* (November 1994).

51. Personal communication with Howard Gardner, March 14, 2013.

52. Ibid.

53. Kenneth A. Leithwood, *Effective School District Leadership: Transforming Politics into Education* (New York: SUNY Press, 1995); Martha Abele Mac Iver and Elizabeth Farley, *Bringing the District Back In: The Role of the Central Office in Improving Instruction and Student Achievement* (Baltimore: Center for Research on the Education of Students Placed at Risk, 2003).

54. Judith Warren Little, "Teachers' Professional Development in a Climate of Educational Reform," *Educational Evaluation and Policy Analysis* 15, no. 2 (1993): 129–151.

55. See, for instance, Hilda Borko, "Professional Development and Teacher Training: Mapping the Terrain," *Educational Researcher* 33, no. 8 (2004): 3–15; Judith Warren Little, "Teachers' Professional Development," 129–151.

56. Dennis Sparks and Stephanie Hirsh, *A New Vision for Staff Development* (Alexandria, VA: Association for Supervision and Curriculum Development, 1997), 1.

57. Edward T. Joyner, "No More 'Drive-By' Staff Development," in *Schools That Learn: A Fifth Discipline Fieldbook for Educators, Parents, and Everyone Who Cares About Education*, ed. Peter Senge et al. (New York: Doubleday, 2000).

58. Personal communication with Howard Gardner, March 14, 2013.

59. "Products and Services," Multiple Intelligences Institute, http://www.miinstitute.info/show/offering.php.

60. Leslie Owen Wilson, "What's the Big Attraction?" *New Horizons for Learning*, http://www.newhorizons.org/strategies/mi/wilson1.htm.

61. See, for instance, "Understanding the Theory of Multiple Intelligences," *Early Childhood Today* 20, no. 3 (November/December 2005).

62. Thomas Armstrong, Multiple Intelligences in the Classroom, 117.

63. Ibid.

64. "Kagan Catalog," Kagan Online, http://www.kaganonline.com/Catalog/index.html.

65. See, for instance, David Jerner Martin and Kimberly S. Loomis, *Building Teachers,* 2nd ed. (Belmont, CA: Wadsworth, 2014).

66. For more on learning styles, see Harold Pashler et al., "Learning Styles: Concepts and Evidence," *Psychological Science in the Public Interest* 9, no. 3 (2009).

67. Gardner, Multiple Intelligences, 33.

68. Armstrong, Multiple Intelligences in the Classroom, 77.

69. Jan Greenhawk, "Multiple Intelligences Meet Standards," *Educational Leadership* 55 (September 1997): 62–64.

70. Howard Gardner, "Reflections on Multiple Intelligences," *Phi Delta Kappan* 77, no. 3 (November 1995).

71. See, for instance, Frances A. Yates, *The Art of Memory* (London: Routledge, 1966).

72. Gardner, "Reflections."

73. James Traub, "Multiple Intelligence Disorder," *New Republic*, October 26, 1998: 22.

74. Howard Gardner, foreword to Multiple Intelligences: Best Ideas from Research and Practice, xii.

75. Howard Gardner, preface to *Multiple Intelligences in the Classroom*, by Thomas Armstrong (Alexandria, VA: Association for Supervision and Curriculum Development, 1994), vii.

76. Howard Gardner, foreword to *Integrating Curricula with Multiple Intelligences: Teams, Themes, and Threads*, by Robin Fogarty and Judy Stoehr (Thousand Oaks, CA: Corwin Press, 2008), vii.

77. Howard Gardner, foreword to *Multiple Intelligences in the Elementary Classroom: A Teacher's Toolkit*, by Susan Baum, Julie Viens, and Barbara Slatin (New York: Teachers College Press, 2005), viii.

78. David Ruenzel, "Two Schools of Thought," *Education Week*, April 1, 1995.

79. Kornhaber, Fierros, and Veenema, *Multiple Intelligences*, xiv.

80. Daniel T. Willingham, "Reframing the Mind," *Education Next* 4, no. 3 (Summer 2004).

81. Lynn Waterhouse, "Multiple Intelligences, the Mozart Effect, and Emotional Intelligence: A Critical Review," *Educational Psychologist* 41, no. 4: 207–225.

82. Personal communication with Howard Gardner, March 14, 2013.

83. Larry Cuban, *How Teachers Taught: Constancy and Change in American Classrooms, 1890–1990*, 2nd ed. (New York: Teachers College Press, 1993); David K. Cohen, "A Revolution in One Classroom: The Case of Mrs. Oublier," *Educational Evaluation and Policy Analysis* 12, no. 3 (1990): 311–329.

84. Maureen Stout, *The Feel-Good Curriculum: The Dumbing-Down of America's Kids in the Name of Self-Esteem* (New York: Perseus Publishing, 2000), 171.

85. Alan Wolfe, "Multiple Intelligences, Book Review," *New Republic*, February 8, 1993.

86. Kornhaber, Fierros, and Veenema, *Multiple Intelligences*.

87. Personal communication with Howard Gardner, March 14, 2013.

Chapter 3

1. Diary of William Heard Kilpatrick, Milbank Memorial Library, Teachers College, New York, NY. Dated January 5, 1936, but unpaginated, January 1, 1917.

2. Diary of William Heard Kilpatrick, August 6, 1915.

3. Herbert M. Kliebard, *The Struggle for the American Curriculum: 1893–1958* (New York: Routledge, 1986), 159.

4. Mendel Everett Branom, *The Project Method in Education* (Boston: Gorham Press, 1919), 44.

5. See, for instance, Michael Knoll, "'I Had Made a Mistake': William H. Kilpatrick and the Project Method," *Teachers College Record* 114, no. 2 (2012).

6. Charles R. Richards, "Department of Manual Training, Teachers College, New York," *Sloyd Bulletin* no. 2 (March 1899): 11.

7. David Snedden, Report of Committee on National Legislation. In *Bulletin No. 15 of the National Society for the Promotion of Industrial Education* (New York: The Society, 1916), 422.

8. Samuel Tenenbaum, *William Heard Kilpatrick: Trail Blazer in Education* (New York: Harper and Bros., 1951), 15.

9. See, for instance, Diane Ravitch, *Left Back: A Century of Battles over School Reform* (New York: Touchstone, 2000).

10. William Heard Kilpatrick, "The Project Method," *Teachers College Record* 19 (1918).

11. William Heard Kilpatrick, *Froebel's Kindergarten Principles Critically Examined* (New York: Macmillan, 1916), 202.

12. Tenenbaum, William Heard Kilpatrick, 29–30.

13. William Heard Kilpatrick, "The Problem-Project Method," (speech at Akron, Ohio, November 6, 1915), box 2, folder 18b, William Heard Kilpatrick Papers, Mercer University (Macon, Georgia), 3.

14. John Dewey, *Democracy and Education* (New York: Macmillan, 1966), 163.

15. Tenenbaum, *William Heard Kilpatrick*, 26. It is important to note here that Kilpatrick actually saw Cornell University professor Charles DeGarmo as more influential in his thinking about interest and effort. As Kilpatrick put it, DeGarmo's book *Interest and Education* "opened up a whole new world," convincing him that "there was no conflict between interest and effort; that they were not divergent forces but that they were inextricably allied; that effort follows interest" (see Tenenbaum, 37).

16. Quoted in Tenenbaum, *William Heard Kilpatrick*, 37.

17. William Heard Kilpatrick, letter to Abraham Flexner, January 25, 1950. William Heard Kilpatrick Papers, Special Collections, Jack Tarver Library, Mercer University, Macon, Georgia.

18. Kilpatrick referred to the "science of education" in one of his first talks on the project method: William Heard Kilpatrick, lecture notes for "Is There a New Education?" May 5, 1917, box 2, folder 3, William Heard Kilpatrick Papers, Mercer University (Macon, Georgia), 7. For the increasing scientific aspirations of educational scholars, see Max van Manen, "Romantic Roots of Human Science in Education," in *The Educational Legacy of Romanticism*, ed. John Willinsky and Aubrey Rosenberg (Waterloo, Ontario: Wilfrid Laurier University Press, 1990), 115–139.

19. Henry Suzzalo, "Editor's Introduction," in *Project Work in Education*, by James Leroy Stockton (Boston: Houghton Mifflin, 1920), vii.

20. William Heard Kilpatrick, lecture notes for "Is There a New Education?" May 5, 1917, box 2, folder 3, William Heard Kilpatrick Papers, Mercer University (Macon, Georgia), 7.

21. Ellen Condliffe Lagemann, *An Elusive Science: The Troubling History of Education Research* (Chicago: University of Chicago Press, 2002), 239.

22. Tenenbaum, William Heard Kilpatrick, 64.

23. Diary of William Heard Kilpatrick, November 20, 1931.

24. Benjamin Fine, "Teacher Remains Progressive at 85," *New York Times*, November 20, 1956, 31.

25. John P. Herring, "Bibliography of the Project Method," *Teachers College Record* 21, no. 2 (1920): 150.

26. Diary of William Heard Kilpatrick, July 29, 1918.

27. J. F. Hosic, "Editorially Speaking," *Journal of Educational Method* 1, no. 1 (1921): 2.

28. J. F. Hosic, "The Supervisor and the Project Method," *Journal of Educational Method* 1, no. 7 (1922): 6–7.

29. "College News and Departmental Notes: Extramural Courses," *Teachers College Record* 22, no. 5 (1921): 443; "College News and Departmental Notes: Extramural Courses," *Teachers College Record* 23, no. 3 (1922): 286.

30. Diary of William Heard Kilpatrick, October 27, 1927.

31. William Heard Kilpatrick, Syllabus and Readings for Dr. Kilpatrick's Course, January 30–February 3, 1922, Milwaukee, WI, box 2, folder 18b, William Heard Kilpatrick Papers, Mercer University (Macon, Georgia); William Heard Kilpatrick, Syllabus in the Philosophy of Education, Teachers College, Columbia University, New York, NY (1922), 75 pages.

32. William Heard Kilpatrick, Foundations of Method Final Exam, 1918, box 3, folder 2, William Heard Kilpatrick Papers, Mercer University (Macon, Georgia).

33. William Heard Kilpatrick, Syllabus and Readings.

34. Action proposed by Teachers Organization in Milwaukee to Board of Education, 1923, quoted in Knoll, "'I Had Made a Mistake.'"

35. William Heard Kilpatrick, Outline of a Course of Five Lectures by William Heard Kilpatrick to Be Held at the Orpheum Theatre in St. Paul, MN, January 28–February 1, 1924, box 2, folder 10b, William Heard Kilpatrick Papers, Mercer University (Macon, Georgia)

36. John Q. Copeland, "School Goal Told by Progressives," *Los Angeles Times*, May 29, 1950.

37. Charles DeGarmo, *Interest and Education: The Doctrine of Interest and Its Concrete Application* (New York: Macmillan, 1902), 23.

38. Bernice Brown McCullar, "Georgia Folkways," *Atlanta Constitution*, June 25, 1944.

39. Kilpatrick, "The Project Method."

40. Ibid.

41. Benjamin Fine, "Kilpatrick, 85, Holds Firmly to 'Progressive' Methods He Impressed Upon the World," *New York Times*, November 18, 1956, 215.

42. William Heard Kilpatrick, speech in Des Moines, Iowa, November 1, 1917, box 2, folder 4a, William Heard Kilpatrick Papers, Mercer University (Macon, Georgia).

43. Branom, The Project Method in Education, 80.

44. Elmer Ellsworth Brown, "The Development of Education as a University Subject," *Teachers College Record* 24 (May 1923): 190–196.

45. "Who Is Dr. Kilpatrick? What Is Teachers College?" *The Bulletin* (December 1921), 12.

46. "Columbia University Woman to Have Charge of Kindergarten to Be Opened at Stanley Hall," *Minneapolis Morning Tribune*, August 6, 1916, D8.

47. Ibid.

48. See, for instance, C. H. Stone, "Making a Match—A Project," *General Science Quarterly* 3 (1919); R. W. Hatch, "Teaching Modern History by the Project Method: An Experiment," *Teachers College Record* 21, no. 5 (1920).

49. Diary of William Heard Kilpatrick, February 24 and 26, 1921.

50. W. W. Charters, "Regulating the Project," *Journal of Educational Research* 5 (March 1922): 245, 246.

51. "Program of the Seventh Annual Meeting of the New Jersey Organization of Teachers of Colored Children," *Philadelphia Tribune*, May 14, 1921, 9.

52. "Teachers Discuss Modern Pedagogy," *Norfolk New Journal and Guide*, January 26, 1924, 10.

53. "Exhibit of Projects Executed by Pupils Arranged to Stimulate School Teachers," *New York Times*, August 30, 1931, E7.

54. "Talkies in the Classroom," *Christian Science Monitor*, June 13, 1931.

55. "Would End 'Fordizing' Pupils," *New York Times*, November 12, 1926, 23.

56. Robinson G. Jones, "School of Today Is Not Like That of Year 1890," *New York Times*, December 12, 1926, 27.

57. Carl Kaestle, *Pillars of the Republic* (New York: Hill and Wang, 1983), 129; Jurgen Herbst, *And Sadly Teach: Teacher Education and Professionalization in American Culture* (Madison: University of Wisconsin Press, 1989); David L. Angus, *Professionalism and the Public Good: A Brief History of Teacher Certification* (Washington, DC: The Thomas B. Fordham Foundation, 2001).

58. Diary of William Heard Kilpatrick, November 20, 1932.

59. William Heard Kilpatrick, letter to Abraham Flexner, January 25, 1950. William Heard Kilpatrick Papers, Special Collections, Jack Tarver Library, Mercer University, Macon, Georgia.

60. Herbert M. Kliebard, "Success and Failure in Education Reform: Are There Historical 'Lessons,'" *Peabody Journal of Education* (1988): 148.

61. Larry Cuban, *How Teachers Taught: Constancy and Change in American Classrooms, 1890–1990* (New York: Teachers College Press, 1993).

62. David Tyack and Larry Cuban, *Tinkering Toward Utopia* (Cambridge, MA: Harvard University Press, 1995).

63. William H. Kilpatrick, "How Shall We Select the Subject Matter of the Elementary School Curriculum," *Proceedings of the National Education Association* (1924): 908.

64. Tenenbaum, William Heard Kilpatrick, 249.

65. Samuel Tenenbaum, "The Project Method: A Criticism of Its Operation in the School System," *School and Society* 49 (1939): 770–772.

66. Charters, "Regulating the Project," 245.

67. This continues to be a criticism. See, for instance, Phyllis C. Blumenfeld et al., "Motivating Project-Based Learning: Sustaining the Doing, Supporting the Learning," *Educational Psychologist* 26, nos. 3 and 4 (1991): 373.

68. David Levine, "The Project Method and the Stubborn Grammar of Schooling: A Milwaukee Story," *Journal of Educational Foundations* 15, no. 1 (2001): 16.

69. W. W. Theisen, "Standards for Judging School Projects," *Projects and Games in the Primary Grades,* 15. Emphasis in original.

70. Daniel R. Hodgdon, "The Psychological and Pedagogical Basis of General Science," *School Science and Mathematics* 19 (July 1923): 321.

71. William H. Kilpatrick, "School Method from the Project Point of View," in *The Classroom Teacher,* ed. Milo B. Hillegas (Chicago: Classroom Teacher, 1927), 229.

72. William H. Kilpatrick, *Remaking the Curriculum* (New York: Newson, 1936); idem, *The Art and Practice of Teaching* (New York: Scott, 1937).

73. Diary of William Heard Kilpatrick, December 8, 1917.

74. David K. Cohen, "Dewey's Problem," *The Elementary School Journal* 98, no. 5 (1998): 445.

75. Arthur Davis, "With a Grain of Salt: Progressive Education Blamed for Weakness of Pupils in Fundamentals in Our Schools," *New Journal and Guide*, November 6, 1948, 8.

76. "Gold Trail Students Build Missions," *Mountain Democrat and Placerville Times*, March 26, 1964, B6

77. "Roynon Students Build Model Mission," *San Dimas Press*, December 4, 1968.

78. "Model Missions on Display at Camino School," *Mountain Democrat*, March 29, 1991, A8.

79. David Templeton, "Model Behavior," *Sonoma County Independent*, August 14, 1997.

80. "The California Mission Project: One Parent's Confession," Bossy Betty blog, August 6, 2010, http://www.bossybetty.com/2010/08/california-mission-project-one -parents.html.

81. Dan C. Lortie, *Schoolteacher: A Sociological Study*, 2nd ed. (Chicago: University of Chicago Press, 2002).

82. Blumenfeld et al., "Motivating Project-Based Learning," 382.

83. In David Templeton, "Model Behavior," *Sonoma County Independent*, August 14, 1997.

84. KimK1ca, "California Mission Vent, Anyone?" February 13, 2011, http:// teachers.net/mentors/profreading/topic6335/2.13.11.18.43.41.html.

85. Jan, comment on KimK1ca, "California Mission Vent."

86. Judy5ca, comment on KimK1ca, "California Mission Vent."

87. Jennifer Eyre White, "Fourth-Grade Mission," *Having Three Kids*, 2006, http://www.havingthreekids.com/onamission.html.

88. PaperModels, Inc., "Paper Models, California Missions," http://www .papermodelsonline.com/.

89. Ibid.

90. Blumenfeld et al., "Motivating Project-Based Learning," 373

91. Ibid., 393.

92. Ibid.

93. Edutopia, "Why Teach with Project-Based Learning?" February 28, 2008, http://www.edutopia.org/project-learning-introduction.

94. Buck Institute for Education, "The BIE Story," http://www.bie.org/about/the _bie_story/.

95. Paul Frysh, "West Virginia Learns Finland's 'Most Honorable Profession,'" CNN.com, http://www.cnn.com/2011/US/08/29/education.wv.finland/index.html?hpt =hp_bn2.

96. "Houghton Mifflin's Project-Based Learning Space," http://college.cengage.com/ education/pbl/background.html.

97. Kilpatrick, "The Project Method."

98. John A. Zahorik, "Elementary and Secondary Teachers' Reports of How They Make Learning Interesting," *Elementary School Journal* 96, no. 5 (1996): 556.

Chapter 4

1. Quoted in Martin A. Kozioff et al., "Direct Instruction: Its Contributions to High School Achievement," *The High School Journal* 84, no. 2 (2000–2001): 66.

2. See, for instance, Urban Education: Approaches That Work: Hearing Before the Subcommittee on Empowerment of the Committee on Small Business, House of Representatives, 105th Cong., Second Session (March 26, 1998).

3. American Federation of Teachers, *Building on the Best, Learning from What Works: Six Promising Schoolwide Reform Programs* (Washington, DC: American Federation of Teachers, 1998).

4. "General FAQs," Association for Direct Instruction, http://www.adihome.org/ 31-faqs/general.

5. Kerry Hempenstall, "The Importance of Effective Instruction," in *Introduction to Direct Instruction*, eds. Nancy E. Marchand-Martella, Timothy A. Slocum, and Ronald C. Martella (Boston: Pearson, 2004), 19.

6. Head Start was first authorized under the Economic Opportunity Act of 1964.

7. Carl Bereiter and Siegfried Engelmann, *Teaching Disadvantaged Children in the Preschool* (Englewood Cliffs, NJ: Prentice-Hall, 1966), 63.

8. Personal communication with Siegfried Engelmann, April 28, 2011.

9. Siegfried Engelmann and Therese Engelmann, *Give Your Child a Superior Mind: A Program for the Preschool Child* (New York: Simon and Schuster, 1966), 24.

10. Siegfried Engelmann and Wesley Becker, *Teaching 3: Evaluation of Instruction* (Chicago: Science Research Associates, 1976), 117.

11. Ibid.

12. Personal communication with Siegfried Engelmann, May 16, 2011.

13. Biloine W. Young, "A New Approach to Head Start," *Phi Delta Kappan* 49, no. 7 (1968): 386.

14. Personal communication with Siegfried Engelmann, June 1, 2011.

15. Barbel Inhelder and Jean Piaget, *The Growth of Logical Thinking from Childhood to Adolescence* (New York: Basic Books, 1958). Jean Piaget, *Play, Dreams and Imitation in Childhood* (New York: Norton, 1962). Jean Piaget and Barbel Inhelder, *The Psychology of the Child* (New York: Basic Books, 1962).

16. Jerome Bruner, *The Process of Education: Towards a Theory of Instruction* (Cambridge, MA: Belknap Press, 1966), 72.

17. Edwina Deans, *Elementary School Mathematics: New Directions* (Washington, DC: U.S. Department of Health, Education, and Welfare, 1963); Joel Frost and Thomas G. Rowland, *Curricula for the Seventies: Early Childhood Through Early Adolescence* (Boston: Houghton Mifflin, 1969); Linda Darling-Hammond and Jon Snyder, "Curriculum Studies and the Traditions of Inquiry: The Scientific Tradition," in *Handbook of Research on Curriculum*, ed. Philip W. Jackson (New York: Macmillan, 1992), 65.

18. Wesley C. Becker, Siegfried Engelmann, and Don R. Thomas, *Teaching: A Course in Applied Psychology* (Chicago: Science Research Associates, 1971).

19. Engelmann and Becker, *Teaching 3*, 302.

20. Personal communication with Siegfried Engelmann, June 1, 2011.

21. Ibid.

22. Brian S. Cittenden, "A Critique of the Bereiter-Engelmann Preschool Program," *School Review* 78, no. 2 (1970): 153.

23. Ibid., 154.

24. Ibid., 155.

25. Siegfried Engelmann, *Preventing Failure in the Primary Grades* (Chicago: Science Research Associates, 1969), 77

26. Stanley Erlwanger, "Case Studies of Children's Conceptions of Mathematics, Part I," *Journal of Children's Mathematical* Behavior 1, no. 2 (1975): 157–283; Barbel Inhelder, Hermine Sinclair, and Magili Bovet, *Learning and the Development of Cognition* (Cambridge, MA: Harvard University Press, 1974).

27. O. M. Ewert and M. Braun, "Ergebnnisse und Probleme Vorschulischer Foerderung," in Struktu Foerderung im Bildungswesen des Landes Nordrhein-Westfalen. Eine Schriften-reihe des Kultusministers, vol. 34: Modellversuch Vorklasse in NW-Abschulssbericht (Koeln: Greven, 1978); W. Winkelmann et al., "Kognitive Entwicklung und Foerderung von Kindergarten und Vorklassenkindern," Bericht uber eine laengsschnittliche Vergleischsuntersuchung zum Modellversuch des Landes Nordrhein-Westfalen, vol. 2 (Kronberg, Germany: Scriptor, 1979).

28. Wesley C. Becker, Siegfried Engelmann, and Don R. Thomas, *Instructor's Manual, Teaching 1: Classroom Management and Teaching 2: Cognitive Learning and Instruction* (Chicago: Science Research Associates, 1975), 69.

29. Personal communication with Siegfried Engelmann, June 15, 2011.

30. Darling-Hammond and Snyder, "Curriculum Studies," 65.

31. Quoted in Frank Riessman, *The Culturally Deprived Child* (New York: Harper and Row, 1962), 93

32. Bereiter and Engelmann, Teaching Disadvantaged Children, 7.

33. Jonathan Kozol, *Death at an Early Age* (Boston: Houghton Mifflin, 1967), 79.

34. Ibid., 165.

35. See, for example, William Labov, *Language in the Inner City: Studies in the Black English Vernacular* (Philadelphia: University of Pennsylvania Press, 1972); Arthur K. Spears, "Institutionalized Racism and the Education of Blacks," *Anthropology and Education Quarterly* 9, no. 2 (1978); John G. Barnitz, "Black English and Other Dialects: Sociolinguistic Implications for Reading Instruction," *The Reading Teacher* 33, no. 7 (1980).

36. Engelmann, Preventing Failure, 152.

37. See, for example, Carl Bereiter, "The Changing Face of Educational Disadvantagement," *Phi Delta Kappan* 66, no. 8 (1985).

38. Personal communication with Siegfried Engelmann, June 9, 2011.

39. Jonathan Kozol, *Free Schools* (Boston: Houghton Mifflin, 1972), 31.

40. Ibid., 35.

41. Thomas Powers, *Diana: The Making of a Terrorist* (Boston: Houghton Mifflin Company, 1971), 66.

42. Carl Bereiter, "Instructional Planning in Early Compensatory Education," *Phi Delta Kappan* 48, no. 7 (1967): 356.

43. See, for instance, Pierre Bourdieu, "The School as a Conservative Force: Scholastic and Cultural Inequalities," in *Contemporary Research in the Sociology of Education*, ed. John Eggleston (London: Methuen, 1974).

44. Bereiter and Engelmann, Teaching Disadvantaged Children, 6.

45. Ibid., 11.

46. Ibid., 42.

47. Ibid., 24.

48. James T. Patterson, *Brown v. Board of Education: A Civil Rights Milestone and Its Troubled Legacy* (New York: Oxford University Press, 2001), xvii.

49. Ibid., 230.

50. Schools Matter, "Why KIPP Is Not a Model for Urban Education," June 17, 2006, http://www.schoolsmatter.info/2006/06/why-kipp-is-not-model-for-urban.html.

51. Personal communication with Siegfried Engelmann, June 9, 2011.

52. See, for instance, Siegfried Engelmann, "Socrates and Education: Bussing," http://www.zigsite.com/PDFs/SocratesAndBussing.pdf.

53. Richard L. Venezky, "The American Reading Script and Its Nineteenth-Century Origins," *Book Research Quarterly* 6, no. 2 (1990).

54. Quoted in Daniel Radosh, "The Pet Goat Approach," *New Yorker,* Talk of the Town Section, July 26, 2004, 34.

55. Siegfried Engelmann, *War Against the Schools' Academic Child Abuse* (Portland, OR: Halcyon House, 1992), 7.

56. Dan Lortie, *Schoolteacher: A Sociological Study*, 2nd ed. (Chicago: University of Chicago Press, 2002), 172.

57. Ibid., 149.

58. Quoted in Young, "A New Approach to Head Start," 388.

59. Ibid.

60. Siegfried Engelmann, Your Child Can Succeed: How to Get the Most out of School for Your Child (New York: Simon and Schuster, 1972), 35.

61. Lortie, Schoolteacher, 228.

62. Engelmann, Your Child Can Succeed, 30.

63. Kenneth S. Goodman, "The Know-More and the Know-Nothing Movements in Reading: A Personal Response" (paper presented at the National Conference on Language Arts in the Elementary School annual meeting, Hartford, CT, March 1979).

64. Siegfried Engelmann and Jerry Silbert, Reasoning and Writing: A Direct Instruction Program (Columbus, OH: SRA/McGraw-Hill, 2001), 7.

65. Siegfried Engelmann and Elaine Bruner, DISTAR Reading I (Chicago: Science Research Associates, 1969); Siegfried Engelmann and Douglas Carnine, DISTAR Arithmetic I (Chicago: Science Research Associates, 1969); Siegfried Engelmann and Jean Osborn, DISTAR Language I (Chicago: Science Research Associates, 1969).

66. Personal communication with Siegfried Engelmann, June 1, 2011.

67. Margaret T. Morgan and Norman Robinson, "The 'Back to the Basics' Movement in Education," Canadian Journal of Education 1, no. 2 (1976): 1.

68. Henry M. Levin, "Back to Basics and the Economy," The Radical Teacher, no. 20 (1982): 8.

69. Ellen Velie Leininger, "Back to Basics: Underlying Concepts and Controversy," The Elementary School Journal 79, no. 3 (1979): 167–173.

70. Vernon Smith, "The Back-to-Basics Movement: A Firmer Stand for English Educators," English Education 9, no. 4 (1978): 195–198.

71. Susan J. Rosenholtz and Elizabeth G. Cohen, "Back to Basics and the Desegregated School," The Elementary School Journal 83, no. 5 (1983): 515.

72. Personal communication with Siegfried Engelmann, May 16, 2011.

73. Linda Stebbins, Education as Experimentation: A Planned Variation Model, vol. 3 (Cambridge, MA: Abt Associates, 1976); Linda Stebbins et al., Education as Experimentation: A Planned Variation Model, vol. 4 (Cambridge, MA: Abt Associates, 1977).

74. David Berliner, "Using Research on Teaching for the Improvement of Classroom Practice," Theory into Practice 19, no. 4 (1980): 307.

75. George F. Madaus, Peter W. Airasian, and Thomas Kellaghan, School Effectiveness: A Review of the Evidence (New York: McGraw-Hill, 1980).

76. Wesley C. Becker and Russell Gersten, "A Follow-Up of Follow Through: The Later Effects of the Direct Instruction Model on Children in Fifth and Sixth Grades," American Educational Research Journal 19, no. 1 (1982): 75–92.

77. Douglas Carnine and Russell Gersten, "Effective Mathematics Instruction for Low-Income Students: Results of Longitudinal Field Research in 12 School Districts," Journal for Research in Mathematics Education 13, no. 2 (1982): 150.

78. Ernest R. House et al., "No Simple Answer: Critique of the Follow-Through Evaluation," Harvard Educational Review 48, no. 2 (1978): 128–160.

79. Personal communication with Siegfried Engelmann, June 9, 2011.

80. National Commission on Excellence in Education, *A Nation at Risk: The Imperative of Educational Reform* (Washington, DC: U.S. Government Printing Office, 1983).

81. Barbara Sizemore, "Pitfalls and Promises of Effective Schools Research," *Journal of Negro Education* 54, no. 3 (1985): 286.

82. Lisa Delpit, "The Silenced Dialogue: Power and Pedagogy in Educating Other People's Children," *Other People's Children: Cultural Conflict in the Classroom* (New York: The New Press, 1995), 28.

83. Lisa Delpit, "Skills and Other Dilemmas of a Progressive Black Educator," *Harvard Education Review* 56, no. 4 (1986): 383.

84. Fran Lehr, "Direct Instruction in Reading," *The Reading Teacher* 39, no. 7 (1986): 708; Siegfried Engelmann, *Direct Instruction* (Englewood Cliffs, NJ: Educational Technology Publications, 1980), 3.

85. Russell Gersten et al., "A Multifaceted Study of Change in Seven Inner-City Schools," *The Elementary School Journal* 86, no. 3 (1986): 273.

86. Virginia Richardson, "Constructivist Teaching and Teacher Education: Theory and Practice," in *Constructivist Teacher Education: Building New Understandings*, ed. Virginia Richardson (Bristol, PA: Falmer Press, 1997), 3.

87. National Research Council, *Everybody Counts: A Report to the Nation on the Future of Mathematics Education* (Washington, DC: National Academy Press, 1989), 57.

88. Douglas Carnine and Jerry Silbert, *Direct Instruction Reading* (Columbus, OH: Charles E. Merrill, 1979), v.

89. U.S. Department of Education, Office of Special Education Programs, Annual Report to Congress on the Implementation of the Individuals with Disabilities Education Act, selected years, 1979 through 2007.

90. Peter Cole and Lorna Chan, *Methods and Strategies for Special Education* (Sydney: Prentice-Hall, 1990); Thomas Scruggs and Bearnice Wong, ed., *Intervention Research in Learning Disabilities* (New York: Springer-Verlag, 1990); Mark Wolery, Melinda J. Ault, and Patricia M. Doyle, *Teaching Students with Moderate to Severe Disabilities* (New York: Longman, 1992); Robert A. Gable and Steven F. Warren, ed., *Advances in Mental Retardation and Developmental Disabilities: Strategies for Teaching Students with Mild to Severe Mental Retardation* (Philadelphia: Jessica Kingsley, 1993); Ronald C. Greaves and Phillip J. McLaughlin, ed., *Recent Advances in Special Education and Rehabilitation* (Boston: Andover Medical, 1993).

91. Barbara Bateman, "Teaching Word Recognition to Slow Learning Children," *Reading, Writing and Learning Disabilities* 7, no. 1 (1991): 11.

92. Hempenstall, "The Importance of Effective Instruction," 21; Engelmann and Engelmann, *Give Your Child a Superior Mind*, 13.

93. Chris Chapman, Jennifer Laird, and Angelina KewalRamani, *Trends in High School Dropout and Completion Rates in the United States: 1972–2008* (Washington, DC: National Center for Education Statistics, 2010).

94. Jean Davidson, "Tests Show City Pupils Still Lagging," *Chicago Tribune*, April 17, 1986, 1.

95. "Tough Talk About New York's Schools," *New York Times*, November 23, 1985, 26.

96. Personal communication with Jerry Silbert, June 9, 2011.

97. See, for instance, Wilma Rimes, "Mabel B. Wesley Elementary," *Behavior and Social Issues* 7, no. 1 (1997).

98. Marcy Stein, Jerry Silbert, and Douglas Carnine, *Designing Effective Mathematics Instruction: A Direct Instruction Approach* (Upper Saddle River, NJ: Merrill, 1997), iii.

99. Gary L. Adams and Siegfried Engelmann, *Research on Direct Instruction: 25 Years Beyond DISTAR* (Seattle: Educational Achievement Systems, 1996), 31–32.

100. Baltimore Curriculum Project, "Direct Instruction and Special Education Fact Sheet," http://www.baltimorecp.org/docs/DI_Special_Ed_Facts.pdf.

101. Daniel M. O'Brien and Anne M. Ware, "Implementing Research-Based Reading Programs in the Fort Worth Independent School District," *Journal of Education for Students Placed at Risk* 7, no. 2 (2002): 168.

102. Quoted in Michael Winerip, "Schools for Sale," *New York Times*, June 14, 1998, 42.

103. Elizabeth Duffrin, "Direct Instruction Making Waves," *Catalyst Chicago*, September 1996, http://www.catalyst-chicago.org/news/2005/07/25/direct-instruction-making-waves.

104. Ibid.

105. Elizabeth Duffrin, "Snapshots from the Different Camps," *Catalyst Chicago*, September 1996, http://www.catalyst-chicago.org/news/2005/07/25/snapshots-different-camps.

106. R. Lucks, "Constructivist Teaching vs. Direct Instruction," December 16, 1999 (unpublished assignment completed for a class).

107. Ibid.

108. American Federation of Teachers, *Building on the Best, Learning from What Works: Five Promising Remedial Reading Intervention Programs* (Washington, DC: American Federation of Teachers, 1999).

109. "School-by-School Reform," Making Schools Work with Hendrick Smith, PBS, http://www.pbs.org/makingschoolswork/sbs/sfa/lessons.html.

110. Bill Honig, *Teaching Our Children to Read: The Components of an Effective, Comprehensive Reading Program*, 2nd ed. (Thousand Oaks, CA: Corwin Press, 2001), 9–10.

111. Daniel Perlstein, "Minds Stayed on Freedom: Politics and Pedagogy in the African-American Freedom Struggle," *American Educational Research Journal* 39, no. 2 (2002): 274.

112. Donald R. Cruickshank, Deborah L. Bainer, and Kim K. Metcalf, ed., *The Art of Teaching*, 2nd ed. (New York: McGraw-Hill, 1999), 230.

113. Debra Viadero, "A Direct Challenge," *Education Week*, March 17, 1999.

114. Geoffrey D. Borman et al., "Comprehensive School Reform and Achievement: A Meta-Analysis," *Review of Educational Research* 73, no. 2 (2003): 168.

115. The Comprehensive School Reform Quality Center, *CSRQ Center Report on Elementary School Comprehensive School Reform Models* (Washington, DC: American Institutes for Research, 2005).

116. Nancy E. Marchand-Martella, Ronald C. Martella, and Kristy Ausdemore, "An Overview of Direct Instruction," *New Horizons for Learning* (September 2005).

117. U.S. Department of Education, "Awards – Comprehensive School Reform Quality Initiatives," http://www2.ed.gov/programs/qualinits/awards.html.

118. Rebecca Herman et al., *An Educator's Guide to Schoolwide Reform* (Washington, DC: American Institutes for Research, 1999).

119. McGraw-Hill Companies, *2006 Investor Fact Book*, (New York: McGraw-Hill, 2006), 22.

120. Ibid.

121. Personal communication with Siegfried Engelmann, June 1, 2011.

122. Marchand-Martella, Slocum, and Martella, ed., *Introduction to Direct Instruction*.

123. Quoted in Radosh, "The Pet Goat Approach."

124. Alan J. Borsuk, "Scores Soar at Siefert School with Aid of Structured Lessons: What's That Slapping Sound?" *Milwaukee Journal Sentinel*, March 2, 2001.

125. Quoted in Marla J. Berry-Johnson, *Advocates' Perceptions of the Direct Instruction Reading Program in One Urban School: The Value of Drill, Rhythm, and Repetition in the Elementary Curriculum* (unpublished master's thesis, Graduate College of Bowling Green State University, May 2006), 45.

126. Personal communication with Dan Robertson, May 27, 2011.

127. Debra Viadero, "A Direct Challenge," *Education Week*, March 17, 1999.

128. Randall J. Rydern, Jennifer Lyn Burton, and Anna Silberg, "Longitudinal Study of Direct Instruction Effects from First Through Third Grades," *Journal of Educational Research* 99, no. 3: 187.

129. Michelle Commeyras, "Scripted Reading Instruction? What's a Teacher Educator to Do?" *Phi Delta Kappan* 88, no. 5 (2007): 405.

130. Sol Stern, "The Bush Education Reform Really Works," *City Journal*, Winter 2007, http://www.city-journal.org/html/17_1_reading_first.html.

131. Ibid.

132. Kate N. Grossman, "City Schools to Ax Scripted Reading Program Despite Gains," *Chicago Sun-Times*, February 21, 2005.

133. Personal communication with Siegfried Engelmann, June 9, 2011.

134. See, for a recent example, responses to Paul E. Peterson, "Eighth-Grade Students Learn More Through Direct Instruction," *Education Next* 11, no. 3 (2011).

135. Mary R. Jalongo, "Editorial: On Behalf of Children," *Early Childhood Education Journal* 26, no. 3 (1999): 139.

136. Quoted in John McWhorter, "We Know How to Teach Black Kids," *The Root*, November 16, 2010, http://www.theroot.com/views/we-know-how-teach-black-kids?page=0,1.

137. Susan G. Magliaro, Barbara B. Lockee, and John K. Burton, "Direct Instruction Revisited: A Key Model for Instructional Technology," *Educational Technology Research and Development* 53, no. 4 (2005): 53.

Chapter 5

1. The taxonomy for the psychomotor domain was never completed by Bloom, Krathwohl, and colleagues.

2. Deane C. Thompson, "What to Do Until Bloom Comes: Behavioral Objectives That Work," *The History Teacher* 7, no. 2 (1974): 217.

3. For more on Google ngrams, see Jean-Baptiste Michel et al., "Quantitative Analysis of Culture Using Millions of Digitized Books," *Science* 331, no. 6014 (2011): 176–182.

4. Eugene H. Cramer and Marrietta Castle, ed., *Fostering the Love of Reading: The Affective Domain in Reading Education* (Newark, DE: International Reading Association, 1994).

5. Henry Ellington, *Educational Objectives: Teaching and Learning in Higher Education* (Aberdeen, Scotland: Scottish Central Institutions Committee for Educational Development, 1984), 8, 9.

6. Ibid.

7. David Tyack, *Seeking Common Ground* (Cambridge, MA: Harvard University Press, 2003), 12.

8. J. Orville Taylor, *The District School* (Philadelphia, 1835), 281.

9. Ibid., 110.

10. A taxonomy for the psychomotor domain was planned as the third volume in the series. It was never completed.

11. Sharon Clark, "The Curriculum Builder's Game Adapted for the Secondary English Program," in *The Growing Edges of Secondary English*, ed. Charles Suhor, John Sawyer Mayher, and Frank J. D'Angelo (Champaign, IL: National Council of Teachers of English, 1968), 39.

12. David R. Krathwohl, Benjamin S. Bloom, and Bertram B. Masia, *Taxonomy of Educational Objectives, Handbook II: The Affective Domain* (New York: David McKay Co., 1964), 17.

13. Carol Kehr Tittle, Deborah Hecht, and Patrick Moore, "From Taxonomy to Constructing Meaning in Context: Revisiting the Taxonomy of Educational Objectives: II, Affective Domain, 25 Years Later" (paper presented at the Annual Meeting of the National Council on Measurement in Education, San Francisco, CA, March 1989), 1.

14. Karin Kirk, "What *Is* the Affective Domain Anyway?" SERC, http://serc.carleton.edu/NAGTWorkshops/affective/intro.html.

15. Izabele Savickiene, "Conception of Learning Outcomes in the Bloom's Taxonomy Affective Domain," *The Quality of Higher Education* (2010), 39.

16. Tyack, *Seeking Common Ground*.

17. Asahel D. Woodruff, "Review II: Taxonomy of Educational Objectives, Handbook II: Affective Domain by D. R. Krathwohl, B. S. Bloom, B. B. Masia," *Journal of Educational Measurement* 1, no. 2 (1964): 176.

18. Onalee McGraw, "Where Is the Public in Public Education," *Phi Delta Kappan* 64, no. 2 (1982): 94.

19. "Bloom's Taxonomy—Learning Domains," Business Balls, http://www .businessballs.com/bloomstaxonomyoflearningdomains.htm.

20. Krathwohl, Bloom, and Masia, Taxonomy of Educational Objectives, Handbook II, 185.

21. Arieh Lewy, "The Empirical Validity of Major Properties of a Taxonomy of Affective Educational Objectives," *The Journal of Experimental Education* 36, no. 3 (1968): 77.

22. Krathwohl, Bloom, and Masia, Taxonomy of Educational Objectives, Handbook II, vii.

23. Sister Trinita Meehan, *The Effects of Instruction Based on Elements of Critical Reading Upon the Questioning Patterns of Preservice Teachers* (Bloomington, IN, and Washington, DC: Indiana University School of Education and National Center for Educational Research and Development, 1970), 60.

24. Robert M. W. Travers, "Taxonomies of Educational Objectives and Theories of Classification," *Educational Evaluation and Policy Analysis* 2, no. 2 (1980): 16.

25. Morton Alpren, "Significance of the Affective Domain," *Theory into Practice* 13, no. 1 (1974): 47.

26. Paul Geisert, *The Dimensions of Measurement of the Affective Domain* (Laramie, WY: University of Wyoming, Center for Research Service and Publication, 1972), 9.

27. Krathwohl, Bloom, and Masia, Taxonomy of Educational Objectives, Handbook II, 80.

28. Lynn W. Glass, "Assessment of Affective Outcomes of Instruction with High School Sophomore Biology Students and Teachers" (paper presented at Annual Meeting of the National Association for Research in Science Teaching, Minneapolis, MN, 1970).

29. Meehan, Effects of Instruction, 64.

30. Deane C. Thompson, "What to Do Until Bloom Comes: Behavioral Objectives That Work," *The History Teacher* 7, no. 2 (1974): 217.

31. Thompson, "What to Do," 217.

32. Martha H. Dillner, "Affective Objectives in Reading," *Journal of Reading* 17, no. 8 (1974): 627.

33. Clark, "The Curriculum Builder's Game," 41.

34. Steven J. Haggbloom et al., "The 100 Most Eminent Psychologists of the 20th Century," *Review of General Psychology* 6, no. 2 (2002): 147.

35. Ibid., 142.

36. Personal communication with Howard Gardner, March 14, 2013.

37. Robert J. Sternberg, *Beyond IQ: A Triarchic Theory of Intelligence* (Cambridge: Cambridge University Press, 1985).

38. Dan Kirby and Carol Kykendall, "Research in the Classroom: Thinking About Research on Thinking," *The English Journal* 76, no. 5 (1987); Samuel Messick, "Multiple Intelligences or Multilevel Intelligence? Selective Emphasis on Distinctive Properties of Hierarchy: On Gardner's Frames of Mind and Sternberg's Beyond IQ in the Context of Theory and Research on the Structure of Human Abilities," *Psychological Inquiry* 3, no. 4 (1992).

39. Robert J. Sternberg, "What Should Intelligence Tests Test? Implications of a Triarchic Theory of Intelligence for Intelligence Testing," *Educational Researcher* 13, no. 1 (1984): 5.

40. Ibid.

41. Ibid.

42. Lee J. Cronbach, "Beyond IQ: A Triarchic Theory of Human Intelligence by Robert J. Sternberg," *American Scientist* 73, no. 4 (1985): 394.

43. Personal communication with Howard Gardner, March 14, 2013.

44. Albert Shanker, "The End of the Traditional Model of Schooling: And, a Proposal for Using Incentives to Restructure Our Public Schools," *Phi Delta Kappan* 71, no. 5 (1990): 349.

45. Robert J. Sternberg and Louise Spear-Swerling, *Teaching for Thinking* (Washington, DC: American Psychological Association, 1996).

46. Ann M. Clarke, "Beyond IQ: A Triarchic Theory of Human Intelligence by Robert J. Sternberg," *British Journal of Educational Studies* 34, no. 2 (1986): 206.

47. Lee Dembart, "Book Review: Measuring Intelligence Beyond IQ Tests," *Los Angeles Times*, August 30, 1988, G6.

48. Robert J. Sternberg, "Frames of Mind: The Theory of Multiple Intelligences by H. Gardner," *American Scientist* 72, no. 4 (1984): 394.

49. Personal communication with Howard Gardner, March 14, 2013.

50. Sternberg, "Frames of Mind," 394.

51. Richard E. Snow, "Frames of Mind: The Theory of Multiple Intelligences by Howard Gardner," *American Journal of Education* 94, no. 1 (1985): 110.

52. Robert J. Sternberg, *Intelligence Applied: Understanding and Increasing Your Intellectual Skills* (San Diego: Harcourt Brace Jovanovich, 1986), v.

53. Kathleen Carlson, "A Useful Addition to the College Classroom," *Phi Delta Kappan* 69, no. 4 (1987): 315.

54. Robert J. Sternberg, *The Triarchic Mind: A New Theory of Human Intelligence* (New York: Viking, 1988), vi.

55. Sternberg, "What Should Intelligence Tests Test," 6.

56. Ibid., 12.

57. Ibid., 13.

58. Samuel Bowles and Herbert Gintis, "IQ in the U.S. Class Structure," *Social Policy* 3: 65–96; Stanley S. Guterman, "IQ Tests in Research on Social Stratification: The Cross-Class Validity of the Tests and Measures of Scholastic Aptitude," *Sociology of Education* 52: 163–173; David Kirp, "Schools as Sorters: The Constitutional and Policy

Implications of Student Classification," *University of Pennsylvania Law Review* 121: 705–797; James R. Flynn, "The Hidden History of IQ and Special Education: Can the Problems Be Solved?" *Psychology, Public Policy, and Law* 6, no. 1 (2000).

59. It also received the Outstanding Book Award from the American Educational Research Association.

60. Robert J. Sternberg, "Applying the Triarchic Theory of Human Intelligence in the Classroom," in *Intelligence, Instruction, and Assessment: Theory into Practice*, ed. Robert J. Sternberg and Wendy M. Williams (Mahwah, NJ: Lawrence Erlbaum Associates, 1998), 4.

61. Alfonso Montuori and Ronald E. Purser, "Deconstructing the Lone Genius Myth: Toward a Contextual View of Creativity," *Journal of Humanistic Psychology* 35, no. 3 (1995): 74.

62. Marie Winn, "New Views of Human Intelligence," *New York Times*, April 29, 1990, SMA16.

63. Dan Kirby and Carol Kykendall, "Research in the Classroom: Thinking about Research on Thinking," *The English Journal* 76, no. 5 (1987): 105.

64. Sternberg, "What Should Intelligence Tests Test," 13.

65. Howard Gardner, *The Disciplined Mind: What Students Should Understand* (New York: Basic Books, 1999).

66. Robert J. Sternberg, "Teaching Critical Thinking: Eight Easy Ways to Fail Before You Begin," *Phi Delta Kappan* 68, no. 6 (1987).

67. Robert J. Sternberg, personal communication, April 30, 2012.

68. Philip N. Johnson-Laird, "Feeling Dumb? Try Mental Self-Management," *New York Times*, September 25, 1988, BR9.

69. Robert J. Sternberg, Bruce Torff, and Elena L. Grigorenko, "Teaching for Successful Intelligence Raises School Achievement," *Phi Delta Kappan* 79, no. 9 (1998): 667.

70. Robert J. Sternberg, "Teaching Critical Thinking, Part 2: Possible Solutions," *Phi Delta Kappan* 67, no. 4 (1985): 278.

71. Robert J. Sternberg, Lynn Okagaki, and Alice S. Jackson, "Practical Intelligence for Success in School," *Educational Leadership*, September 1990: 36.

72. Personal communication with Howard Gardner, March 14, 2013.

73. Sternberg and Spear-Swerling, *Teaching for Thinking*, 38, 56, 71, 85, 130.

74. Gardner, "Reflections of Multiple Intelligences," 202.

75. Ibid., 209.

76. Robert J. Sternberg, "Assessing What Matters," *Educational Leadership* 65, no. 4 (2007): 20–26.

77. Robert J. Sternberg, "Applying Psychological Theories to Educational Practice," *American Educational Research Journal* 45, no. 1 (2008): 163.

78. "Generative Learning," NASA-Dryden Learning Technologies Project, http://www.ed.psu.edu/nasa/genetxt.html.

79. Richard E. Mayer, "Merlin C. Wittrock's Enduring Contributions to the Science of Learning," *Educational Psychologist* 45, no. 1 (2010): 47.

80. See Lawrence A. Cremin, *The Transformation of the School: Progressivism in American Education, 1876–1957* (New York: Knopf, 1961).

81. Merlin C. Wittrock, "The Cognitive Movement in Instruction," *Educational Psychologist* 13 (1978): 15.

82. Richard E. Mayer, "Merlin C. Wittrock's Enduring Contributions to the Science of Learning," *Educational Psychologist* 45, no. 1 (2010): 48.

83. Marilyn Kourilsky and Merlin C. Wittrock, "Generative Teaching: An Enhancement Strategy for the Learning of Economics in Cooperative Groups," *American Educational Research Journal* 29, no. 4 (1992): 863.

84. Hyeon Woo Lee, Kyu Yon Lim, and Barbara L. Grabowski, "Generative Learning: Principles and Implications for Making Meaning," in *Handbook of Research on Educational Communications and Technology*, ed. J. Michael Spector et al. (New York: Taylor & Francis, 2008), 112.

85. Lyn Corno and Edys Quellmalz, "Mentor: Inside and Out," *Educational Psychologist* 45, no. 1 (2010): 70.

86. Michele Linden and Merlin C. Wittrock, "The Teaching of Reading Comprehension According to the Model of Generative Learning," *Reading Research Quarterly* 17, no. 1 (1981): 45.

87. Thomas A. Romberg, "Wittrock's Influence on Mathematics Education: Some Personal Comments," *Educational Psychologist* 45, no. 1 (2010): 62.

88. Wittrock, "The Cognitive Movement in Instruction," 9.

89. Ibid., 10.

90. Kourilsky and Wittrock, "Generative Teaching," 869.

91. Aaron Fried et al., "From Design *Theory* to Development *Practice*: Developing a Stronger Understanding of Our Field," AECT 2006 presentation proposal, http://web.cortland.edu/frieda/html/pdfs/fried2006AECT.pdf.

92. Barbara L. Grabowski, "Generative Learning Contributions to the Design of Instruction and Learning," in *Handbook of Research for Educational Communications and Technology*, ed. David H. Jonassen (New York: Simon & Schuster Macmillan, 1996), 739.

93. Roger Osborne and Merlin Wittrock, "The Generative Learning Model and Its Implications for Science Education," *Studies in Science Education* 12, no. 1 (1985): 66.

94. Grant Wiggins and Jay McTighe, *Understanding by Design* (Alexandria, VA: ASCD, 2005), 123.

95. James M. Applefield, Richard Huber, and Mhnaz Moallem, "Constructivism in Theory and Practice: Toward a Better Understanding," *The High School Journal* 84, no. 2 (2000/2001): 36.

96. Linda B. Stebbins et al., *Education as Experimentation: A Planned Variation Model, Volume IV-A: An Evaluation of Follow Through* (Cambridge, MA: Abt Associates, 1977).

97. Wesley Becker and Douglas Carnine, "Direct Instruction: A Behavior Theory Model for Comprehensive Educational Intervention with the Disadvantaged," in *Contributions of Behavior Modification in Education*, ed. S. Bijon (Hillsdale, NJ: Laurence Erlbaum, 1981).

98. Donald M. Baer, Montrose M. Wolf, and Todd R. Risley, "Some Current Dimensions of Applied Behavior Analysis," *Journal of Applied Behavior Analysis* 1, no. 1 (1968): 91–97.

99. University of Kansas, Lawrence, Department of Human Development, and Far West Laboratory for Educational Research and Development, *The Behavior Analysis Model, Program Report* (Berkeley, CA: Far West Laboratory for Educational Research and Development, 1971), 6.

100. Milton Goldberg, Gerald Knowles, and Leontine Scott, "Project Follow Through in Philadelphia," *Educational Leadership* 29, no. 1 (1971): 21.

101. American Institutes for Research, *Behavior Analysis Model of a Follow Through Program, Oraibi, Arizona* (booklet prepared for the White House Conference on Children, Washington, DC, December 1970).

102. Judy Goodwin and Anne M. Lukshus, *Follow Through Expansion Pre-Program Data, 1975*. Report Number 7642, Philadelphia School District Office of Research and Evaluation, October 1975.

103. Dan Lortie, *Schoolteacher: A Sociological Study*, 2nd ed. (University of Chicago Press, 2002).

104. Ibid., 106.

105. Ibid., 114.

106. Ibid., 114.

107. B. F. Skinner, *Science and Human Behavior* (Upper Saddle River, NJ: Pearson, 1953), 403.

108. Carl V. Binder, "Marketing Measurably Effective Instructional Methods," *Journal of Behavioral Education* 1, no. 3 (1991): 322.

109. Donald Bushell Jr., Patricia Ann Wrobel, and Mary Louise Michaelis, "Applying 'Group' Contingencies to the Classroom Study Behavior of Preschool Children," *Journal of Applied Behavior Analysis* 1, no. 1 (1968): 61.

110. American Institutes for Research, *Behavior Analysis Model*.

111. Binder, "Marketing Measurably Effective Instructional Methods," 324.

112. Ernest R. House et al., "No Simple Answer: Critique of the Follow-Through Evaluation," *Harvard Educational Review* 48, no. 2 (1978): 128–160; personal communication with Siegfried Engelmann, June 9, 2011.

113. Wesley Becker and Douglas Carnine, "Direct Instruction: An Effective Approach to Educational Intervention with the Disadvantaged and Low Performers," in *Advances in Clinical Child Psychology*, vol. 3, ed. B. B. Lahey and A. E. Kazdin (New York: Plenum, 1980), 429–473.

114. Wesley Becker and Russell Gersten, "Follow-up of Follow-Through: The Later Effects of the Direct Instruction Model on Children in Fifth and Sixth Grades," *American Educational Research Journal* 19, no. 1 (1982): 75–92.

115. Russell Gersten, "Follow Through Revisited: Reflections on the Site Variability Issue," *Educational Evaluation and Policy Analysis* 6 (1984): 109–121; Russell

Gersten, "Direct Instruction with Special Education Students: A Review of Evaluation Research," *Journal of Special Education* 19 (1985): 41–58; Russell Gersten and Douglas Carnine, "Direct Instruction in Reading Comprehension," *Educational Leadership* 44 (1986): 69–78; Russell Gersten and Thomas Keating, "Long-Term Benefits from Direct Instruction," *Educational Leadership* 44 (1987): 28–31; Russell Gersten, Thomas Keating, and Wesley Becker, "Continued Impact of the Direct Instruction Model: Longitudinal Studies of Follow Through Students," *Education and Treatment of Children* 11 (1988): 318–327.

116. Education Consumers Foundation, *Direct Instruction: What the Research Says* (Arlington, VA: Education Consumers Foundation, 2011).

117. University of North Carolina Wilmington, "Hillcrest Reading Program," http://uncw.edu/wha/hillcrest/ResearchBaseforDIand100Easy.html.

118. S. Brederkamp, ed., *Developmentally Appropriate Practice in Early Childhood Programs Serving Children from Birth Through Age 8* (Washington, DC: National Association for the Education of Young Children, 1987), 67–78.

119. Edward K. Morris, "History of Applied Behavioral Science" (University of Kansas syllabus, 2011).

120. National Institute of Neurological Disorders and Stroke, National Institutes of Health, "Autism Fact Sheet," http://www.ninds.nih.gov/disorders/autism/detail_autism.htm.

121. National Institute of Mental Health, "A Parent's Guide to Autism Spectrum Disorder," http://www.nimh.nih.gov/health/publications/a-parents-guide-to-autism-spectrum-disorder/how-is-asd-treated.shtml.

Conclusion

1. Ellen Condliffe Lagemann, *An Elusive Science: The Troubling History of Education Research* (Chicago: University of Chicago Press, 1990); David F. Labaree, *The Trouble with Ed Schools* (New Haven: Yale University Press, 2004); Geraldine Clifford and James Guthrie, *Ed School: A Brief for Professional Education* (Chicago: University of Chicago Press, 1988).

2. See, for instance: Carl Kaestle, "The Awful Reputation of Education Research," *Educational Researcher* 22, no. 1 (1993): 27; David K. Cohen, "A Revolution in One Classroom: The Case of Mrs. Oublier," *Educational Evaluation and Policy Analysis* 12, no. 3 (1990): 311–329.

3. James Hiebert, Ronald Gallimore, and James W. Stigler, "A Knowledge Base for the Teaching Profession: What Would It Look Like and How Can We Get One," *Educational Researcher* 31, no. 5: 3–15.

4. Eleanor Duckworth, "Teaching as Research," *Harvard Educational Review* 56, no. 4 (1986): 481–496.

5. Fred N. Kerlinger, "The Influence of Educational Research on Education Practice," *Educational Researcher* 6, no. 8 (1977): 10.

6. Cynthia E. Coburn, Meredith I. Honig, and Mary Kay Stein, "What's the Evidence on Districts' Use of Evidence?" in *The Role of Research in Educational Improvement*, ed. John D. Bransford (Cambridge, MA: Harvard Education Press, 2009), 71.

7. Jack Schneider, "Rhetoric and Practice in Pre-Service Education: The Case of Teach For America," *Journal of Education Policy* (2013).

8. Linda Darling-Hammond, Ruth Chung-Wai, and Alethea Andree, *How High-Achieving Countries Develop Great Teachers* (Stanford, CA: Stanford Center for Opportunity Policy in Education, August 2010).

9. Craig D. Jerald, *On Her Majesty's School Inspection Service* (Washington, DC: Education Sector, 2012).

10. National Center for Educational Statistics, *Revenues and Expenditures for Public Elementary and Secondary Education: School Year 2005–06* (Washington, DC: Institute for Education Sciences, U.S. Department of Education, 2008).

11. Heather C. Hill, "Fixing Teacher Professional Development," *Phi Delta Kappan* 90, no. 7 (2009).

12. Ian Westbury et al., "Teacher Education for Research-Based Practice in Expanded Roles: Finland's Experience," *Scandinavian Journal of Educational Research* 49, no. 5 (2005).

13. Lee S. Shulman et al., "Reclaiming Education's Doctorates: A Critique and a Proposal," *Educational Researcher* 35, no. 3 (2006).

14. Anthony S. Bryk, Louis M. Gomez, and Alicia Grunow, "Getting Ideas into Action: Building Networked Improvement Communities in Education," Carnegie Foundation for the Advancement of Teaching, http://www.carnegiefoundation.org/sites/default/files/bryk-gomez_building-nics-education.pdf.

15. Ruth Chung-Wai et al., Professional Learning in the Learning Profession: A Status Report on Teacher Development in the United States and Abroad (Dallas: National Staff Development Council, 2009).

16. An interesting model that might be borrowed from the field of nursing is the "Magnet" designation, which indicates a level of research-based practice among nursing staff at hospitals.

17. Louise Stoll et al., "Professional Learning Communities: A Review of the Literature," *Journal of Educational Change* 7, no. 4 (2006): 221–258.

18. An interesting example here is Darryl Yong, who spent a research sabbatical teaching in a large urban school district. Darryl Yong, "Adventures in Teaching: A Professor Goes to High School to Learn about Teaching Math," *Notices of the AMS* 59, no. 10 (2012): 1408–1415.

19. Stanford History Education Group, "Reading Like a Historian," http://sheg.stanford.edu/rlh.

20. Personal communication with Howard Gardner, March 14, 2013.

21. Ben Levin, "Making Research Matter More," *Education Policy Analysis Archives* 12, no. 56 (2004): 12.

Epilogue

1. *What People Think About Youth and Education*, National Education Association Research Bulletin no. 5, November 1940 (Washington, DC: NEA, 1940).

2. William J. Bushaw and John A. McNee, *Americans Speak Out: The 41st Annual Phi Delta Kappa/Gallup Poll of the Public's Attitudes Toward the Public Schools* (Bloomington, IN: Phi Delta Kappa, 2009).

ACKNOWLEDGMENTS

This project, like all scholarly ventures, is the result of many hands lifting. As such, its entrance into the world must begin with acknowledgment of their strength and generosity.

Because histories cannot be written without records of the past, thanks are owed to the librarians at Mercer University and the University of Chicago—home to the William H. Kilpatrick and Benjamin S. Bloom papers, respectively—who helped discover hidden gems in their collections. In a similar vein, I am grateful to Howard Gardner, Mindy Kornhaber, Carl Bereiter, Jerry Silbert, Robert Sternberg, Edward Morris, and Vivian Fueyo for sharing their time with me, and particularly to Siegfried Engelmann, who spent hours on the phone talking openly and honestly about the past and present.

True thanks, however, must be directed to a small but dedicated group that helped hoist this project up several flights of figurative stairs. David Labaree, who has made good on his promise to continue advising long after the end of my formal apprenticeship to him, provided keen insight and steady encouragement. My friends, Scott Gelber and Ethan Hutt, read several versions of the manuscript and still managed to remain on speaking terms with me. Bob Hampel made several excellent suggestions for framing the book, and offered sage counsel throughout the process. Larry Cuban provided timely and critical feedback, and like any great mentor, always challenged me to reach beyond what I had done but not beyond what is possible. And David Tyack, my role model, served throughout the project as a source of inspiration; I know no one with more dignity or humanity than him.

I owe a particular debt to my friend and colleague, Sivan Zakai, who has become my most trusted reader over the past several years. An ideal intellectual sparring partner, she not only read the manuscript in its various states of insufficiency, but also provided feedback with such grace that it was almost possible to believe I had not burdened her. She is a treasure.

A separate note of thanks must be written to my parents, whom I have to thank for nearly all that I do. As I have written before, it is a great gift to be the child of a poet and a librarian. Each taught me to love language, ideas, truth, and beauty. But such lessons hardly tip the scales when weighed against what each taught me about what it is to take the gift of hours and make a day, to take the blessing of existence and make a life. I strive under the banner of my mother's love, with the great hope that I may someday match my father's honor and courage. And I do so, always, with the deepest gratitude.

And finally, I must thank my wife, Katie, and my daughter, Annabelle—the great loves of my life. I wrote this book because I believe in our collective power to learn, to grow, and to shape the future. But I move through each day because of them. We make a world, we three.

A B O U T   T H E   A U T H O R

JACK SCHNEIDER is an assistant professor of education at the College of the Holy Cross. He holds a BA in political science from Haverford College, an MA in history from Stanford University, and a PhD in education from Stanford University. A former high school teacher, he lives in Somerville, Massachusetts, where he is active in the public schools.

Project Follow Through, 172
psychology, 172–175
receding from mainstream
    literature, 177
scripted programs, 171
similarity with counterparts,
    178–179
socially valued knowledge and
    behavior, 173
student achievement gains, 176
teacher professionalism, 174
teacher training, 180
terminology, 175
tokens reinforcing desired
    behaviors, 172–174
transportability, 175
what token is worth, 175–178
behaviorism
    attacks on, 115, 118
    behavior analysis model and,
        173–174
    challenging teaching techniques, 117
    criticisms of, 116
    decline in 1960s and 1970s, 173
    Direct Instruction and, 121
    progressive educators and, 116
    rejection of, 39, 153
behaviorists, 115
Bellanca, James, 66
Bereiter, Carl, 111, 116, 118–120
Bereiter-Engelmann model preschool,
    111–112
Bereiter-Engelmann Program, 111
Berliner, David, 126
Berman, Sally, 66
Bernard Van Leer Foundation, 53
Best Evidence Synthesis program, 201
Bestor, Arthur, 28, 29
best practices, vii

*Beyond IQ: A Triarchic Theory of
    Intelligence* (Sternberg), 153, 155,
    156, 159
Bijou, Sidney W., 172
Biological Science Curriculum Study,
    25
Bloom, Benjamin, 15–16, 18–20, 25,
    27, 36, 46–47, 142, 158, 170, 189
Bloom, Sophie, 34
Bloom's taxonomy, ix, 2, 11, 141, 143,
    179
    add-on to existing curriculum, 40
    affective domain, 142
    aligning with research in domains,
        24
    American education, 44–45
    broad appeal of, 26–31
    classifying behaviors by complexity,
        41
    classroom practice, 23–24
    cognitive domain, 142
    commonsense terms, 38
    content in curriculum, 29
    creation of, 16–23
    critical thinking, 29, 40–41
    curricular traditionalists and
        progressives, 29
    curricular unity, 39
    curriculum developers, 25–26
    curriculum guides, 15, 37
    cycles of legitimacy, 43–46
    defense of traditional liberal
        education, 30
    differences in students ability,
        34–35
    difficulty disproving, 43
    district-specific exposures to, 37
    ease of implementation, 38–39, 43,
        46, 148

Kilpatrick, William Heard, 79–108,
  163, 169, 197
Kirby, Dan, 159
KISS [Keep It Simple, Stupid]
  principle, 38
Klein, M. Frances, 34
Kliebard, Herbert, 95
Kloss, Robert, 41
knowledge, 15, 147, 158
  acquisition components, 154
  categories of, 20–21
  constructing, 163
  means of acquisition, 33
  nature of, 10
  systematic differences in absorbing,
    24
  for teaching, 191
Kornhaber, Mindy, 73, 76–77
Kourilsky, Marilyn, 167
Kovacs, Edna, 67
Kozol, Jonathan, 118–119
Krathwohl, David, 20, 36, 38,
  44–46, 142, 145–146, 158
Krathwohl's taxonomy, 11, 142–143
  affective domain, 148–149
  classroom practice, 179
  coordination across grades, 180
  difficulty understanding, 147–148
  hierarchical levels, 148
  inappropriateness of, 147
  negative feedback loop, 150–151
  occupationally unrealistic, 148
  philosophical compatibility, 180
  reimagining nature of teaching,
    148–149
  similarity with counterparts,
    178–179
  storing and sharing among
    educators, 148

  structuring, 181
  as works of scholarship, 179
Kreitzer, Amelia, 44
Kropp, Russell P., 24
K-12 teachers and Bloom's taxonomy,
  26

L
Labov, William, 119
Lagemann, Ellen, 85
law of effect, 115
Lazear, David, 66
Leadership Training Project, 37
learners
  establishing relationships with
    information, 166
  self-explanatory labels of, 52
learning
  by doing and independent schools,
    56
  law of effect, 115
  objectives broken down into
    component parts, 112
  teacher-guided, student-pursued
    activities, 98
  universality of, 39
  what is learned in school, 145–147
learning circles, 199
learning projects, 97
learning styles and theory of multiple
  intelligences, 71
Lehr, Fran, 128
Lessinger, Leon, 24
lesson plans and Bloom's taxonomy,
  15
lesson study, 199
Levin, Henry, 126
Levine, David, 97
linguistic intelligence, 54

NFDI. *See* National Institute for Direct Instruction (NIFDI)
No Child Left Behind Act (2001), vii,
63, 133
North Sacramento Education Association, 132

O
occupational realism, 8–9, 97–98,
107, 188
disregard for, 160
improving, 200–202, 206
occupational status and educational
attainment, 30
O'Connor, Anna T., 66
Ontario Institute for Studies in
Education, 112
Open Education Model, 113
Organisation for Economic Cooperation and Development, 9
organization, 147

P
PaperModels, Inc., 103
parents
classroom practices, 102
Project Follow Through, 113
well-rounded education, 59
Parker, Samuel Chester, 92
Parrish, William Clay, Jr., 197
Paul, Richard, 41
pedagogical progressivism, 83–84,
164, 166
perceived significance, 7–8, 185–186,
206
actors supporting teachers, 195
educational research, 194–197
intermediaries, 196

proxies and, 194
researchers, 196–197
teacher capacity for vetting
research, 194–195
performance components, 154
Perini, Matthew, 67
Pestalozzi, Johann, 83–84
Phi Delta Kappan, 72, 114, 159, 167
philosophical compatibility, 8, 187,
206
actors role, 198–199
importance of, 180
improving, 197–200
teacher preparation programs, 198
Piaget, Jean, 115, 128, 171
Piagetian perspective of intelligence,
53
policy makers
affects on instructional core, 4–5
benchmark level of proficiency, 61
blaming teachers for failure to
implement plans, 209
connections to scholarship, 206
discord over, 13
Howard Gardner's criticisms of, 62
low standardized test scores, 127
overgeneralization about student
potential, 61
uniform schools, 62
portfolio assessment, 56
Portland Public School System, 26
practical, 156, 158
practical education, 29–30
practical intelligence, 158
Practical Intelligence for School
program, 160
practice-based research, 191
Praxis exam, 37

students, *continued*
  differences in abilities, 34–35, 57, 71
  high criterion of learning, 34
  intellectual growth, 27–28
  intellectual strengths and weaknesses, 61
  maintaining interest, 89
  matching learning needs, 34
  meeting needs of individual, 57
  motivation and accountability, 17
  non-college-bound students, 32–33
  slower learners, 35
  social capital, 33
  specialized training for work force, 30
  thinking analytically, 158
  thinking creatively, 158
  thinking practically, 158
  tracking, 33
  what they should be doing in classroom, 10
Studies in Science Education, 170
Success for All program, 133
"Suggested Method for Introducing Bloom to Students-15 days, 15 minutes a day," 26
Sullivan Programmed Phonics, 172
Suzzalo, Henry, 85
synthesis, 15, 147, 158
  categories of, 20–22

T
Tasker, Sandy, 67
taxonomy, levels of, 15
"Taxonomy of Educational Objectives," 20
Taxonomy of Educational Objectives, Handbook II, 142–143

Taxonomy of Educational Objectives: The Classification of Educational Goals, Handbook I: Cognitive Domain, 20–27, 142
Taxonomy of Educational Objectives for the Affective Domain, 11, 141
Taxonomy of Educational Objectives for the Cognitive Domain. *See* Bloom's taxonomy
Taylor, Orville, 145
Teach21, 105
teacher-directed verbal instruction, 111
teacher education
  Bloom's taxonomy, 26, 44
  re-orienting toward research, 204
teacher-guided, student-pursued activities, 98
teacher preparation programs
  colleges and universities, 195
  philosophical compatibility, 198
teachers
  accountability scores and, 135–136
  actors supporting, 195
  advanced degrees, vii
  autonomy, 207
  benefits of research for, 4
  best practices, vii
  Bloom's taxonomy, 36–37, 41–42, 147
  chief duty of, 145
  content delivery, 5
  culture of practice, vii
  curricular and pedagogical policy control, 184
  development, 5
  Direct Instruction, 109–110, 121–125, 137
  domain-specific knowledge, 4